Foundations of Data and Digital Journalism

C000157022

This accessible, step-by-step guide is written for students and working professionals who want to better understand data journalism, web design, and the visualization of information.

Foundations of Data and Digital Journalism recognizes a growing need for general data knowledge in newsrooms across the globe, including an understanding of what's possible for both data reporting and presentation and how it can be achieved. It serves as a roadmap for students and working journalists who seek to understand what data is and how to find it; how to harness it most effectively for news; how to think critically about analysis results, potential shortcomings in the data, and the inclusion of appropriate context; and how to present compelling, data-driven stories online. Interviews with a diverse range of current practitioners help the reader gain a deeper understanding of how these tools and techniques are used in digitally focused newsrooms today. Taking a holistic approach to data journalism, this book enables readers to:

- Assess a data set with a critical eye, understanding what it shows, how it was created, and for what purpose.
- Master prominent and easily accessible software tools, including Google Sheets and R.
- Translate findings and conclusions into plain English for a news audience without overstating what the data can show or being misleading.
- Create impactful, attractive visualizations for an audience to explore.
- Understand how the modern web works, including HTML5, CSS3, and responsive webpage frameworks, like Bootstrap.

This is an ideal textbook for undergraduate and postgraduate journalism students and for working professionals looking to expand their skillset.

The book is supported with online student resources, including example datasets to support the material covered, available at Routledge.com.

Alex Richards is an assistant professor at Syracuse University's S.I. Newhouse School of Public Communications. Richards was a Pulitzer Prize finalist in 2011, and his reporting has been honored with the Goldsmith Prize for Investigative Reporting and the Taylor Family Award for Fairness in Journalism, among others. He previously worked as a data reporter and editor for the *Chicago Tribune*, Nerdwallet, *The Chronicle of Higher Education*, and the *Las Vegas Sun*. Richards is also a former training director for Investigative Reporters & Editors, where he taught in-depth reporting and data journalism techniques in newsrooms across the country.

Foundations of Data and Digital Journalism

Alex Richards

Routledge
Taylor & Francis Group

NEW YORK AND LONDON

Designed cover image: © Floriana/ iStock via Getty Images

First published 2023
by Routledge
605 Third Avenue, New York, NY 10158

and by Routledge
4 Park Square, Milton Park, Abingdon, Oxon, OX14 4RN

Routledge is an imprint of the Taylor & Francis Group, an informa business

© 2023 Alex Richards

The right of Alex Richards to be identified as author of this work has been asserted in accordance with sections 77 and 78 of the Copyright, Designs and Patents Act 1988.

All rights reserved. No part of this book may be reprinted or reproduced or utilised in any form or by any electronic, mechanical, or other means, now known or hereafter invented, including photocopying and recording, or in any information storage or retrieval system, without permission in writing from the publishers.

Trademark notice: Product or corporate names may be trademarks or registered trademarks, and are used only for identification and explanation without intent to infringe.

ISBN: 9781032017778 (hbk)
ISBN: 9781032017747 (pbk)
ISBN: 9781003182238 (ebk)

DOI: 10.4324/9781003182238

Typeset in Goudy
by codeMantra

Access the Support Material: www.routledge.com/9781032017747

For Meg, without whom none of this would have been possible.

Contents

List of figures xi

Acknowledgments xvi

1 Introduction: Why data journalism? 1
Finding data 3
Working with data 4
Representing data 6
Why data journalism? 7

2 Data, numeracy, and how to bulletproof information 10
Gaining a better understanding of your data: first steps 10
What is each row in my data? 12
Spotting common data problems 13
Problems with the data universe 16
Understanding your data: an early checklist 17
Three ways to talk about your data 18

3 Where data comes from—and how to get it 21
Routes to public data 22
Open records in action 23
Record retention schedules: a guide to what governments keep 24
Writing an official request 26
Non-public data 30
Sticking to what's "gettable" 31

4 Starting with spreadsheets 35
Four ways spreadsheets excel 35
Where spreadsheets (traditionally) lag 36
Some background on Google Sheets 36
Getting started with Google Sheets 37

Basic spreadsheet concepts   38
Other important interface features   41
Getting data into Google Sheets   42
Navigating the data display and controlling its structure   44
Exploring a data set to learn something new   46

5   Sort, filter, pivot: The building blocks of data analysis   51
Reordering your data table with sorting   51
Focusing on the most relevant information with filter   54
Filtering by values   55
Filtering by condition   56
Working with filtered data   57
Other things to know about filtering   58
Summarizing data sets with pivot tables   58
Finding meaningful groups in your data   59
Creating a pivot table   59
Building a simple pivot table from a question   61
Pivot table summary types   63
Sorting a pivot table   65
Leaning into the flexibility of pivot tables   65
Filtering a pivot table   67
More than one way to group data   68

6   Clean and repair: Techniques for more advanced analysis   70
The filter menu and frequency tables   70
Adding columns for cleaned values   72
Functions to help you clean text   74
Using functions in a cleaning column   75
Getting your changes to stick with "Paste Special"   75
Using more than one function at the same time   76
Combining and separating cell contents   76
Using "Split text to columns"   77
Merging values   80
Splitting cells at specific positions: focus on dates   81
Adding new categories based on a condition   83

7   Simple tools for everyday data visualization   86
Common types of visualizations and when to use them   86
The process of creating a data visualization   92
Beyond the data visualization: other critical things to consider   97
Using color in data visualizations   98
What can go wrong?   100

8 Introduction to R and the tidyverse   104
   The best way to work with R   105
   Overview of the RStudio interface for R   105
   Using R: understanding variables   107
   Expanding base R with outside packages   108
   Installing and loading packages within RStudio   109
   Importing a simple data table from CSV   111
   Where is R looking for files?   112
   An example with `read_csv()` *112*
   Data tables, tibbles, and adjusting data types   113
   Putting it all together in an R script   115

9 Using R for data analysis   117
   Changing the data's column headers   118
   Sorting and filtering data in RStudio and the tidyverse   118
   Using "pipes" in the tidyverse to keep your data analysis straight   122
   Expanding your analysis into new columns   123
   Summarizing a data set by different groups   125
   *A tidyverse superpower: joining data sets using a column with
      shared values   129*
   The types of joins   130
   Returning to the crash data: merging it with populations   134
   Joining perils: ending up with duplicated data   136
   Next steps in R   137

10 Making the modern web with HTML and CSS   139
    An HTML primer   139
    What you need to create HTML   141
    The parts of an HTML element   142
    Basic webpage structure and other common HTML elements   143
    Where CSS fits in, and how it works with HTML   146
    Writing a CSS selector   147
    Some common CSS properties   148
    Giving your CSS selectors more specific targets   150
    Styling HTML based on classes and IDs   150
    When CSS selectors clash   152

11 More advanced CSS: Layouts, Bootstrap, and more   154
    Block vs. inline display   155
    The "box model" in HTML   155
    Simple responsiveness for block elements using width   158

Content divisions   160
Repositioning a content division element using margins   161
Nesting div elements   163
Keeping images in check   165
Shorthand properties for margins, padding, and borders   166
Content divisions and the semantic web   167
Creating more complex webpage layouts with the Bootstrap Grid   167
What is Bootstrap?   168
Adding Bootstrap to your webpage   169
How the Bootstrap grid works: using containers, rows, and columns   169
Column classes   171
Giving instructions for more than one breakpoint   176
Aligning and distributing content   177
Next Bootstrap steps   179

12 Where to learn more   181

Index   185

Figures

2.1 An example of so-called "dirty data, " where the "nature_of_complaint" field suffers from a lack of standardization 14

3.1 A screen capture of the New York State Archives website 25

3.2 A screen capture of the Chicago Police Department's online records retention schedule 26

4.1 A brief tour of Google Sheets' interface components. 1: The spreadsheet grid; 2: A highlighted cell; 3: Tabs to access different sheets within the file; 4: The quicksum box; 5: the formula bar; and 6: the name box 38

4.2 Using cell references in a formula to calculate New York's population change between 2010 and 2020 in cell D2 40

4.3 A highlighted range with the corresponding cell references (cell A2 through cell C10) appearing in the name box 42

4.4 A CSV file of census data in the Sublime text editor. In this case, commas are the delimiting character used to signify column breaks in the data table, and double quotes are the text qualifier that prevent the population values from being broken up improperly 43

4.5 After autofilling all the population differences in column D 47

4.6 Calculating a percentage change in population for Northeastern states by taking the population change in column D and dividing it by the base population value in column B 48

4.7 Using the SUM() function to find total population figures for all Northeastern states in 2010 and 2020, as well as autofilling the raw population difference and the population percentage change for these new values in cells D11 and E11 50

5.1 Ensuring the correct range (A1:G52) has been selected prior to any sorting 52

5.2 The dialogue box with options for controlling a sort. The population data has a header row, so that option has been checked, and the sort will occur in descending order (Z → A) based on the values in the "Change" column 53

5.3   Filtering enabled on the state population table, along with the
      dropdown filter menu on the "Division" column   55
5.4   Creating a new pivot table. The full extent of the data table is
      selected, so the range for the pivot table is already completed   60
5.5   The pivot table editor on the right side of the window has two
      sections: a list of all column headers in the selected data table,
      and four pivot table elements where those columns can be
      added. When changes are made here, they are reflected in the
      pivot table itself on the left side of the window   61
5.6   The "Sector" column added to "Rows." All unique values found
      in that column appear on their own row in the pivot table   62
5.7   A pivot table grouping colleges based on their sector and
      showing the average student fees for each group in column B.
      The average values have been formatted as currency   64
5.8   Adding another summary column to the pivot table   66
5.9   A pivot table showing the average cost of room and board
      at different types of institutions, using the "Filter" option to
      remove schools that don't offer meal plans or housing from the
      summary   68
5.10 A crosstabulation using "Rows" and "Columns" together to
      group the data by state and sector at the same time, showing a
      count for each   69
6.1   The unique values present in a column can be seen using the
      filter menu; here, there are multiple spellings of "Park Ave."
      that may need to be fixed   71
6.2   The process for creating a cleaning column: First, add a new
      blank column next to the one you're trying to clean. Then,
      duplicate the values from the original column and give it an
      appropriate column header. Finally, target values that need to be
      standardized using filter and correct them in the cleaning column   73
6.3   Rather than having different parts of a mailing address appear
      in separate columns, this data table keeps them together,
      making it difficult to group by city or state   77
6.4   Adding blank columns to the right of Column L provides open
      space for the values impacted by "Split text to columns" so that
      you won't overwrite existing data   78
6.5   The "Separator" dropdown is how you control where Google
      Sheets creates a split in the values. Here, it's detecting the
      comma character automatically   79
6.6   The "Split text to columns" process is repeated on Column N,
      using a space character, separating state and postal zip code   80
6.7   The CONCATENATE function is combining three things
      together into one value: The first name and middle initials in
      Column B; a space character to separate the values contained
      in Columns B and A; and the last name in Column A   81

6.8   Taking different date components from the value in Column E;
      with the MID function, the extraction is beginning with the
      seventh character present in the cell and moving forward four
      characters to capture the year   83

6.9   An example of different compensation components for Boston
      Police and Fire Department employees   84

7.1   A column chart showing the monthly Consumer Price Index
      for housing costs in the Los Angeles metropolitan area through
      the end of 2021; data from the Bureau of Labor Statistics   87

7.2   A stacked bar chart showing total baseball player salaries for
      the 10 teams that spent the most on pitchers in 2021. The fall
      length of the bar represents their salary roster for the year,
      while the components of the bar divide the players into two
      overall groups: pitching positions and all others. Data from
      Major League Baseball and USA Today   88

7.3   A time series line chart showing monthly natural gas prices to
      residential consumers in New York; data from National Grid   89

7.4   An area chart showing seven decades of electricity generation
      in the U.S., split into three primary modes of creation; data
      from the Energy Information Administration   90

7.5   A scatter chart where each point represents a U.S. county in
      2010. The vertical axis, or height of the point, corresponds
      with the median household income in that county. The
      horizontal axis shows the life expectancy for men in years.
      Shown together, you can see how they're related to each other.
      Data from the U.S. Census Bureau and the Institute for Health
      Metrics and Evaluation   91

7.6   The same life expectancy data shown in geospatial form   92

7.7   Year-over-year monthly inflation data shown in two different
      ways: As a column chart and as a line chart. Data from the
      Bureau of Labor Statistics   94

7.8   A line chart using (1) a highlighted range to show the period
      during coronavirus pandemic before vaccines were widely
      available in the United States and (2) a text annotation with a
      line to describe what the audience is seeing   95

7.9   Tooltips can show more information about a data visualization.
      Life expectancy and median household income are the values
      being visualized using the scatter chart, but a pop-up for each
      point shows more specifics for each county   96

7.10 A data visualization complete with a headline, chatter, notes,
      credit, and source. Note the difference in the headline, which
      is a more literal description of the chart, and the chatter,
      which helps the viewer understand the point being made; they
      complement one another. The note here gives more detail
      about which electricity sources are considered renewable,
      something that might not be immediately apparent   99

8.1   The RStudio interface on initial startup. 1. The Console pane,
       where you can enter R code. 2. The Environment pane, where
       defined variables—like imported data sets—will appear. 3.
       This pane allows you to see your present working directory
       and navigate the filesystem on your computer, as well as access
       installed packages that extend what base R can do   106

8.2   The Packages pane, which allows you to install, update, and
       activate outside packages through the RStudio GUI   110

8.3   The imported data set, stored in the variable "example," open
       for view within RStudio   113

9.1   In a left join, the contents of the first table remain, along with
       any matching records from a second table. Only Jane, Reginald,
       and Megan from Table 1 have a matching record in Table 2.
       The entirety of Table 1 appears after the join, along with new
       columns from Table 2. Vera and Madge aren't shown because
       they don't have a match in Table 1; Dane and Robert only
       appear because they were already present in Table 1   131

9.2   The primary difference for an inner join when compared to a
       left join is that only rows that have a match will appear in the
       result. Only Jane, Reginald, and Megan appear in both tables,
       therefore they're the only records that are present in the
       resulting join   132

9.3   In a full join, all records from Table 1 and Table 2 appear,
       whether or not a match is present. In the resulting join, we see
       Dane, Robert, Vera, and Madge, along with the values that are
       present for them, even though they don't appear in both tables   133

10.1   The homepage of the Flatwater Free Press, a nonprofit
       newsroom based in Omaha, Nebraska   140

11.1   A diagram of the box model, showing where padding, the
       border, and margins are situated around content in an
       HTML element   155

11.2   A paragraph with 50 pixels of padding on all sides, creating space
       between the text content and its outside edge. Above, another
       paragraph that has no padding property defined, for comparison   157

11.3   A paragraph with 50 pixels of margin on all sides, creating
       space between its outside edge (in this case, a dashed black
       border) and its enclosing element. Above, another paragraph
       that has no specific margin property defined, for comparison   158

11.4   Top: An example of HTML rendered in full-sized web browser;
       with a width or max-width property for paragraphs and a
       headline set to 600 pixels, the text content will stop at 600
       pixels, even though more horizontal space is available. Bottom
       left: On mobile, a width of 600 pixels is wider than the screen,
       so text content will spill off to the right, forcing a user to scroll.
       Bottom right: A max-width of 600 pixels, though, means that
       the paragraphs and headline will narrow along with the screen   162

11.5   Text content inside of two div elements with different max-
       width sets. The outside div is wider at 750 pixels (colored
       gray for emphasis); the inside div is 600 pixels wide, has an
       automatic left margin and a zero-pixel right margin, right-
       justifying itself within the outside div. On a narrower mobile
       screen, the margins fall away and both divs conform to the
       available browser width   165

11.6   An example of a webpage layout using the Bootstrap grid;
       on a desktop or laptop screen, content elements are arranged
       horizontally as well as vertically. On a smaller mobile screen,
       the layout collapses to a simpler, vertical arrangement, making
       for a better scrolling experience   168

11.7   A simple two-row layout using the Bootstrap grid: By
       default, column divs (shaded gray for visibility) will share the
       available 12 columns of horizontal space equally. Where two
       are present, each will take up six columns of space; three will
       use four columns; etc.   171

11.8   Column divs can have their classes modified to conform to
       a specific width. In the top row, column divs will share the
       space equally; in the bottom row, a specific width has been set
       on each of the column divs. A class of "col-3" means that the
       column div will take up three of the 12 available columns   172

11.9   Column breakpoints set the threshold for which column divs
       will change from stacking vertically to appearing side by side.
       With a small ("sm") breakpoint set, on a screen narrower than
       576 pixels, the columns will stack; on one wider, they will
       appear next to each other   174

11.10 If column divs within a row div have been set up to take up
       more than 12 columns of space, they will wrap below   176

11.11 Top left: Below the "small" breakpoint, the column divs will
       stack. Top right: On a larger mobile device screen, like a tablet,
       that falls between the "small" and "large" breakpoints, the
       column divs will share the space equally. Bottom: On a full-size
       display, wider than the "large" breakpoint, the column divs will
       follow the instructions in the other class that's been applied,
       resizing their widths accordingly   177

Acknowledgments

Thank you to the S.I. Newhouse School of Public Communications at Syracuse University, especially my department chairs Profs. Melissa Chessher and Aileen Gallagher, who greatly encouraged me during this process.

Much credit is due to Investigative Reporters & Editors, an organization that launched me forward on the path of investigative data journalism as a student. Without their incredible community and essential resources, I don't know that I would have been able to write this book; my first steps into many of these spaces were at one of IRE's conferences or in the classroom of Prof. David Herzog at the University of Missouri.

Thanks, too, to Prof. Adam Peruta and Kevin Crowe, who kindly agreed to review portions of the book for me, and to my colleagues, Profs. Dan Pacheco and Nausheen Husain, who piloted portions of this text at Newhouse before publication.

I am forever grateful to my wife, Megan Craig, for her support and assistance throughout this entire project. Her astute editing—with a reporter's eye—made the whole text much better. She also ensured that this book even reached fruition.

Finally, this text stands on the shoulders of many journalists who were willing to share their hard-earned knowledge with others. Without that spirit of goodwill and generosity, the entire profession would falter. I am forever in their debt.

1 Introduction

Why data journalism?

* * *

The world is awash in data.

This likely comes as no surprise. We live in an era when people everywhere are connected both to and through the invisible glue of the internet. Data—some private, some not—is constantly being handed back and forth between faraway servers and digital storage centers by our personal devices as we navigate everyday life.

Nearly everyone leaves some sort of electronic trail, and this larger digital transformation has fundamentally altered how we interact with information channels, government services, and one another.

But that trail doesn't always begin with what you might immediately think of as data, which may conjure stereotypical images of bits and bytes zipping through the ether; perhaps lots of ones and zeros, long numbers, and inscrutable formulas.

Ask yourself: Is a handwritten parking ticket stuck on someone's windshield data? What about a court case? A nursing license?

Whether these items can be treated as data comes down to the form they take, which data elements or details compose them, and how it's all organized.

Let's go back to the parking ticket: The layout of the ticket itself may look different from jurisdiction to jurisdiction, but we would probably expect to find a standard set of fundamental details contained within each, like the date and time the ticket was issued; the make, model, and license plate number for the offending vehicle; the nature of the violation; and the fine amount.

These are all data points within a larger "record:" the ticket itself. Even if a parking violations employee jotted down those ticket details by hand, chances are that a copy of that ticket and its associated data points will make its way back to a central office, and someone will enter its details into a database that helps the municipality keep track of fines and issue overdue notices.

A district attorney's office may have a comparable system to hold its court case records, which can contain elements like the number of criminal charges that a defendant faces, if those charges passed through a felony review process, and the judge's final ruling on each. A nursing license could include the renewal date and the name and address of the medical facility where the licensee works.

DOI: 10.4324/9781003182238-1

These data points that we encounter daily, and in some cases that help describe our lives, can take countless forms: a credit card number, a temperature reading, a college's first-year enrollment count, a birth date, a campaign donation amount, a medical diagnosis code, a set of geographic coordinates, or a surname.

Making sense of disparate bits of data may seem like a daunting task, and entire scientific and academic disciplines are built around the analysis, interpretation, and deep understanding of data. But there's a purpose driving this careful attention to data: Its thoughtful examination can help illuminate aspects of the world around us.

That's why the use of data fits together naturally with journalism.

If the practice of journalism is intended to allow its practitioners to weave together fact, observation, expert perspective, personal experiences, and historical context into a compelling portrait of the truth, then by harnessing data, journalists can sharpen that portrait and reveal information that would otherwise be hidden away.

Fundamentally, **data journalism** is about asking questions—something every journalist is trained and expected to do—and then discovering ways to provide answers through measurable and testable means. Instead of seeking out some statistics in a report that might help drive home a point or relying solely on the research and findings of other sources, data journalists cut out the middleman. Using data journalism tools, they analyze the raw data on their own to arrive at some conclusion that helps answer a question as clearly and comprehensively as possible. Journalists can use these techniques to uncover new stories on the beat, refute conventional wisdom, and expose wrongdoing.

The process of answering those questions doesn't need to be overly complex or involve weighty mathematical formulas, either. It can be as straightforward as summarizing a data set: organizing data into groups, counting things up, and adding items together or examining some measure of central tendency, like an average.

Data journalism is this act of quantification. Boiled down, a data journalist measures something in order to answer a question and then presents the results to a news audience.

Questions themselves can be asked in numerous ways and different forms, but the ones at the heart of data journalism stories frequently revolve around:

- How much, or how often?

- Who or what is affected the most—or the least?

- How has it changed over time?

- How does it compare with other situations or places?

These may sound like questions you'd ask a person during a conversation. In reality, data analysis is not dissimilar. In fact, it's sometimes helpful to think of it as an interviewing process, much like the one a journalist would undertake with a human source for a news story.

Returning to the parking ticket example, let's say you've heard that few enforcement employees are out on the street and making the rounds to write tickets across the city after 2 p.m., even though pay-to-park hours technically run until 7 p.m.

Here we have the beginnings of a couple of reporting questions, and ones that can be verified through some simple analysis of parking ticket data: Are the fewest parking tickets issued late in the day, but before the end of traditional business hours? Do different streets or neighborhoods have peak issuance times or days during the week?

Maybe another way to ask this question: Does that data help confirm what we've been told, or is it in some way contradictory?

Answering these questions may lay the groundwork for the central premise of a news story, but the reporting work does not begin and end there. Depending on the data, the nature of the answers that come back usually addresses the "what," "where," and "when" components of news reporting much better than the "why." In this way, data journalism isn't meant to wipe away or replace other news-gathering skills. It serves to complement and enhance shoe-leather reporting rather than replace valuable techniques, like interviewing and research. The answers a journalist is able to extract from data can lead to better story ideas—in this case, by checking out a news tip from a source to see whether anecdotal evidence matches with what the data shows—but also sharper questions for further reporting. Without interviewing experts, government officials, and real people, it's very difficult to get that sense of why something is happening and how it's all playing out in the real world.

Finding data

Where do all these data points come from and how are they gathered? Data journalists frequently use federal and state open records laws, including the **U.S. Freedom of Information Act** (FOIA), to retrieve portions of the vast trove of records created and maintained by government authorities at every level. Sometimes that data is readily available to download from public websites: Cities like Chicago[1] and Boston[2] offer civic portals where any user can peruse data sets on a range of topics, including public employees' pay, reported crimes, and property tax assessments. These municipalities, as well as certain states and U.S. counties, have followed in the footsteps of federal agencies including the Social Security Administration, which began placing publications and other informational resources online in earnest during the early 1990s.[3] But these resources typically reveal only the tip of the iceberg in terms of the recorded data that various agencies, departments, and bureaus generate while interacting with the public and fulfilling their assigned missions.

Data journalists also frequently create data sets that they can then analyze themselves. In some cases, they do this to fill a void where the data set doesn't readily exist or simply isn't sufficient to answer the question at hand.

In recent years, journalists have built important databases to monitor the use of deadly force by police around the country[4] and track mass shooting events[5] because the information from official sources wasn't complete or it simply wasn't tracked in a comprehensive way.

Building data sets from scratch can also help journalists confirm results found in government records or refute the conventional wisdom on a subject. In a 2018 series, reporters working for the Philadelphia Inquirer asked School District of Philadelphia employees to help collect environmental samples inside more than a dozen schools so that they could conduct lab testing for toxins like lead, mold, and asbestos. They did all this to both independently check and supplement existing building maintenance records that the newspaper had already analyzed, providing a clearer window into a sluggish response from district administrators and the risks of classroom exposure to environmental hazards.[6]

This can also be achieved through core social science methods, like the creation and execution of surveys meant to capture trends, attitudes, and experiences that are representative of a larger population. A pioneer of this practice, Philip Meyer, a journalist and professor emeritus at the University of North Carolina at Chapel Hill, undertook this sort of research to better understand the seething discontent among members of the Black community in Detroit after multiday riots and civil unrest rocked the city in the late 1960s.[7,8] Some of the conventional wisdom at the time blamed outside agitators for unrest and violence—migrants coming into the city from the southern U.S. Meyer's survey work not only refuted those allegations but provided insight into what Detroit's Black community thought fueled the riots.

Surveys can be more qualitative in nature, too, and shine light in spaces where it's dangerous for journalists to tread. A recent example: As part of a larger story, Al Jazeera English reporters conducted a mobile telephone survey in South Sudan to gain insight into the number of citizens who reported being forced off their land, often by members of the South Sudanese military.[9]

When journalists assemble data sets themselves—organizing pieces of information to be analyzed or reviewing survey responses from a questionnaire they crafted—it's much easier to understand the data's inherent problems and limitations.

That's not always the case with data that comes from other sources. As much as solidly crafted data can offer a wellspring of answers to relevant journalistic questions, data that's weak, inconsistent, or created without much rigor can steer the reporting process in the wrong direction.

For that reason, journalists must approach data with some of the same healthy skepticism that they would have for information from a human source, with a firm understanding of why data exists, how it's normally used, and what its limitations are.

Consider this as another part of the interview process for data. Reporters seek information from people every day; the answers given not only provide the details needed for news, but can also help journalists understand the boundaries of a source's knowledge of a subject. If the data being used can't provide clear answers to the questions being asked during the analysis process, those limitations and problems can be revealing all on their own.

Working with data

To interrogate data and find these answers, journalists have borrowed data tools from other disciplines, with other purposes in mind.

For example, the foundation for the different ways to analyze data for news stories is built on the back of readily available spreadsheet software, like Microsoft Excel and Google Sheets, which can be used to count, sort, filter, group data together, and track changes over time. The programmers who first conceived of these computer applications didn't design them with the editorial side of the news industry in mind; they were an adaptable space meant for financial modeling and accounting work that garnered wide appeal in the early days of personal computing,[10] in part because that flexibility and powerful efficiency meant that they could be used for a wide range of purposes.

Journalists also saw promise in relational database software, meant to hold large amounts of information. These programs make it easier to sort, align and connect different data sets that share common data elements between them, like names, birth dates, and identification numbers.

Database applications, like Microsoft Access and MySQL, can also hold far more data than a spreadsheet would reasonably permit. Prior to 2007,[11] Microsoft Excel could only hold about 65,000 rows of data in a single spreadsheet—a figure that may sound like it accommodates plenty when thinking through much of the data encountered on a day-to-day basis.

But what if a journalist is working with a massive set of records that exceeds these limits? Encountering data like this isn't uncommon—reporters often plumb data collections that include millions of individual records.

Consider this example of government data: Over the years, reporters at different news outlets have shown how loan approval disparities affect communities of color around the nation[12,13] using the records contained within the Home Mortgage Disclosure Act data, which span millions of detailed home loan applications each year.[14] To analyze data of this size, a spreadsheet won't cut it.

These programs have also allowed journalists to create novel matches between data sets that were never originally meant to be connected with one another—again, all in the service of answering questions about the world around them. Cross-referencing names and identities has provided the foundation for many investigative stories. As an example, a newspaper in Wisconsin used this method to figure out the number of convicted felons who had been granted gun hunting licenses by the Department of Natural Resources, something that stood in direct conflict with the state's firearm ownership laws.[15]

For the most part, these database programs lack a graphical user interface, so the journalists who use them use lines of computer code to reshape, summarize, and connect data together.

These two primary tools don't make up all the ways that journalists have analyzed data with different pieces of software. Journalists have used statistical computing programs, including SAS and SPSS, to assess how data elements may be correlated with one another and grasp the uncertainty present in estimates. Geographic Information Systems help journalists meld data points with physical space, providing visual representations of data to accompany stories on elections, climate change, and the census. Other programs help reporters digitize paper records or search for frequent topics and keywords that may appear within multivolume government document dumps that run thousands of physical pages.

Representing data

Among these seemingly miraculous technical abilities, it's hard to underestimate how important the standard technologies that underlie the internet, including HTML, CSS, and JavaScript, have been to the field of data journalism.

In the past, when data analysis uncovered findings, the presentation in traditional media outlets was conventional. These newly derived statistics would wind up written into a story top or printed in static charts on a newspaper page or spoken on-air as part of a broadcast script. The stories may have fresh angles and ideas, but the final news product for the audience did not change much. News stories across these different media channels looked very much like they always had.

The internet, though, transformed what journalists could show as part of the story, offering innovative ways to represent news online in both an interactive and visual manner, freed from the constraints of set pages in printed media or precious broadcast time during primetime news.

Suddenly, it was possible to publish whole databases on news web pages for audience members to page through or search at will. For example, news organizations have put these reporting efforts online to accompany government accountability stories about high salaries and overtime pay and to share average standardized test scores across public school districts in a state or region.

A notable facet of this development: Instead of relying solely on journalists to guide them to important pieces of data, audience members were able to find the most personally relevant or interesting details on their own.

Adrian Holovaty, a journalist and developer who worked for the Lawrence Journal-World and The Washington Post,[16] created early forays into this interactive style of data journalism for news outlets and his own online projects.

One such website, the now-defunct chicagocrime.org, is a good example of how data analysis and data presentation began to fit together. Launched in 2005, Holovaty had automated the process of gathering reported crime events by Chicago Police on a weekly basis.[17] After "scraping" this data, which generally included a set of geographic coordinates or an approximate address associated with each crime, he connected it to another service that was gaining traction at the time: Google Maps. The audience could not only explore reported crimes laid out on a dynamic map online, but also view summaries by zip code and crime type.

In this way, the presentation of data became the news story; it's an entirely different way of thinking about what journalism can look like. Instead of the more traditional method of publishing a daily or weekly crime blotter in print, with short descriptions of crimes and where they occurred, the audience could track crime in their own neighborhoods by the time of day or along a route they frequent.

The same sort of interactivity has come to pervade charts and graphs online, where findings from data analysis are represented by color, position, length, and size. Today, these data visualizations are aided by the same fundamental computer code that renders and updates web pages. Instead of those charts being plotted through a manual process, journalists can use an array of programming packages and web tools that can ingest a data set and automatically visualize it in a publication-ready format.

This has played out in different ways since these early steps. The ideas behind many data-heavy web experiences in support of journalism have had to adapt to the rise of the mobile web, where screen sizes can vary, internet connectivity can be spotty, and controls may be limited by the lack of a mouse and cursor.

As news organizations field an increasing amount of their reporting to a mobile audience,[18] they have adapted data visualizations and interactive storytelling to these smaller screens, at times making the resulting news product akin to a guided visual tour of information. In 2015, the Tampa Bay Times blended these elements together into a responsive "prologue" for their investigative series "Failure Factories,"[19] which charted the fallout from Pinellas County's abandonment of school integration in the mid-2000s and how it created stark racial divides among students in the district. To open the series, a reader swipes, clicks, or taps through a set of maps and charts that show the yawning divergence for Black students and their declining test scores in reading and math.

Why data journalism?

As you can see, data journalism doesn't mean reinventing journalism completely, but rather complementing traditional skills. When data is used to answer questions and test hypotheses, it's treated much like any other journalistic source; interviewing and understanding it is just a process that largely takes place with a computer cursor or lines of code. The techniques discussed in this book should be used in conjunction with traditional reporting methods to uncover new stories on a beat, refute conventional wisdom, and expose wrongdoing by powerful interests.

By presenting large data sets in easily digestible formats, data journalism has helped create a deeper understanding of the information—offering stories and insights people can grasp in a wholly different way. This holds true not only for the audience, but for the journalist as well.

It's helpful to think about data journalism as a path, one through which you find data, understand it, analyze it, and present it in some fashion. Creating harmony among these competing steps and the ability to bridge them is of growing importance as newsrooms continue to evolve.

Among the topics this book will discuss:

- How to assess data with a critical eye to understand what it shows and where it may be lacking.

- How to use prominent software tools, including spreadsheets like Google Sheets, with their flexibility and user-friendly graphical interface, and R, with its power for data analysis.

- Ways to translate what you've found into compelling news reports without overstating what the data can show or misleading the audience.

- Understanding how modern web technologies work together, including HTML5, CSS3, as well as ways to create and publish clear data visualizations on online platforms.

In essence, the purpose behind this book is to help you better understand the necessary steps along the path of data analysis and presentation, as well as a framework for how to practice sound, ethical data journalism using many of the same tools used by professional data journalists.

* * *

Samah Assad tells human stories using data

Samah Assad is passionate about exposing systemic issues with investigations.

When Assad first started reporting in college, she covered sports. She loved it, but she also was drawn to hard news. She had the opportunity to attend a data bootcamp hosted by the nonprofit Investigative Reporters and Editors, and that's how she found investigations and data reporting.

"I realized that there were all these different story ideas that I knew that I would need to work with data to be able to tell them," Assad said. "I thought, I want to do that."

She got a job at a local TV news station that had an impressive investigations team and started trying to earn her way onto that team. And during that time, she quickly learned how important data is to telling important stories.

> It was more than just investigations and journalism, more than just doing research or uncovering something. It's like, you really need to hone and have that skill of being able to work with data so that you can find and tell these impactful stories that I wanted to tell and be a part of, and also to bring about change, Assad said.

She sees data as a door to stories she wouldn't otherwise be able to tell. Now an investigative producer for WBBM, Chicago's CBS affiliate, Assad works to expose issues in the city and beyond.

But she also makes a point never to forget what's behind the millions of datapoints she examines every year: the people she's trying to help. That allows her to humanize the data and use it to tell intimate but far-reaching stories.

Notes

1 City of Chicago. (n.d.). *City of Chicago Data Portal.* Retrieved September 25, 2020, from https://data.cityofchicago.org/.
2 City of Boston. (n.d.). *Analyze Boston.* Retrieved October 23, 2020, from http://data.boston.gov/.

3 Mahler, J., & Regan, P.M. (2002, September 1). Learning to Govern Online: Federal Agency Internet Use. *The American Review of Public Administration, 32* (3), 326–349. https://doi.org/10.1177/0275074002032003004.

4 Tate, J., Jenkins, J., Rich, S., Muyskens, J., & Fox, J. (2020, January 22). Fatal Force: Police Shootings Database. *The Washington Post.* www.washingtonpost.com/graphics/investigations/police-shootings-database/.

5 The Associated Press. (2019, December 28). US Mass Killings Hit a Record High in 2019: 'This Seems to Be the Age of Mass Shootings'. *USA Today.* www.usatoday.com/story/news/nation/2019/12/28/us-mass-shootings-killings-2019–41-record-high/2748794001/.

6 Laker, B., Ruderman, W., & Purcell, D. (2018, May 3). Danger: Learn at Your Own Risk: Many Philadelphia Schools Are Incubators for Illness, with Environmental Hazards that Endanger Students and Hinder Learning. *The Philadelphia Inquirer.* www.inquirer.com/news/inq/lead-paint-poison-children-asbestos-mold-schools-philadelphia-toxic-city-20180503.html.

7 Rosegrant, S. (n.d.). Revealing the Roots of a Riot. *Institute for Social Research.* Retrieved October 23, 2020, from isr.umich.edu/news-events/insights-newsletter/article/revealing-the-roots-of-a-riot/.

8 Meyer, P. (1967, August 20). The Non-Rioters: A Hopeful Majority. *Detroit Free Press,* 4.

9 Thompson, C., van Schie, K., & Lagu, J. (2019, September 12). Forced Out: Measuring the Scale of the Conflict in South Sudan. *Al Jazeera English.* interactive.aljazeera.com/aje/2019/south-sudan-forced-out/index.html.

10 Karaian, J. (2015, December 22). This Is the Man Who Invented the Spreadsheet. But Don't Hold That against Him. *Quartz.* qz.com/578661/dan-bricklin-invented-the-spreadsheet-but-dont-hold-that-against-him.

11 Microsoft. (n.d.). *Excel Specifications and Limits.* Microsoft Support. Retrieved October 24, 2020, from https://support.microsoft.com/en-us/office/excel-specifications-and-limits-1672b34d-7043-467e-8e27-269d656771c3.

12 Glantz, A., & Martinez, E. (2018, February 15). Modern-Day Redlining: Banks Discriminate in Lending. *Reveal.* www.revealnews.org/article/for-people-of-color-banks-are-shutting-the-door-to-homeownership/.

13 Dedman, B. (1988, May 1). Atlanta Blacks Losing in Home Loans Scramble. *The Atlanta Journal-Constitution.* https://www.ajc.com/news/atlanta-blacks-losing-home-loans-scramble/RA3uapfwkWlChDq2fHsZ2L/.

14 Consumer Financial Protection Bureau. (n.d.). *Download Historic HMDA Data.* Consumer Financial Protection Bureau. Retrieved October 24, 2020, from www.consumerfinance.gov/data-research/hmda/historic-data/.

15 Poston, B. (2007, October 31). Felons Issued Gun Hunting Licenses: Law Bars Them from Possessing Guns but Doesn't Prevent License Purchase. *Milwaukee Journal Sentinel,* A1.

16 Niles, R. (2006, June 5). The Programmer as Journalist: A Q&A with Adrian Holovaty. *Online Journalism Review.* www.ojr.org/the-programmer-as-journalist-a-qa-with-adrian-holovaty/.

17 Holovaty, A. (2008, January 31). In Memory of Chicagocrime.org. *Holovaty.com.* www.holovaty.com/writing/chicagocrime.org-tribute/.

18 Walker, M. (2020, May 30). Americans Favor Mobile Devices over Desktops and Laptops for Getting News. *Pew Research Center.* www.pewresearch.org/fact-tank/2019/11/19/americans-favor-mobile-devices-over-desktops-and-laptops-for-getting-news/.

19 Lash, N. (2015, August 12). Why Pinellas County Is the Worst Place in Florida to Be Black and Go to Public School. *Tampa Bay Times.* projects.tampabay.com/projects/2015/investigations/pinellas-failure-factories/chart-failing-black-students/.

2 Data, numeracy, and how to bulletproof information

* * *

Back in 2009, a fledgling effort by journalists at the Los Angeles Times to map and analyze local crime incident data was running into an oddity, if not a significant problem: There seemed to be an overwhelming number of crimes happening in the shadow of City Hall.[1]

The Los Angeles Police Department reported dozens of offenses, including robberies and aggravated assaults, just a block away from the building on a weekly basis. Reporters found that over a six-month span, about one in 25 crimes were connected to this seemingly unfortunate location, near the intersection of 1st and Spring streets in downtown L.A.

Reporters learned that a government contractor's mistake led to a troubling situation: When the computer system couldn't successfully match a specific incident's street address to geographic coordinates, it would default to the downtown location. The outlet notified the city of the errors and adjusted their reporting accordingly.

While data skills can empower journalists, the underlying reporting still must be done carefully. Taking abnormal findings at face value or not thoroughly vetting a data source threatens to pollute the information ecosystem with potentially misleading journalism, regardless of its creator's intent.

Verification is part of the everyday journalism process. Reporters size up sources and learn about their motivations and the experiences that shape their perspectives. And when people go on the record and state things as fact, journalists are expected to follow up with questions that uncover how these sources know something to be true. Taking a similar approach is critical when working with data.

Gaining a better understanding of your data: first steps

Asking a couple of questions early on about the data you use for reporting can stave off potential problems down the line:

- What or who is this data's source, and are they a trustworthy and reliable source for this kind of information?

- Why does this data exist and how is it used?

DOI: 10.4324/9781003182238-2

At times, the answers will be obvious, but even in the most clear-cut situations, a little research will likely be involved.

When we talk about a data source, we almost always mean the creator of the data set—the entity that determined what to record and collected it somehow. This is an important distinction, especially when looking for data to download from the internet. Because much of the data out in the world is digital, it can be easily copied or modified and then hosted in different locations throughout the internet.

Performing an online search for data on a particular topic may bring many relevant results, but some of these websites are simply third parties that traffic in data and statistics originated by others. Check their references or citations. If they didn't create the data, who did? Be especially wary when these sorts of details aren't present. When they are, follow the thread back as far as you can take it. You want as little distance as possible between you (the journalist) and the original source.

Identifying the original source for data will not only help ensure that you have some point of contact for an unadulterated copy of the data, but will offer a potential source you can question about the information. Those responsible for overseeing the data's creation and publication should have answers about the collection process and methods; they should be able to explain specific details about anything you find contained within.

Government bureaucracies and researchers generally don't create data because they're bored or looking for something to do, either. There's typically a purpose behind it. Understanding why a data set exists can help gauge whether it's reliable.

For example, the several thousand degree-granting colleges and universities that take federal funding from the government through Title IV[2] student financial aid have to share many different facts about their institutions with the U.S. Department of Education each year. If schools don't comply with these annual surveys, or report inaccurate details about their institution, which include information about student demographics and school finances, they risk fines.[3]

But schools also have something potentially larger at stake—their public profile compared to competitors. In 2018, eight schools were removed from the U.S. News and World Report's "best colleges" rankings for misreported data,[4] including inflated graduation rates. It's unlikely that any of the chief administrators for these institutions were ecstatic about being shut out from this form of marketing.

There are certainly exceptions to every rule, but journalists can have greater confidence in data where consequences exist for significant errors and inaccuracies.

It also helps to understand how the data or records are used day-to-day during regular business. Go back to the example of the city parking enforcement system: Each day, individual tickets are fed in; plates or vehicle identification numbers need to be matched against state motor vehicle records to find registered owners, reminder notices are sent, and penalties increase when they aren't paid in a timely manner. It's part of the bureaucratic machinery that discourages illegal parking and guarantees the city a stream of revenue—it's vital for that agency.

Not everything that gets collected is nearly as integral nor has such a clear purpose. Data can be created haphazardly, or because a law demands it even though it's never really used for anything meaningful. That can jeopardize its accuracy and completeness.

When reporters in Arizona tried to analyze data on the state's "Empowerment Scholarship" program, which gave vouchers for families to spend on private school tuition and other education expenses, they found it to be "opaque, incomplete and riddled with errors."[5]

A big reason for the problems: The state's education department said that parents were supposed to be submitting details about how they used those funds to the state. But officials had few mechanisms in place to ensure that the data being collected was even remotely complete, resulting in a financial blind spot for residents, journalists, and state legislators.

What is each row in my data?

A data set can be organized in myriad ways, even though you largely experience it as a row-and-column structure using spreadsheet software, laid out as a data table of information within the spreadsheet grid.

Take time to understand and discern the "unit" of each data set you use, which should correspond with an individual row or record. What each row in your data represents—and it could be a person, place, event, or some other thing entirely—impacts how you go about analyzing the data and what you are able to say about it. Any documentation linked to the data can help with this, as can the advice of expert sources or those who work with the data on a regular basis.

This sort of misunderstanding crept into a FiveThirtyEight piece in 2014 that cataloged a rising wave of violent kidnappings in Nigeria.[6] The story used an ongoing project called the Global Database of Events, Language, and Tone (GDELT) to identify abductions in that part of the world, showing an explosion of kidnappings in recent years that dwarfed the number in the 1980s and 1990s.

The problem was that the original story confused data that described media reports about kidnappings with the kidnappings themselves—GDELT is created and updated from a variety of international media sources. The distinction is important: there's the possibility that a single event could be reported multiple times, ending up in the data set more than once.[7] And over the decades, the number of media sources GDELT is able to draw from has grown considerably. A larger number of news organizations leads to more media reports.

Problems like this can be a bit more subtle, too, where rows seem to represent the same thing and appear directly comparable to one another but ultimately have differences that affect any findings.

The Voice of San Diego, a nonprofit newsroom in Southern California, analyzed personnel records and student enrollment data that showed declining student-teacher ratios across the San Diego Unified School District[8]—having fewer instructors per student is typically seen as a good thing for a community.

But the reporting overcounted the number of teachers working for the district, skewing the annual ratios to make them seem a bit better than they really were. Student–teacher ratios had moved slightly higher in years prior to publication.

The overcounting stemmed from not quite understanding what each row in the data set meant. Instead of being limited only to full-time instructors working for schools operated by the school district, it also included part-timers, as well as teachers who worked in area charter schools.

Spotting common data problems

No data is perfect—far from it. But part of the job with any data set you to work with is swiftly recognizing and diagnosing show-stopper issues that will twist or invalidate what you learn through data analysis. Some issues fall to you as the journalist to wade through with a magnifying glass, while others can only be overcome by working with the original source or creator of the information.

Data can frequently have:

- Problems with standardization

- Significant outlier values

- Blanks or zeros

- Duplicated rows/records

These problems are generally sitting in the data for you to find. While they may speak to larger underlying issues to address over the course of reporting, straightforward sorting, filtering, and grouping should be able to bring most of them to the forefront.

Data is not standardized

A standard is when the same things are described in the same way.

The beauty of creating groups around a common value within data is that it provides an easy route to classify and then summarize those items.

But the existence of groups depends on those values being identical—for the most part, a computer program is going to see stark differences where your eyes might gloss over slight variations to be able to recognize them as the same thing.

In a column of data that lists the names of different U.S. football franchises, you'd likely know that the "Los Angeles Rams" and the "LA Rams" were members of the same group; that "Walmart" and "Wal-Mart" aren't different companies; and that "Main St." and "Main Street" is a single road.

Even small differences in capitalization or additional spaces between words can create a rift where one group becomes two—or more.

	A	B	C	D	E	F
	ObjectId	property_address	property_zip	case_number	case_open_date	nature_of_complaint
1	1	1012 Wolf St	13208	L00035	2014-06-04T00:00:00.000Z	Lead Paint Violations/Health OCHD RENT STOP Unit #1 10/13/17
2	2	707 Turtle St	13208	L00130	2014-12-31T00:00:00.000Z	Lead Paint Violations/Health
3	3	2234-36 Grant Blvd	13208	L00609	2019-01-31T00:00:00.000Z	Lead Paint Inspection
4	4	200-02 Dale St & Hillside St	13208	L00518	2018-09-26T00:00:00.000Z	Lead paint Inspection/Health
5	5	2309 Grant Blvd	13208	L00015	2016-11-23T00:00:00.000Z	Lead Paint Violations/Health OCHD STOP RENT 10/24/17
6	6	2402 Lodi St	13208	L00748	2019-12-06T00:00:00.000Z	Lead Paint Inspection/Health
7	7	819 Danforth St & First North	13208	L00543	2018-10-22T00:00:00.000Z	Lead Paint Inspection/Health
8	8	807 Danforth St	13208	L00647	2019-06-05T00:00:00.000Z	Lead Paint Inspection
9	9	806 Carbon St	13208	L00225	2015-03-30T00:00:00.000Z	Lead Paint Violations/Health Unit #1 Inspected. OCHD STOP RENT 8/29/17
10	10	1004 Spring St	13208	L00693	2019-07-19T00:00:00.000Z	Lead Paint Inspection/Health
11	11	1004 Spring St	13208	L00727	2019-09-23T00:00:00.000Z	Uncorrected lead paint hazard violations/Referral to NBD Case Management for relocation
12	12	138 Lawrence St	13206	L00571	2018-12-28T00:00:00.000Z	Lead Paint Inspection/Health
13	13	1228 Park St	13208	L00752	2019-11-01T00:00:00.000Z	Lead Paint Inspection/Health
14	14	735 Alvord St N	13208	L00132	2013-01-04T00:00:00.000Z	Lead Paint Violations/Health Unit #1 Inspected. OCHD STOP RENT 8/29/17
15	15	1807 Lodi St	13208	L00184	2014-03-27T00:00:00.000Z	Lead Paint Violations/Health OCHD STOP RENT Unit 1F 10/24/17
16	16	924 State St N	13208	L00290	2017-08-31T00:00:00.000Z	Lead Paint Violation/Health
17	17	911 Townsend St N	13208	L00749	2019-11-12T00:00:00.000Z	Lead Paint Inspection/Health
18	18	412 Division St E	13208	L00773	2019-10-24T00:00:00.000Z	Lead Paint Inspection/Health
19	19	110 Pond St & Lilac St	13208	L00774	2019-12-04T00:00:00.000Z	Lead Paint Inspection/Health
20	20	113-15 Lilac St	13208	L00044	2015-01-14T00:00:00.000Z	Lead Paint Violations/Health OCHD STOP RENT 113 Lilac, 1st floor 10/13/17
21	21	402 Pond St	13208	L00630	2019-04-09T00:00:00.000Z	Lead Paint Inspection
22	22	111 Neutral Ct	13208	L00754	2019-11-25T00:00:00.000Z	Lead Paint Inspection/Health
23	23	1113 Park St To Neutral Ct	13208	L00718	2019-09-06T00:00:00.000Z	Lead Paint Inspection/Health
24	24	530 Carbon St & Herbert St	13208	L00488	2018-07-06T00:00:00.000Z	Lead Paint Inspection/Health
25	25	720-22 Pond St	13208	L00756	2019-11-22T00:00:00.000Z	Lead Paint Inspection/Health
26	26	624 Division St E	13208	L00780	2019-12-20T00:00:00.000Z	Lead Paint Inspection/Health
27	27	131 John St	13208	L00442	2018-06-06T00:00:00.000Z	Lead Paint Inspection/Health

Figure 2.1 An example of so-called "dirty data," where the "nature_of_complaint" field suffers from a lack of standardization.

Why is this problematic when analyzing data? Not having standard values means that members of a group won't be included.

This is where the concept of "cleaning" comes in, which will be explored later: Ways to modify the data to correct these issues.

Significant outliers are present

The previous example involving so many crimes happening on one Los Angeles block is an outlier—a value within the data set or findings that are so far outside of what's expected that it needs scrutiny.

It can be an error repeated within a data set multiple times—which was the case in L.A.—rising to the top of the list when journalists counted recorded crimes by street address. It can also be an extremely high or low value that just doesn't fit with the others or doesn't make sense in the given context. In a database of public salaries, you wouldn't expect an administrative assistant to make $650,000 a year, but it would be much less of a stretch for the chief of neurosurgery at a state-run hospital. What's more likely is that an extra zero was added to the value when it was being input into the personnel records system.

Don't assume one way or the other, though. Seeing an outlier like this doesn't necessarily mean the data is incorrect, but an element that sticks out deserves healthy skepticism and investigation. This is where data analysis work becomes data journalism—striving to do the reporting that resolves inconsistencies.

Outliers can enter data in a variety of ways, and they happen often, like transcription errors when converting paper copies of records to their digital counterparts.

Mystery blanks or zeros in the data

Don't ignore empty cells in a data table or places with a value of zero where you would not expect it. Assessing this missing information is an important crossroads for moving forward with analysis.

Several questions to ask when considering how to proceed: Is it blank because the value isn't known (so it wasn't entered at all)? Or is there some other overarching and readily explained the reason for it? In certain data sets, like those involving public health information, values representing too few people may be suppressed for confidentiality reasons.[9]

And what impact will the blanks have on some type of analysis? At what point will the story's audience need to be clued into the fact that a portion of the data has been excluded because of missing information?

Also, blank values are typically ignored by spreadsheet functions. For example, AVERAGE will leave the blank cells in a reference out of a calculation; if those are supposed to be the equivalent of zero instead, the result will be wrong.

There aren't hard or fast rules around a threshold for comfort to guide you— it's not as though having 10% of the values in a column turning up as blanks will always be fine for publication, while 40% should be considered dangerous or alarming.

Work with the data set's creators and other experts who regularly use the data. Even when a data set has been well-vetted and seems credible enough to use, some columns may have inconsistent or incomplete information.

Data has been duplicated erroneously

There's a chance that rows may appear more than once in a data set; the important thing in this case is figuring out whether it's occurring—and how—so you can isolate duplicates from the rest of the data so that it doesn't end up impacting the analysis. Duplicated data can take a few different forms:

- **Full duplication:** One or more rows are completely identical when that should not be the case.

  Some data may have a column devoted to unique identifiers for its rows and records—usually a string of numbers that isn't repeated. Those identifiers can have multiple purposes in a data set, but they can also help distinguish data that's been repeated that, when analyzed, could inflate results.

  Google Sheets also has the built-in ability to remove duplicate rows if they are exactly alike. In its "Data" menu, under "Data Cleanup," there's an option to "Remove duplicates." The program will look across all columns selected in the dialog box for repeated combinations of values among the data table's rows. It will tell you how many were removed and how many unique records remain; the downside is that it won't let you see the duplicated rows before their removal.

- **Mixing of levels:** Granular data, pieces of a larger whole, occupy the same table as rows that contain subtotals and totals.

  This is common with data from places like the U.S. Census—a table may have state totals or percentages in addition to the breakdown of various geographic places, like cities or counties within that state. Bundling those into summary analyses can lead to dramatic errors in results.

- **Partial duplication:** Certain rows are unusually similar to one another and may represent the same information captured more than once.

  This one can be trickier to figure out. Say there's a police database that shows more than one reported crime happening at the same date, time, and street address. This may be a clue that single events are getting repeated somehow.

  It could be some type of easily explained issue: Perhaps if an exact time wasn't captured in the system, it defaults to 12:00 a.m., so there are multiple instances where crimes appear to happen simultaneously even though they were separated by hours. Or it could have something to do with the data's structure, where if more than one type of criminal statute was violated during a single event, they appear on separate rows, which may require a rethinking of what each row in the data table represents.

Problems with the data universe

When buying a car, it's easy enough to spot mismatched paint or a giant hole in an exterior panel. Those problems can be identified and addressed more directly.

What's harder is when the car looks complete inside and out—and all seems well—but there's a major design flaw hidden inside that only reveals itself later, if at all, and makes the vehicle unsafe to drive.

That's one way to think about issues with your data's "universe," where decisions that were made behind the scenes about the design and collection of data aren't readily apparent. Records could be missing from the data, or the standards of collection may have evolved over time; it's easier to find flaws with what's in front of you than figure out which rows never even made it to the data table.

The case of the missing data

If records are missing from a data set that should be there, how can you go about figuring that out?

First, confirm an understanding of what each row in the data represents—it's always possible that that data represents a subset of a larger group.

Find an outside benchmark when possible. Facts backed by hard data are frequently discussed in the aggregate in news media and press releases, i.e., "budgeted expenditures were $121 million," "inspectors visited 1,200 eateries," "7,000 motorists were stopped by county police," "890 people are licensed chiropractors." If what you're finding in the data doesn't approximate some of these overarching figures for the same time frame, there has to be a reason for it.

The Chicago Police Department's crime data almost always contains fewer homicides than comparable stats from the Cook County Medical Examiner because it excludes cases that the other entity counts.[10] For example, even if a murder's location is inside Chicago's city limits, those that take place on one of the city's expressways are considered the jurisdiction of the Illinois State Police, so those crimes are not included.[11]

Collection standards have changed

In 2014, Chicago officials touted the efficacy of their automated ticketing program, saying it cut the overall number of dangerous traffic collisions roughly in half from 2005 to 2012.[12]

But about five years prior, the whole state experienced an abrupt drop in motor vehicle crashes, per data maintained by the Illinois Department of Transportation. If all parties were insured, any crash that resulted in less than $1,500 in property damage did not need to be reported to the state anymore, a sizable increase over the old $500 threshold.[13]

The fender-benders resulting in $500–$1,500 in damage were still happening, but they were no longer being collected (or reported) by state authorities.

When data collection standards change, it can create a situation where accurate comparisons over time are difficult, if not impossible. The real differences are washed out, overwhelmed by missing data.

The policy shifts and internal decision-making that shape data are not always obvious or explicitly stated. Be on the lookout for a different kind of an outlier in the data: an abrupt shift over time that defies existing trends.

Understanding your data: an early checklist

Approaching a new data set with a process is helpful; it's a bit like an opening move in a chess game that can then adapt based on what you find. It can help familiarize you with a data set and push you to confront any oddities. Plus, for a larger data set that extends far beyond the range of a device screen, scrolling through pages won't be especially useful.

1   **What does each row in the data set represent?** And be as specific as possible, which may mean consulting documentation or reaching out to expert sources.

2   **Do the column headers describe the values that appear below them in the column?** For example, for a column header like "age," the expectation would be whole numbers, likely falling somewhere between 0 and 120.

3   **In each column:**

a   **What are the largest and smallest values present (or the first and last, alphabetically)?** This is a way to highlight unexpected values, like punctuation at the beginning of a cell value or text mixed with numbers.

b   **Which values occur the most and least frequently?** If missing values dominate the column, there might be a problem.

c   **For non-numeric columns, how many different unique or distinct values are present? What are they?** Looking at these in alphabetical order can reveal standardization issues to correct, like the same city name spelled in various ways.

Three ways to talk about your data

It's probably becoming clear that gaining a solid understanding of your data can be a laborious process at times that rewards attention to detail and a lot of questions. But at the end of it all, you need to be able to turn around and tell people what you've learned concisely.

Use approximations when possible

Stories and scripts are loaded with terms like "about," "roughly," "almost." It's a recognition that the actual number or statistic is more precise than the audience is being told, but the level of exactness is not important—at least, not important enough for them to be bothered with. They can fully understand the reporting's premise without a long string of digits.

Studies have shown that people take longer to process numbers that aren't round—like the difference between 50 and 52.433—forcing them to make these sorts of approximations anyway.[14,15]

In journalism, it's rare that a story needs a level of precision beyond a tenth (0.1) unless comparing two figures with a very minute yet significant difference.

To help your audience understand prevalence and proportion, lean on approximations.

Instead of saying that something happened "41,311 times," find a balance for approximating or rounding the figure: "about 41,300," "about 41,000," or "more than 40,000 times" would all be acceptable.

Absolute vs. relative

Giving people enough context is frequently about offering comparisons; with raw or absolute numbers, a point of reference can be challenging.

If data analysis shows that about 14,000 people a week were diagnosed with COVID-19, is that value large or small? An important point of comparison becomes how it compares relative to the whole. If it happened in Denver, a city of more than 700,000 people, that's about 2% of the entire population. But if it happened in Grand Junction, Colorado, it would represent more than 20% of residents—a huge difference.

Some common ways to express how something relates to the whole:

- Percentages, which express values as a rate per 100. For Denver, it would be the number of coronavirus cases divided by the total number of residents.

  14,000 / 715,522 = 0.0196, or about 2%.

- A unit fraction, which would turn a relative figure like "10%" into "1 in 10." Dividing one (1) by a percentage expressed as a decimal gives the denominator.

  1 / 0.0196 = 51.02, or 1 in 51 (which could also be expressed as about 1 in 50).

- As a rate per a figure larger than 100, like 10,000 or 100,000. This is useful for relative figures that would be too small to work well as a percentage. If there were only 100 COVID-19 cases in Denver, it would represent 0.01% of the population. It makes more sense to expand the base.

  100 / 715,522 = 0.00014

  0.00014 × 100,000 = 14 per 100,000 people

The power of thresholds

You should always make clear to your reader that some records could be missing from a data set. Data can inadvertently exclude things, so it's helpful to use the words "at least" to describe a finding that comes from a data set with potential holes.

As an example, a New York Times story found that police officers had shot and killed *at least* 2,100 people in U.S. cities over a five-year span, using a data set created by journalists at the Washington Post.[16]

Adding "at least" acknowledges that there may have been more fatal shootings that happened over this period, but it's possible that those events weren't able to be properly identified and added to the full data. Thus, we have records that total up to about 2,100, and we know there were at least this many—the figure could not be smaller.

Notes

1 Welsh, B., & Smith, D. (2009, April 5). Highest Crime Rate in L.A.? No, Just an LAPD Map Glitch. *Los Angeles Times*. https://www.latimes.com/local/la-me-geocoding-errors5–2009apr05-story.html.

2 U.S. Department of Education National Center for Education Statistics. (2021–2022). *IPEDS Data Collection System*. IPEDS. https://surveys.nces.ed.gov/ipeds/public/participation-in-the-surveys.

3 U.S. Department of Education National Center for Education Statistics. (2012–2013). *IPEDS New Keyholder Handbook*. IPEDS. https://surveys.nces.ed.gov/ipeds2k12_13/downloads/New_Keyholder_Handbook_2012_all.pdf.

4 Morse, R., Mason, M., & Brooks, E. (2018, August 22). Updates to 8 Schools' 2018 Best Colleges Rankings Data. *U.S. News & World Report*. https://www.usnews.com/education/blogs/college-rankings-blog/articles/2018-08-22/updates-to-8-schools-2018-best-colleges-rankings-data.

5 O'Dell, R., & Wingett Sanchez, Y. (2017, April 8). Why Arizona Officials Don't Know Which Private Schools Benefit from Expanding Voucher Program. *The Arizona Republic*. https://www.azcentral.com/story/news/politics/arizona-education/2017/04/08/arizona-voucher-expansion-private-schools/100147404/.

6 Chalabi, M. (2014, May 13). Mapping Kidnappings in Nigeria (Updated). *FiveThirtyEight*. https://fivethirtyeight.com/features/mapping-kidnappings-in-nigeria/.

7 Chalabi, M. (2014, May 6). Kidnapping of Girls in Nigeria Is Part of a Worsening Problem (Updated). *FiveThirtyEight*. https://fivethirtyeight.com/features/nigeria-kidnapping/.

8 Kyle, K. (2012, August 1). Teachers Story Contained Major Errors: Fact Check. *Voice of San Diego*. https://www.voiceofsandiego.org/topics/education/teachers-story-contained-major-errors-fact-check/.

9 Centers for Disease Control and Prevention. (n.d.) *FAQs – Frequently Asked Questions*. CDC Wonder. Retrieved October 24, 2021, from https://wonder.cdc.gov/wonder/help/faq.html.

10 Mitchell, C. (2021, December 16). Chicago Has Exceeded 800 Homicides in 2021. *WBEZ Chicago*. https://www.wbez.org/stories/chicago-has-exceeded-800-homicides-in-2021/f5518836-b3a2-490f-8cf3-ca503b6640ba

11 Bernstein, D., & Isackson, N. (2015, May 11). New Tricks: One Year after We Reported that the Chicago Police Department Was Undercounting the City's Murders, the Problem Persists – and Top Brass Are Up to Some. *Chicago Magazine*. https://www.chicagomag.com/Chicago-Magazine/June-2015/Chicago-crime-stats/.

12 Kidwell, D., & Richards, A. (2014, December 19). Tribune Study: Chicago Red Light Cameras Provide Few Safety Benefits. *Chicago Tribune*. https://www.chicagotribune.com/suburbs/lake-county-news-sun/ct-red-light-camera-safety-met-20141219-story.html.

13 Illinois Department of Public Health. (n.d.). *Traffic Crash Report Database*. EMS Data Reporting System. Retrieved October 24, 2021, from http://www.idph.state.il.us/ems-rpt/crash.asp.

14 Jain, G., Gaeth, G.J., Nayakankuppam, D., & Levin, I.P. (2020, July 1). Revisiting Attribute Framing: The Impact of Number Roundedness on Framing. *Organizational Behavior and Human Decision Processes, 161*, 109–119. https://doi.org/10.1016/j.obhdp.2020.04.006.

15 D'Agostino, S. (2020, November 7). Why Researchers Are 100 Percent Sure We Love Round Numbers. *The Washington Post*. https://www.washingtonpost.com/science/humans-love-round-numbers/2020/11/06/c1d29b38-08ac-11eb-859b-f9c27abe638d_story.html.

16 Santo, A., & Dunlop, R.G. (2021, August 13). Where Police Killings Often Meet With Silence: Rural America. *The New York Times*. https://www.nytimes.com/2021/08/13/us/police-shootings-rural.html.

3 Where data comes from—and how to get it

* * *

It's a significant act of faith when parents send their children to school; there's a blanket assumption of safety, and that everyone working there has been thoroughly vetted. They don't expect their child to wind up in a classroom with a teacher who has a history of serious misconduct, including the physical and sexual abuse of students.

But that's precisely what had been happening in some U.S. schools. Journalists found that thousands of educators had slipped through cracks in the computerized systems meant to stop them from being able to move on to new school districts in other states. Teachers were returning to the classroom after discipline or being stripped of their teaching credentials altogether.[1]

The reporters working on this story would not have been able to figure out the scale of the problem or the risk to families nationwide without open records laws and the government transparency they are designed to create.

By sending public information requests to state education departments, reporters were able to obtain copies of internal databases for licensed teachers and disciplinary actions. In comparing them, they were then able to see where certain teachers reappeared in another state's data set with a new teaching license.[2]

Since the world is teeming with data and information, an important skill to develop is being able to find and ask for the data you need to tell a story. But the larger question becomes: What's out there? And how do I get it?

No one expects you to amass some encyclopedic knowledge that details where every sort of data set is kept and by whom. Like many aspects of journalism, you can travel a long way toward your ultimate goal of getting data by following a process; the series of steps starts with that all-important question, followed by a bit of detective work on where that information is most likely to be kept, before making a formal and targeted request for data.

And when we talk about finding data, much of the emphasis is on what journalists can get from the public sector—government agencies, offices, bureaus, and departments with different roles and responsibilities, financed with tax dollars. These entities make up the public trust, and having the ability to examine their activities is important in government oversight.

DOI: 10.4324/9781003182238-3

Your county's office for aging services, your state's election division, the Center for Medicare & Medicaid Services, the local police department—these groups sit upon a trove of information that helps them fulfill their duties, and it forms a foundation of information and organizational systems that keeps civilization humming along (albeit imperfectly). Journalists frequently use these records to examine the wheels of bureaucracy as they turn.

Parking tickets need to be paid, so there are records systems in place to track scofflaws and issue fine reminders by mail. City restaurant inspectors issue safety demerits and health grades, making sure to return to check whether deficiencies have been corrected. U.S. Citizenship and Immigration Services monitors asylum seekers who've been granted temporary protected status. Hospitals may have to report administrative data, like what they charge for inpatient care, to state regulators. Government employees are issued paychecks and collect benefits. Students in K-12 classrooms take standardized tests, and those results are reported to district offices, sometimes to be used as measures of teacher effectiveness.

And journalists, along with all other residents, have a legal right to inspect or obtain copies of these public records—with some limits—based on state and federal laws.

Routes to public data

When journalists obtain full public data sets—so not something they've collected themselves from disparate sources or tracked on their own to analyze—it typically comes from one of three places:

1   **In response to a formal open records request.** Since the late 20th century, all 50 states have had laws in place that control the availability of records generated in the course of conducting public business (which accounts for much of what they do), and a similar law that applies to the federal government has existed since 1960.[3]

2   **From a government or civic data "portal" online.** In recent years, an "open data" movement has helped spur U.S. cities, counties, and states, as well as the federal government, to make downloadable versions of data available to whoever is interested.[4] In some places, like New York City, making information available this way is governed by local law.[5] These websites can offer a central access point for a variety of data sets created by many different departments or offices under the same jurisdiction—a state data portal could contain data from the state's department of motor vehicles or environmental protection division. But data available from these online systems really only represent the tip of the iceberg in terms of what public records exist.

3   **From a website operated by specific government agencies or public research institutions.** Some agencies disseminate data and records directly from their own websites. At the federal level, there may even be divisions

and bureaus tailored specifically for this purpose. For example, the Bureau of Labor Statistics, which is part of the U.S. Department of Labor: they exist to make detailed data on employment, wages, and related topics available to lawmakers and the public.[6]

Open records in action

New Jersey police departments have been required to document the use of force among their police officers since the early 2000s; this was done with the intention that officials would use the information to root out officers who wield force too frequently or in troubling ways. But without a centralized system in place to monitor and track these reports, the information remained fragmented and little used.

In 2018, journalists at New Jersey Advance Media set out to understand how regularly individual sworn law enforcement officers across the state used force— any force—in the line of duty and whether police departments were properly scrutinizing the work histories and backgrounds of the officers they hire.[7]

To fill this void in public understanding, the journalists filed separate open records requests for the use of force forms from hundreds of different municipal police departments in New Jersey, including the state police.

They found that only 10% of officers were responsible for nearly 40% of force instances across all the departments examined, and that force was used disproportionately against people of color.[8]

This series is just one example of data journalism that relies on freedom of information laws—without them, none of these questions would have been properly answerable, and the impact of the reporting would have been limited.

To make all of this happen, the journalists involved had to do three big things:

1   They had done enough pre-reporting to know that these mandatory use of force forms existed, and that a recent New Jersey Supreme Court decision meant that the records' contents were available to the public in a largely unredacted manner (meaning that certain important details on the form, like the officer's name, weren't blanked out or removed before disclosure).

2   They knew how to ask for copies of these forms from police departments in a systematic and formal way, using the New Jersey Open Public Records Act (OPRA) to produce a response under the law.

3   They knew how to turn information from paper forms into an organized, usable data set.

As a journalist, finding your way through the wilderness to accomplish these major steps won't always fall to you—at times, the data you need will already be online or readily accessible in some form or requested frequently enough by members of the public that mechanisms exist to ask for the data and get a prompt reply.

Record retention schedules: a guide to what governments keep

The public sector can start to feel like a maze of opaque interlocking systems, tracking internal and external information, old paper records mixed with fresher, digital data. Life would certainly be easier for journalists if there were some sort of list available that cut through the noise, giving you a sense of what these agencies actually keep.

This is where **records retention schedules** can come in handy.

Governments don't have infinite space to store all the information they produce while going about their business. Even as the cost of digital storage space has dropped to mere pennies per gigabyte—and will undoubtedly continue to decrease in the future—there must be limits on what governments are required to archive from the past once it's no longer considered relevant.

These schedules serve as guidelines for how long governments should store different types of information, and they can be incredibly valuable to reporters trying to gain a deeper understanding and a better sense of the possibilities for news coverage.

Quite simply, these schedules are about the closest thing that exists to that list, menu, or map—an outline that shows what records agencies keep, what they're called and how far back in time they go.

There are two types you're most likely to encounter: **General schedules** are frequently produced by a state archivist agency in concert with state and local governments to help them determine how long they need to keep records before disposing of them. They provide a high-level view of the types of documents and data that are usually generated by different departments and offices as they operate and provide services to residents.

Agencies themselves may also keep **specific schedules** of their own that give a more complete accounting of everything they have, including the edge-case records that are unique to that particular office or department and would not make sense to include as part of a general records retention schedule.

For example, nearly all law enforcement agencies have systems in place to track arrests—even if they're just written by an officer on a standard paper form and stored in a filing cabinet. So, it makes sense that records of this nature would be captured on a general schedule, with all police departments in agreement about standards when it comes to how long they keep that kind of information before destroying it. (In New York state, the guidance is to retain criminal arrest and incident logs permanently.)

But the Chicago Police Department has two different official records described in their forms retention schedule that are specifically for police ride-along approvals: one for city employees, and another document for everyone else. This is an example of highly specific records—unique to an agency—that would not exist for police downstate in a place like Peoria or Champaign, Illinois. Now, a description of how to handle records related to police ride-along programs for different law enforcement agencies could appear in a general schedule, and police in other jurisdictions may have their own internal documents for ride-along approvals. But

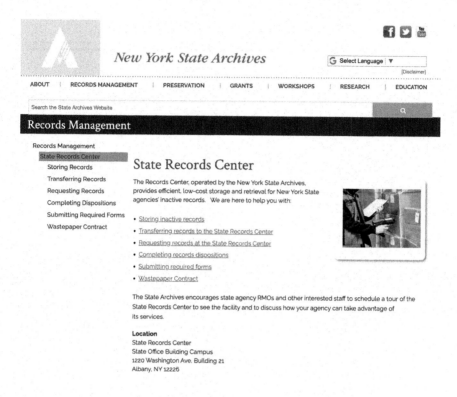

Figure 3.1 A screen capture of the New York State Archives website.[9]

an agency-specific schedule will give you an added level of precision and insight when requesting copies of data or documents.

If you're wondering where to start viewing general records retention schedules, the Brechner Center for Freedom of Information at the University of Florida keeps an online repository of state websites for the entity responsible for records retention (https://brechner.org/records-retention-schedules-by-state/), as does the Council of State Archivists (https://www.statearchivists.org/about/state-archives/state-archives-directory?Execute=1). Specific schedules may be posted online, or they can be formally requested through the normal open records process.

While these schedules describe hundreds of different types of records used, it's important to remember that the limits of open records laws still apply. Not everything you see listed in a records retention schedule is obtainable; some will be covered by exemptions written into the laws governing public information. You can certainly ask for it, but it doesn't mean that the agency has to fork it over. The specific reasons for something to be held back or redacted vary from place to place, but the records you want could contain highly personal or sensitive

FORMS RETENTION SCHEDULE - Alphabetical Listing

Form Title / Record	Form No.	Retention	Rev. Date	Item No.	Online
"Hot Spot" Designation Application	21.372	Pending	9/17		Y
A Communication Guide for Police Officers	51.100	Not Applicable	5/06		N
A/V Repair Request	32.706	2 years	1/01	79.37	N
Acknowledgement of Loss of Exemption Upon Termination	63.114	Pending	9/04		N
Acting in a Higher Rated Position (Civilian)	11.646	2 1/2 years	4/02	11.66	Y
Active Criminal Warrants	DPOL 9258	Until superseded		97.67	N
Additional Witness Information-Personal Service Citation	22.114	None	2/03		Y
Administrative Alcohol/Drug Influence Report	44.130	Pending	8/16		Y
Administrative Citation Control Sheet	11.495	6 months	11/01	11.113	Y
Administrative Message	11.490	orig. 1 year	2/18	78.34	Y
Administrative Notice of Ordinance Violation (ANOV)	11.497	3 years	1/06	11.98	N
Administrative Notice of Ordinance Violation Hearing Date/Hearing Time Change(s)	11.566	Pending	7/12		Y
Administrative Proceeding Rights/Notification of Charges/Allegations	44.105	File (C.R.) File (Drug Test)	8/16	10.4	Y
Affidavit of Employment	31.563	W./Gun Registration.	10/13	97.56	Y
AFIS Documentation Worksheet	31.858	Pending	3/15		Y
Alcohol/Drug Influence Report	22.118	10 years	12/14	28.18	N
Alternate Response Call Screening Volume	32.524	6 months	7/97	78.31	Y
Ammunition Report	63.340	Until no longer useful	1/08	60.15	Y
Animal Inventory (pink)	ACC-3230-34	30 days		11.72	N
Announcements For The Daily Bulletin	11.464	5 years	1/14		Y
Annual Furlough Application - Exempt Personnel	11.610	Until return from furlough	11/11	39.12	Y
Annual Lockup Inspection Summary Report	21.976	Pending	9/19		Y
Applicant Fingerprint Card	62.168	File (Pers. Jacket)	2/17	74.96	N
Application for a Limited Duty Assignment	62.473	Pending	9/15		Y
Application for Appointment of Special Police	62.252	2 years after termination of employment/5 years after revocation or denial	7/14	74.20	N
Application for Authority to Dispose of Local Records	31.408	Permanent	2/04	97.17	Y
Application for District Advisory Committee and Subcommittee Membership/Officer positions, Beat Faci	21.707	Pending	1/10		Y
Application for Police Certificate	31.420	6 periods	10/15	100.34	Y

Figure 3.2 A screen capture of the Chicago Police Department's online records retention schedule.[10]

information that would violate the privacy of an individual if disclosed, business trade secrets that private companies are only required to share with government regulators, or something else that may be prohibited from release because of another law entirely.

Writing an official request

Once you know what kinds of records are kept and how they're kept by a specific agency, you're ready to file a request. Over time, reporters who file open records requests usually hone their template for a formal letter. When asking for public information, you don't have to start from scratch each time, and several prominent online services have request letter generators online—some state agencies that deal with public records, like Iowa,[11] even offer fill-in-the-blank letters for people who want to request information.

But here are seven elements to consider; some of these will need to be changed for each request depending on the nature of the information you're seeking or where you're trying to get it from, while others can remain the same every time.

Where and to whom am I sending this request?

At this point, you've done the requisite pre-reporting to understand which segment of government keeps the data you seek. Some states have created online directories of public records contacts for each individual agency, including their name and contact information.[12]

Who's responsible for responding to these kinds of requests? It's not always the same type of employee. At the federal level, the U.S. government employs thousands of full-time workers who handle federal FOIA requests,[13] while for state and local agencies, a number of people can fill that role other than those who strictly deal with open records, like legal counsel or the head of a department.

Do your best to figure out who, specifically, is responsible for processing requests. If it's not online, call the agency to find out. The reasons here are two-fold: Ideally, they're going to have a dedicated email address for request letters so that you can send a digital copy. Making a guess here could leave your request in an inbox that never gets checked, with no hope of getting a response. And it also helps to know who to directly address the content of your letter to, though it's certainly not a requirement.

Which open records law am I using for this request?

Every state has its own law to govern the release of public records, and it's best to cite your legal right to the information upfront and outright, along with a reference to the specific statute or code. Do the same with a federal FOIA request.

For example, in New Jersey, public records are governed by OPRA: the Open Public Records Act, which is recorded in a specific part of the state's statutes: *N.J.S.A. 47:1A-1, et seq.* Missouri calls theirs the "Sunshine Law,"[14] while in New York, it's known as FOIL, which stands for Freedom of Information Law.[15]

In practice, a formal request letter should open with a sentence like this: *Pursuant to the New York Freedom of Information Law (N.Y. Pub. Off. Law, § 84–90), I would like to request the following records.*

What records do I want?

This is where you should focus most of your energy and attention. Being able to describe the records you want as precisely as possible is key; it helps to be able to call a record by the same name they use internally. While online research is great, don't be afraid to ask officials and other department employees about the forms, databases, and other systems they use to track different aspects of their work.

Let's say you're working on a story about residential construction in your community and ask the city for their "buildings data." This big problem here is, if you ask for something in a vague way or without sufficient detail, the onus is then on the agency or department to try and interpret your request. In reality, they probably won't spend much time deciphering it—the letter will be denied on the grounds that it's overly broad, producing too many responsive records to be possible, or that it's not specific enough for them to be able to find anything that matches at all.

So be sure to research what you want. In this case, it might be a digital copy of building permit issuance data, which contains details from the original application, the dates that the city inspected the building site, and other information from the final occupancy certificate. This sort of data could not only allow you to see where new home-building projects are springing up locally, but which construction companies have had delays or problems along the way.

In this section of the letter, make sure you're answering these questions sufficiently:

- What are the records called?

- What important details should they contain?

- How far back in time should the data go?

What format do I want it in?

Without a doubt, you want to get copies of data in a digital format that can be easily ingested by spreadsheet software or some other analysis tool. Ask for the data in a common electronic format—most, if not all, database systems used by the public sector can export copies of raw data tables as Microsoft Excel files or character-delimited text files like CSVs, which will be discussed in more detail in the next chapter.

It's also worth specifying here how you want that information delivered, though you may not have much control over this part. Some agencies insist on fulfilling open records requests by saving the responsive data or documents to physical media, like a disc, and then sending it through the mail. Others will be receptive to emailing copies of the data or making it available for download through cloud-based online storage or other means.

An element that can be tricky to navigate is a common digital export not conducive to data analysis—Portable Document Format (PDF) files. These files are intended to preserve the way content is laid out on a virtual page, divorcing a document's presentation from specific hardware or software needs. These are great for printing, but they can also be a serious stumbling block for data journalists. Ultimately, if data arrives in PDF form, it will have to be unlocked for use in some way, which can be an extremely onerous and time-consuming process as you try to convert structure and spacing meant for a printed page into a data file.

A paragraph like this will make your interests clear: *Please provide all the requested information in a common electronic format, such as a Microsoft Excel spreadsheet or a plain text file of comma-separated values. I would also prefer to have the completed request sent to me electronically by email or similar means.*

If the agency can charge money for the data, how should they proceed?

Governments may be allowed to recoup their costs for the time and resources that they expend producing responsive data and documents. This can include charges for copying the data to discs, redacting information considered exempt from disclosure under the law, and specialized programming to export a subset of a larger data set.

It can help to set a reasonable cost limit right off the bat. If the agency determines that it will be more expensive than your threshold, ask them to confirm with you first before proceeding.

It's also important to remember that you're asking for this data as a journalist for the purpose of newsgathering; while many news organizations are owned and operated by for-profit companies, their editorial mission is to inform the public. What you're doing with the data should not be equated with typical commercial endeavors, where a company may be trying to use public information for something like making targeted business decisions. Because you're working in the public's interest, you can request a waiver of fees. It doesn't mean that the department or agency will oblige that request, but you'll never know if you don't ask.

Unfortunately, sky-high cost estimates on the part of public entities can have a chilling effect, effectively blocking requesters from accessing information. When a Massachusetts attorney asked for Breathalyzer data from the Massachusetts State Police in 2012, the agency quoted a price of $2.7 million,[16] insisting on basing the cost of the work on manually copying millions of pages of test results and tens of thousands of hours redacting personal information from documents. The same attorney had managed to get similar data files from other states for free.

This sort of price tag is an extreme outlier, but an agency may quote you fees of hundreds or thousands of dollars to produce responsive records. If that happens, ask them for an itemized breakdown that shows how they've estimated the charges.

A paragraph like this should suffice: *I ask that you waive any applicable fees; this information is for newsgathering purposes. If you are entitled to charge fees, please confirm them with me before you fulfill this request.*

What should the agency do if some or all of the information is exempt from disclosure?

For one thing, you don't want them to deny the request in full because certain sections of the data may need to be deleted. Be clear about your expectations for their formal response, including what information should be shared with you about a decision to withhold copies of the records.

At a minimum, the agency needs to be able to explain which exemptions apply and the legal reasoning behind why they should apply for this particular data set.

Because you're asking for electronic records in the form of data, exempt information should be easy to segregate from nonexempt information. Redaction should be a relatively painless process for the agency, often as simple as not selecting a column of data before exporting or deleting it from a data table before sending it along to you.

A sample paragraph: *If my request is denied in whole or part, please justify all deletions with references to specific exemptions of the law, including an explanation of why the exemption is applicable. If your agency believes that certain parts of this request are legally exempt, please furnish the elements that are not exempt.*

How can they contact me with questions or for clarifications?

It's important to give the agency several ways to reach you, as well as a mailing address where they can send correspondence or a physical copy of any responsive records—some will insist on it. Close your letter by thanking them for reviewing your request, along with your telephone number, email address, and a mailing address (if it wasn't included at the top of the letter or within letterhead, if applicable).

Non-public data

This is not to say, however, that all data worth using is publicly available. Many types of commercial data also exist, appearing online in droves and being used for myriad purposes, including marketing and business intelligence.

But data created by private companies may have preset conditions on its use that journalists are forced to abide by because it's the company's intellectual property, and it may cost money to get a hold of or republish in some way. The data itself could also exist specifically to promote a particular brand, company, or product in such a way that it compromises journalistic independence.

While reporters need to remain vigilant when using any kind of information in their stories, it's especially important to consider the source and purpose of commercial data.

Take something like professional sports statistics, for instance. Depending on what you're interested in knowing about players, teams, or individual games, this kind of data can be found in numerous locations online: It's collected by different news outlets, the leagues themselves, or through private companies that offer them for sale to groups like sports betting and fantasy leagues. While each set of data—like the current National Football League player roster—may exist in varying levels of completeness or may contain different details depending on the source, all are likely to mirror one another to an extent and have a considerable amount of overlap. There are few questions about how it's generated under the watchful eyes of fans or whether it's accurate; that Patrick Mahomes of the Kansas City Chiefs had 4,740 passing yards during the 2020 season is not in dispute.[17]

But heightened scrutiny is necessary when data comes from a "black box" situation, where the source and methods are murkier. Reporters should constantly be asking about the process through which the records were created and the methods used to produce them. When a commercial trade group releases a set of statistics or data for use, it's important to get a sense of how reliable the information is and how the organization went about achieving those findings. Just because the data exists and is available doesn't automatically make it accurate or mean that you should lend it credibility by using it as part of a story.

Sticking to what's "gettable"

It's also important to ground your data journalism process in the records or information that actually exist and are accessible to you, or that you could reasonably assemble on your own or with a team of other people.

In terms of accessibility, certain types of information are exempt from disclosure under open records laws. While the specifics can and will be different, here are some examples of items that may be denied:

- Sensitive personal identifiers, like social security numbers, or personal information that could be considered an invasion of privacy to produce.

- Data or documents about an active or ongoing law enforcement investigation.

- Information on the negotiation process between governments and other entities, including collective bargaining with public-sector unions and contracts with private companies.

- Trade secrets or proprietary financial information that businesses have to disclose to regulators in order to operate.

The Reporters Committee for Freedom of Press (RCFP) maintains an "open government" guide for freedom of information laws in each state (https://www.rcfp. org/open-government-guide/) which typically discuss not only specific exemptions, but the legal precedent for different types of data being available to the public.

It can also be a helpful resource for understanding the local availability of common types of records, including those kept by law enforcement, public utilities, state colleges and universities, and emergency dispatch, among others.

In other situations, the data you want may not be accessible because it doesn't exist at all. For example, let's say you've recently spoken with a couple of local LGBTQ business owners, and you want to know how many members of that community own and operate establishments, as well as whether those numbers have expanded in recent years. While you may be able to find a coalition of these business owners, perhaps, who keep tabs on their membership, there's not some master register of U.S. citizens available that contains their sexual preference or gender identity—for very good reason. That demographic information isn't collected as part of a census questionnaire, on licensing forms or through federally backed small business loan applications, either. So how many of these businesses are there? It could be quite difficult to put hard numbers to it with confidence without doing a tremendous amount of legwork to collect your own data.

Similarly, it can be quite resource-intensive for journalists to capture people's attitudes, feelings, and behaviors in a quantitative way, even though in many cases it would be useful data for reporting.

This is not to say that it does not happen, but it can be a challenging endeavor for even a group of journalists to undertake. In the earlier Al Jazeera example about conflict and displacement in South Sudan, journalists enlisted the help of a private company to randomly call over 35,000 mobile numbers, ultimately capturing complete survey answers from several hundred people. The survey itself was created with the help of experts and translated into six languages.[18]

To get a representative sample—a quality group of survey respondents whose answers to different questions can be generalized to a larger population, like a state or country—can cost thousands of dollars; Pew Research Center, for example, spends millions each year[19] on research related to national public opinion. For various reasons, experts and scholars don't always make the raw data from their research available. Political polling partnerships that involve news organizations are expensive and utilize specialized personnel.

Recognizing and returning to this data with reasonable expectations for what's realistically knowable (or gettable)—because it's been accurately recorded in some fashion and you have access to it—will help refine your reporting ideas and keep you from spinning your wheels. It can also potentially spur creativity in your use of data. Sometimes there's more than one way to get an answer to a question.

* * *

Ron Nixon uses public records, data to find answers

Ron Nixon is the global investigations editor for the Associated Press. He stumbled into journalism by accident – a music major who used the military to help fund his education, he didn't have any idea he'd eventually use data to tell stories. At the AP, Nixon encourages his reporters to use data so they can identify patterns they wouldn't necessarily otherwise see in the documents.

But don't call him a data journalist.

"I hate the term data journalism ... It's just journalism," Nixon said. "Once you get people beyond the idea that you're doing some high-level calculation, then I think they are more relaxed and we can just incorporate it into what they do already."

One of Nixon's first leaps into investigative journalism came after a woman at a public meeting introduced him to open records and the Freedom of Information Act (FOIA). She wanted to prove a point and came with a huge stack of documents. After the meeting, he asked her how she got all that information.

"She was like, 'Well, I got it from FOIA,' and I was like 'Who's he?'" Nixon said.

He realized a world of information was available – and all he had to do was write a letter to access it.

"After that, I was just on a tear," he said.

He's been using open records laws to get documents and data for investigative analysis ever since.

Notes

1 Reilly, S. (2016, February 14). Broken Discipline Tracking Systems Let Teachers Flee Troubled Pasts. *USA TODAY.* https://www.usatoday.com/story/news/2016/02/14/ broken-discipline-tracking-system-lets-teachers-with-misconduct-records-back-in-classroom/79999634/.

2 Reilly, S., & Kelly, J. (2016, February 14). How USA TODAY Audited the Country's Broken Systems for Tracking Teacher Discipline. *USA TODAY.* https://www.usatoday. com/story/news/2016/02/14/how-usa-today-audited-countrys-broken-systems-tracking-teacher-discipline/80357584/.

3 United States Department of Justice. (n.d.) *What Is FOIA?* Retrieved August 19, 2021, from https://www.foia.gov/about.html.

4 Data Coalition. (2019, March 8). What's Next for Open Data in the U.S.: A Look Ahead Following the Passage of the OPEN Government Data Act. *DataCoalition.org.* https://www.datacoalition.org/blog/12844955.

5 Accessibility to Public Data Sets, Local Laws of the City of New York § 5.23–501– 506 (2012). https://codelibrary.amlegal.com/codes/newyorkcity/latest/NYCadmin/ 0-0-0-42710.

6 United States Department of Labor. (2020, January 2). *U.S. Bureau of Labor Statistics.* https://www.bls.gov/bls/blsmissn.htm.

7 Nelson, B. (2018, November 29). Frequently Asked Questions about The Force Report. *NJ.com.* Retrieved August 6, 2021, from https://www.nj.com/news/2018/11/frequently_ asked_questions_about_the_force_report.html.

8 Stirling, S., & Sullivan, S.P. (2018, November 29). Hundreds of N.J. Cops Are Using Force at Alarming Rates. The State's Not Tracking Them. So We Did. *NJ.com.* Retrieved August 6, 2021, from https://www.nj.com/news/2018/11/nj_police_use_of_ force_punch_kick_pepper_spray_sho.html.

9 New York State Archives. (n.d.). *Records Management.* Retrieved August 19, 2021, from http://www.archives.nysed.gov/records/local-government-record-schedule/building-and-property-regulation.

10 Chicago Police Department. (n.d.). *Forms Retention Schedule.* Retrieved September 1, 2021, from http://directives.chicagopolice.org/forms/CPD-11.717-Numerical.pdf.

11 Iowa Public Information Board. (n.d.). Sample Records Request Letter. *State of Iowa.* Retrieved September 1, 2021, from https://ipib.iowa.gov/sample-records-request-letter.

12 State of Illinois. (n.d.). *FOIA Contacts.* Retrieved September 1, 2021, from https:// www.illinois.gov/about/foia-contacts.html.

13 Bridis, T. (2017, March 14). Obama's Final Year: US Spent $36 Million in Records Lawsuits. *Associated Press.* https://apnews.com/article/business-lawsuits-united-states-government-0b27c4d4b23b436d805328694e58c605.

14 Schmitt, E. (n.d.). Sunshine Law. *Missouri Attorney General's Office.* Retrieved September 1, 2021, from https://ago.mo.gov/missouri-law/sunshine-law.

15 Committee on Open Government. (n.d.). Freedom of Information Law. *New York State.* Retrieved September 1, 2021, from https://opengovernment.ny.gov/freedom-information-law.

16 Wallack, T. (2015, July 18). Mass. Agencies Often Limit access to Records. *Boston Globe.* https://www3.bostonglobe.com/metro/2015/07/18/often-national-leader-massachusetts-ranks-near-bottom-government-transparency/HfjFvRd4RJI6QYIHBAobEP/story.html?arc404=true.

17 National Football League. (n.d.). *Patrick Mahomes.* Retrieved September 1, 2021, from https://www.nfl.com/players/patrick-mahomes/stats/career.

18 Thompson, C. (2020, May 11). Using a Mobile Phone Survey to Investigate South Sudan's Conflict. *Global Investigative Journalism Network.* https://gijn.org/2020/05/11/how-they-did-it-using-a-mobile-phone-survey-to-investigate-south-sudans-conflict/.

19 Pew Research Center. (2019). *Return of Organization Exempt from Income Tax* (Form 990). Retrieved September 1, 2021, from https://www.pewresearch.org/wp-content/uploads/2021/04/YE2020-Pew-Research-Ctr-990-990T-public-inspection.pdf.

4   Starting with spreadsheets

* * *

At first, hauling a spreadsheet into your reporting process may feel like the antithesis of journalism. Or, if not the opposite, maybe a distinctly different sort of journalism, only to be rolled out for special situations—one that's less concerned with knocking on doors, gaining the trust and respect of critical sources, or crafting a compelling story.

But it's important to see spreadsheets for what they are: more of a constant companion in modern reporting, just like the web or a voice recording app on your phone.

Like those other tools, spreadsheets are inherently powerful; you could examine data in nothing but a spreadsheet program and be able to pinpoint facts that lead to better, deeper stories or stumble upon new ideas you never would have known existed.

Journalists have been using them in earnest since the early 1980s, and the software we're accustomed to today evolved from what was essentially a visual calculator arranged in a grid of rows and columns meant for businesses and households. But the killer feature of those early spreadsheets, and one of the things that fueled their adoption, was that the user didn't need to come equipped with even a basic understanding of computer programming to get the software to do what they wanted.[1] This was fairly revolutionary in the early days of personal computing, when the experience of using a computer wasn't refined or seamless.

Four ways spreadsheets excel

Part of the power of spreadsheets is that they take the complicated and sometimes tedious process of working with data and make it accessible to nearly everyone. In that way, they're a good first step for data analysis and a training ground to gain comfort with data before moving on to more complex or specialized data journalism tools.

They provide a graphical user interface (GUI) to navigate and make changes to the data. The ability to point, click and drag makes the barrier to entry much lower for new users. It turns the analysis process into a series of actions rather than a set of explicit written instructions you must create.

DOI: 10.4324/9781003182238-4

They offer a flexible and forgiving space to work with data. Individual spreadsheets can function more like a scratchpad for exploration. When data is tied up in a database manager or parsed by code, it isn't treated in such a mutable way. The structure is rigid and modifying the original data is more difficult. But if you want to have a single spreadsheet hold multiple tables, rearrange its columns, add new rows of data, or change the contents of individual cells on the fly, you can. Errors usually are obvious and won't bring everything to a screeching halt.

They come with a significant amount of functionality. While spreadsheets aren't the only "multitool" program for data analysis that can be used to do a variety of things, they do give journalists quick access to many common tasks, like reordering and filtering data, summarizing it by groups, repeating calculations across rows or columns, and making common types of charts and graphics. And these abilities can be extended to include more heavyweight statistical testing if necessary.

They are used far and wide. Spreadsheets are an integral part of any productivity suite of programs, which most computers already have. Data files frequently come in formats native to spreadsheets or that spreadsheets are designed to interpret.

Where spreadsheets (traditionally) lag

In journalism, reporters typically make a big deal not only about what they know but how they know it. That hallmark of transparency is meant to engender trust and credibility with the audience.

They aren't as useful for replicability: The ability for others to examine an analysis process with the same data and repeat it. Even though spreadsheets are an accessible, adaptable canvas for data, if you share one, the other user can only really see the result of your saved work. The steps you've taken from start to finish will largely be a mystery. Sure, they would be able to see hints of what may have been changed or added, but unless you carefully document each individual thing that you do to the data in some fashion, the step-by-step information is lost.

Why does that matter? For some news organizations, one method of transparency is allowing the public to peer inside the data analysis process. At ProPublica[2] and BuzzFeed News,[3] journalists regularly post collections of online files that document their data analysis methods so that any curious party, like another journalist, an academic, or a public official, can fully understand how they arrived at their conclusions.

Some background on Google Sheets

Google Sheets is part of an online suite of tools offered by Google, which you can gain access to by creating a Google account (Google support has step-by-step instructions on how to do this: https://support.google.com/accounts/answer/27441).

Why Google Sheets as opposed to a traditional application that runs directly on the computer, like Microsoft Excel? Google Sheets is free to use, has millions of users,[4] and is accessible through just about any modern web browser.

A single Google Sheets spreadsheet can also be used and edited by multiple people at once. Because it's a cloud-based service, it's perpetually handing information back and forth between your browser and Google's servers while open, so it requires internet connectivity. And instead of having to periodically save like you would with a desktop program, software in the Google Docs Editors suite saves automatically as you make changes, creating a series of past versions of the file that you can revert to if necessary.

A Google account comes with an online storage space service called Google Drive, which you also interact with through the browser. As you create new spreadsheets and import data, those files will be stored in Google Drive automatically. The platform uses the same organizing principles as any computer desktop, whether macOS, Microsoft Windows, or something else—it's a system of files and folders.

A note on data sensitivity and cloud-based storage: While data security and privacy fall outside the scope of this book, keeping sensitive data on the web and working with it using online tools carries some risk, even though it may be small. If you find yourself at some point analyzing a confidential data set that could potentially cause harm if it were inadvertently disclosed—think medical information or something with social security numbers—it's probably best done on a local machine.

Google Sheets offers a comparable user experience for much of what journalists need to do with a spreadsheet, and nearly everything covered here will also apply to competing spreadsheet products. While some functionality may be called something else, and the program's interface may look a little bit different, the central concepts are the same.

It's a capable program with some limitations compared to its desktop counterparts because it's based online. Currently, a spreadsheet is limited to 5 million cells[5]; if you have a 5-column spreadsheet that runs 1 million rows, or a 250,000-row spreadsheet with 15 columns, you'll bump up against these restrictions. Even with a data set in the million-cell range, you may notice some pauses in the interface as data is loaded into your browser's memory.

Getting started with Google Sheets

Once you're logged into your Google account, there are a few different pathways to creating a new spreadsheet or working with an existing one.

The primary way is to use the Google Drive web interface:

1   Visit https://drive.google.com in your web browser.

2   To create a new spreadsheet, click on the "New" button in the top left corner. From the resulting drop-down menu, choose "Google Sheets."

3   To work with an existing spreadsheet, select it from the files and folders within Google Drive.

You can take similar steps using the Google Sheets website directly: https://sheets.google.com or https://docs.google.com/spreadsheets.

Alternatively, Google has a shortcut URL to create a new spreadsheet and open it immediately under the primary Google account logged into the web browser: https://sheets.new.

Basic spreadsheet concepts

Upon opening a spreadsheet, the first thing that probably stands out is the "grid" that takes up most of the interface: a series of horizontal **rows** and vertical **columns** composed of individual **cells**, which act as containers for data points.

Rows have numbers and columns have letters to distinguish them from one another. Combine these, and you have a **cell reference** or address that points to the contents of a single spreadsheet cell, like "A1" or "D6."

Clicking on any cell gives you the ability to modify those contents, and cells can hold different types of data in the form of **values**, including:

- **Text** strings, which aren't limited to letters of the alphabet. They may be a combination of letters and numbers, or numbers treated as text, like a postal zip code or a PIN. These are values you can't realistically perform a basic math operation upon. For example, it will never make sense to multiply zip codes.

- **Numbers**, which are quantities and measurements that can be used in mathematical operations. It's a little counterintuitive, but this also includes values represented as dates and times, which can be compared to one another to determine spans of time, like the number of days between two different dates.

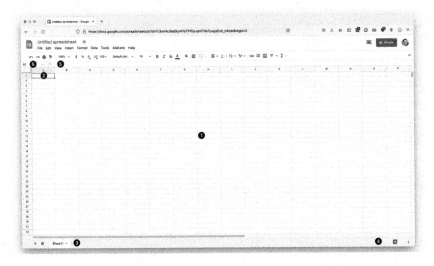

Figure 4.1 A brief tour of Google Sheets' interface components. (1) The spreadsheet grid; (2) A highlighted cell; (3) Tabs to access different sheets within the file; (4) The quicksum box; (5) the formula bar; and (6) the name box.

- **Booleans**, which are the result of a logical evaluation, where an expression can either be one of two things: true or false. The number four equals the number four (4 = 4)—this expression is true because those numbers have equal values. But the number one is not greater than the number four (1 > 4), so that evaluation would be false. While these are simplistic examples, the use of Booleans winds up being integral in situations where you want to take different actions with your data depending on the values in a specific cell.

But cells can also hold another critical kind of information instead of values: **formulas.** And this is where the whole idea of a spreadsheet being a visual calculator begins to come into play.

A formula is a series of operations for the spreadsheet to carry out within a cell. They can range from being as simple as a brief mathematical operation, like adding two numbers together, to lengthy sprawl of interlinked calculations, functions, and logical evaluations.

In any case, they always begin with an equals sign (=)—this is the overarching cue to Google Sheets that any input that follows should be treated like a formula rather than a value. After typing return or enter, what ends up being displayed within the cell is the result of the formula rather than the formula itself.

So, for example, by selecting cell A1 and then typing =1+2, you'll see the result of that formula displayed in cell (3), even though the contents of the cell are still the formula (=1+2).

How can you tell? Double-clicking within the cell will reveal the formula sitting behind the scenes. It's also present in the **formula bar** directly above the column labels, aligned with column B. If a formula is present in a cell rather than a value, you'll see it there when the cell is selected.

Using formulas in conjunction with cell references is where spreadsheets really shine—it's this combination that allows you to analyze the data you have.

Let's say you are trying to figure out how much the population in New York state increased over the previous decade. You have the official U.S. Census count on April 1, 2010, entered in cell B2 and the corresponding number for 2020 directly to the right of it in cell C2.

If we were to employ a formula to handle this calculation in cell D2, the next cell over, you would not have to retype the population values contained in cells B2 and C2 as part of the calculation to get an answer. Instead, you can use the cell references to target the cells that contain the values you want. So, entering =C2-B2 would yield the same result as =20201249-19378102, displaying the outcome of the formula (823147).

For one simple math operation like this, it may seem like a spreadsheet isn't doing much more than what you'd get by manually punching numbers into a calculator. But by unleashing the combination of formulas and cell references across dozens, hundreds, or thousands of different data points at once, analyses that would have been tedious at best and impossible at worst are within reach.

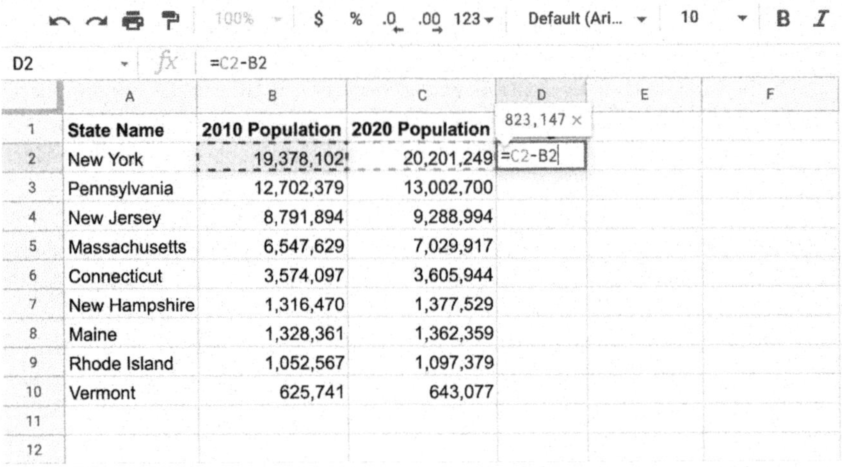

	A	B	C	D	E	F
1	State Name	2010 Population	2020 Population	823,147 ×		
2	New York	19,378,102	20,201,249	=C2-B2		
3	Pennsylvania	12,702,379	13,002,700			
4	New Jersey	8,791,894	9,288,994			
5	Massachusetts	6,547,629	7,029,917			
6	Connecticut	3,574,097	3,605,944			
7	New Hampshire	1,316,470	1,377,529			
8	Maine	1,328,361	1,362,359			
9	Rhode Island	1,052,567	1,097,379			
10	Vermont	625,741	643,077			
11						
12						

D2   *fx*   =C2-B2

Figure 4.2 Using cell references in a formula to calculate New York's population change between 2010 and 2020 in cell D2.

There are other couple of things to note from the example above. Some of the cells have values entered within this larger spreadsheet; calling this collection of cells "data" is certainly accurate, but they also make up what's known as a data **table**.

A table is a contiguous set of values in adjacent rows and columns—usually, no gaps or empty spaces exist between them. The values within a table represent orderly, connected pieces of information, too. Here, each row represents a single U.S. state, and each column contains a piece of information about that state. And for this particular table, we know three things about each one: its name, its population in 2010, and its population in 2020.

Data tables can be designed in myriad ways, but many tables you'll analyze are organized around rows representing a thing, like a person, an event, a place, or an item. Columns then hold information about whatever's in the row: the person's age, the date and time the event occurred, the place's street address, or an item's cost.

Tables also have **header rows**, which hold short text descriptions of the values represented in each column. These are important indicators for people working with data to know what they're looking at; while you could probably puzzle out the fact that "New York" and the other values in column A are states without any information from the header row, the other numerical values in other columns could represent anything. A header row won't always appear on the first row (row 1) of a spreadsheet—remember, it's a flexible space, and a data table can appear almost anywhere within the spreadsheet grid—but it is expected to be directly above the subsequent rows of data.

Other important interface features

Google Sheets files can include multiple **sheets**—you're not limited to just one. At the bottom of the browser window, below the spreadsheet grid, there's a single tab called `"Sheet1."` Much like the values in a header row, these are intended to have brief descriptive (and differentiating) names to describe the contents of the sheet.

Clicking on the plus icon (+) to the left of `Sheet1` will create a new tab; clicking on the tabs themselves allows you to switch between different sheets in the file.

Using separate sheets can be useful for holding copies of your data analysis at different stages or storing different related sets of data you plan to examine together.

You're not limited to creating new blank spreadsheets in a file. Each tab has a small downward-facing arrow icon that brings up a contextual menu of options. A key feature here is the ability to **duplicate** an entire sheet and its data contents.

Duplicating a spreadsheet to keep an untouched, original copy of a data table saved before you analyze or alter it in any way can rescue you from potential missteps and can allow you to start over in Google Sheets, where modifying the structure of a table or changing values in cells is easy to do inadvertently.

The **quicksum menu** appears in the bottom right corner of the interface when more than one cell is selected and will show instant summaries for any highlighted group of cells, giving you the ability to pinpoint important facts quickly. For a set of numerical values (or formulas that result in numerical values), these appear in the form of simple descriptive statistics, including the sum, average and highest number within the group. For non-numerical values, it will show a count of the cells that aren't blank.

Groups of cells are called **ranges**, and any cell or cells that are selected together appear in the **name box** to the left of the function bar. A range is denoted by the cell references of the first cell in the series and the last, separated by a colon (:) character.

So, clicking on cell `E5`, dragging the cursor down to cell `E12` and then to the right into column `F` will highlight the range `E5:F12`, which will appear in the name box. Alternatively, typing in a cell reference or range will highlight the corresponding cells in the spreadsheet.

Ranges can also capture entire rows or columns. Clicking on the number of a row or letter of a column will select its full extent; to capture everything in the third row of a spreadsheet, the range to enter in the name box would be `3:3`.

Like other types of files generated by the Google Docs Editors suite, they exist online and have a unique URL. The blue button located toward the top right of the interface controls sharing and access options for the spreadsheet. By default, files are private; access will be limited only to your Google account.

Finally, you probably don't want your spreadsheet to be called "Untitled spreadsheet," which is the blanket name for all new Google Sheets files. Any name given here will be reflected in the Google Drive file listing.

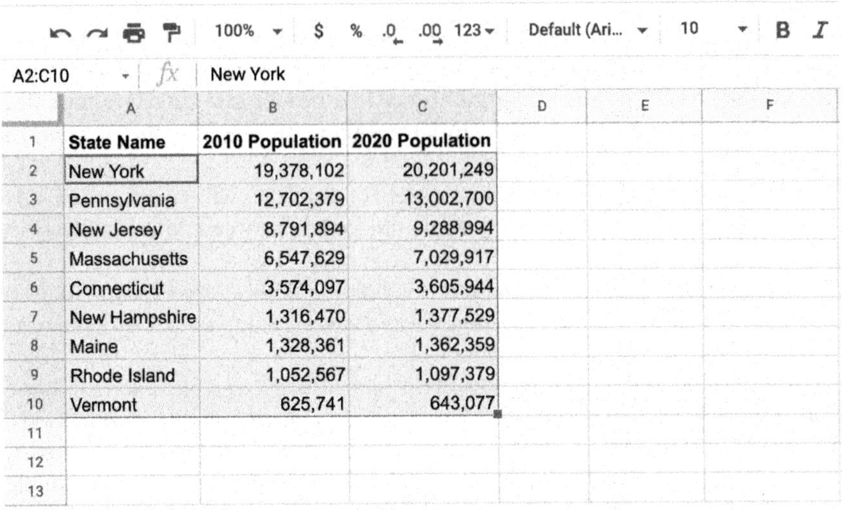

Figure 4.3 A highlighted range with the corresponding cell references (cell A2 through cell C10) appearing in the name box.

Getting data into Google Sheets

While Google Sheets has achieved ubiquity in the spreadsheet world, much of the data you'll encounter online or obtain from sources won't be in its native file format. Because the program is based in the cloud and interacted with purely through browsers or mobile apps, it doesn't really have a format in the traditional sense. If the desktop version of Google Drive is installed to manage the online storage space, Google Sheets files will appear with the extension **.gsheet**, but this is essentially a web link rather than a local file.

It has the ability, though, to open, import, and export common file types used for the interchange of data. There are two prominent ones to know:

1   The Microsoft Excel format, which uses a **.xlsx** or **.xls** extension, depending on which version of the software it was created with. These files are Excel **workbooks,** and each one contains one or more separate **worksheets,** much like Google Sheets files can hold multiple spreadsheets.

2   **Delimited text,** where the file extensions can vary depending on the type of text format it uses.

In the case of delimited text, each line in the file represents one row of data. Because these text files don't have columns the way a spreadsheet does, the text itself must hold some set of indicators to show a program like Google Sheets where,

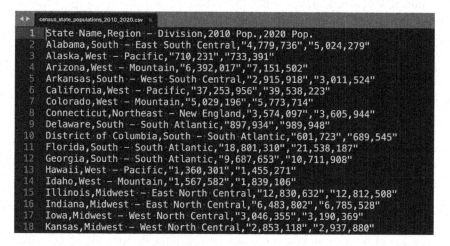

```
census_state_populations_2010_2020.csv  ×
 1  State Name,Region — Division,2010 Pop.,2020 Pop.
 2  Alabama,South — East South Central,"4,779,736","5,024,279"
 3  Alaska,West — Pacific,"710,231","733,391"
 4  Arizona,West — Mountain,"6,392,017","7,151,502"
 5  Arkansas,South — West South Central,"2,915,918","3,011,524"
 6  California,West — Pacific,"37,253,956","39,538,223"
 7  Colorado,West — Mountain,"5,029,196","5,773,714"
 8  Connecticut,Northeast — New England,"3,574,097","3,605,944"
 9  Delaware,South — South Atlantic,"897,934","989,948"
10  District of Columbia,South — South Atlantic,"601,723","689,545"
11  Florida,South — South Atlantic,"18,801,310","21,538,187"
12  Georgia,South — South Atlantic,"9,687,653","10,711,908"
13  Hawaii,West — Pacific,"1,360,301","1,455,271"
14  Idaho,West — Mountain,"1,567,582","1,839,106"
15  Illinois,Midwest — East North Central,"12,830,632","12,812,508"
16  Indiana,Midwest — East North Central,"6,483,802","6,785,528"
17  Iowa,Midwest — West North Central,"3,046,355","3,190,369"
18  Kansas,Midwest — West North Central,"2,853,118","2,937,880"
```

Figure 4.4 A CSV file of census data in the Sublime text editor. In this case, commas are the delimiting character used to signify column breaks in the data table, and double quotes are the text qualifier that prevent the population values from being broken up improperly.

exactly, to make splits. Those indicators are the **delimiters** (or separators), usually a single character and frequently a comma (,) or a tab.

These are CSVs or TSVs, which stand for "comma-separated values" and "tab-separated values," respectively, and often use those abbreviations as a file extension.

There are also situations where cell values in a delimited text file contain the delimiter. You might have a data table where a column with first and last names has a comma before a generational suffix (e.g., Freddie Prinze, Jr.), or a column that contains a narrative description of an event that uses full punctuation. In those situations, spreadsheet software must be able to parse these text files in a way where some rows don't end up misaligned, containing more columns than others because the line was split in places where it wasn't supposed to be.

The preventive measure here is what's known as a **text qualifier** wrapped around each value in the delimited text file. These characters, usually double or single quotation marks, cause the program to ignore any delimiters found between them, keeping the value intact in its own column.

There are two primary ways to get your data into a Google Sheet: uploading it to Google Drive and then using Google Sheets to open it or importing it into a new or existing spreadsheet.

Google Sheets can edit uploaded Excel files in their native format, meaning that they will retain their extensions after being added to Google Drive and remain Excel files if you download them to a computer. Delimited files like CSVs can be opened with Google Sheets by double-clicking on them in Google Drive.

It will show a preview of the file in spreadsheet form and give a prompt for how to open the file at the top of the browser window.

For existing spreadsheets, whether they're full of data or not, selecting the "File" menu and then choosing "Import" will allow you to pick a file already in Google Drive or upload one from your computer.

With either type of file, you can control whether the new data is added to whatever's already there, replaces it wholesale or generates a brand-new spreadsheet file entirely. For delimited text, you're also prompted to choose the separator (by default, Google Sheets will scan the file and attempt to detect the correct character automatically) and whether it should recognize numbers, dates, and formulas in the file and format them as such.

While this seems like the sort of helpful feature you'd want to use, leaving this decision up to a simple algorithm isn't always the right choice—it really depends on the data you have.

As mentioned previously, sometimes a number isn't intended to be treated like a numerical value. In the case of a column containing zip code values, for example, having Google Sheets recognize them all as numbers will cause any leading zeros to be stripped away for addresses in areas like the Northeast. In this situation, it's best to leave this option unselected and handle column formatting after the data is imported.

Navigating the data display and controlling its structure

No surprises here: you're able to move between cells within the spreadsheet grid using a cursor and a keyboard. From a highlighted cell, arrow keys will move the selection in appointed directions; the tab key functions like a right arrow, moving the selection along a given row.

For data tables that stretch beyond the extent of the browser window—and many will—a quick way to jump to the first or last row (or column) without having to scroll through it all is by using the command key and an arrow key together (in Microsoft Windows, use the control key and an arrow key together).

One point of caution: If you start typing anything while a cell is highlighted, you will overwrite the value currently in the cell. To modify a value without replacing it entirely, double-click on the cell or edit the value through the formula bar.

When it comes to restructuring data within a spreadsheet, there are three major actions you can take:

- **Clear:** Values are removed from cells, rows, or columns, but the empty space remains.

- **Delete:** The cells, rows, or columns are removed, and surrounding data values shift to fill the void. For a cell or group of cells, you also have to choose whether other existing data will move up from the rows below or fill in from the columns to the right.

- **Insert:** The inverse of deletion, where new cells, rows, or columns are added. For cells, a similar choice: you can either nudge existing cells downward or to the right to make space for these new additions.

These actions can be accessed through the "Format" menu in conjunction with selected cells, columns, or rows, or by right-clicking (potentially command-clicking in macOS, depending on your mouse or trackpad setup).

Returning to the table of Northeastern states and their population counts, let's say you wanted the column holding 2020 population counts, currently in column C, to precede the values from 2010 instead—effectively having them switch places:

1   *Select* column C; *cut* the column using the drop-down menu denoted with a downward arrow icon that appears when your cursor is over the **column reference** letter, by using the "Edit" menu, or a keyboard shortcut.

2   *Select* column B; choose "Insert 1 left" from the column reference's drop-down menu or by using the "Insert" menu and choosing "Column left."

3   *Select* the now-blank column B and *paste* the cut column.

Unless cell values used in a calculation are deleted or cleared, Google Sheets will attempt to preserve the cell references used in formulas to account for the restructuring, changing them automatically. But it's always a good idea to check and make sure formulas are still fetching values from the proper cells when you make any modifications like this.

You may also notice that if the value in a cell is longer than the width of the column, it spills into the next cell or gets cut off if there's a value in the cell immediately to the right. To fix this, columns and rows can be resized to accommodate lengthier values. Move the cursor to the short vertical line that separates column references at the top of the spreadsheet grid; click and drag there when the cursor's icon changes to make a column wider or thinner. Double-clicking will automatically resize the column to fit its longest value. And by highlighting everything in the grid (selecting the blank box above row 1 and to the left of column A) and then double-clicking between column references, every column with data will be resized at once.

Finally, rows and columns can be locked in place so that they don't disappear from the interface while scrolling through data that exceeds the size of your screen. This is helpful when examining data tables with many columns, for instance, so that you're always able to see the header row above the column values, saving you from having to leave what you're doing and return to the top of the table.

This ability is called **freezing** and can be achieved by using the "View" menu and choosing "Freeze." From there, you can select a preset number of columns or rows to freeze, or you can use the currently highlighted cell as the freezing guidepost.

Exploring a data set to learn something new

Having the ability to access and control data sets within Google Sheets is critical, but these skills are only the first steps in the analysis process—they set the table for the real work to begin.

As stated previously, analysis allows you to tease out the answers to different questions about data. And journalists often concern themselves with how something has changed over time. Is it higher? Lower? Does the difference matter—is that shift significant? And if so, what's the most important thing for people to know?

Applying a few simple formulas to a data table, combined with some of your own natural curiosity and judgments about what you see in the results, can help answer these questions.

Let's jump back to a query raised earlier while using census data: You want to know how much the population in New York and other Northeastern states has increased since 2010.

(We'll use a data table unadulterated by previous structural changes, where column B holds the 2010 populations and column C holds their 2020 counterparts.)

First, in column D, you'll want to extend the table's header row, adding a value to cell D1 to describe the column's contents. Entering something along the lines of "Change" or "Difference" is probably most appropriate.

To find this change, begin with New York state on row 2. Subtract the older population value from the more recent one; a positive result from this simple math operation will represent growth in population over the ten-year span: =C2-B2

You may notice that Google Sheets creates visual cues around the cells referenced in the formula while it's being edited—a dashed line is drawn around cells B2 and C2, with a different color assigned to each. For those less inclined to go through the hassle of typing different cell references into a formula and would rather use the cursor, simply clicking on a cell while a formula is in progress will insert the cell reference; the same is true for highlighting a range. There's no difference between the two methods; it's really just a matter of personal preference.

After hitting enter or return, Google Sheets will likely suggest to **autofill** the formula, extending it down the column and automatically adjusting the row number for each cell reference. (On the next row, in cell D3, the formula would be =C3-B3, and so on.)

It makes little sense to retype the formula yourself; the autofill ability in spreadsheet software is almost always used to repeat formulas among different rows or columns in a data table.

Google's best guess at what you're trying to accomplish can be accepted in this case. If there's no prompt, or for more manual control over the autofill process, you have a few options at your disposal.

Whenever a cell is selected in Google Sheets, it has a thicker blue bar around it, and a small square in the bottom right corner. Hovering over the square with your cursor will cause its icon to change from a normal pointer arrow to a thin,

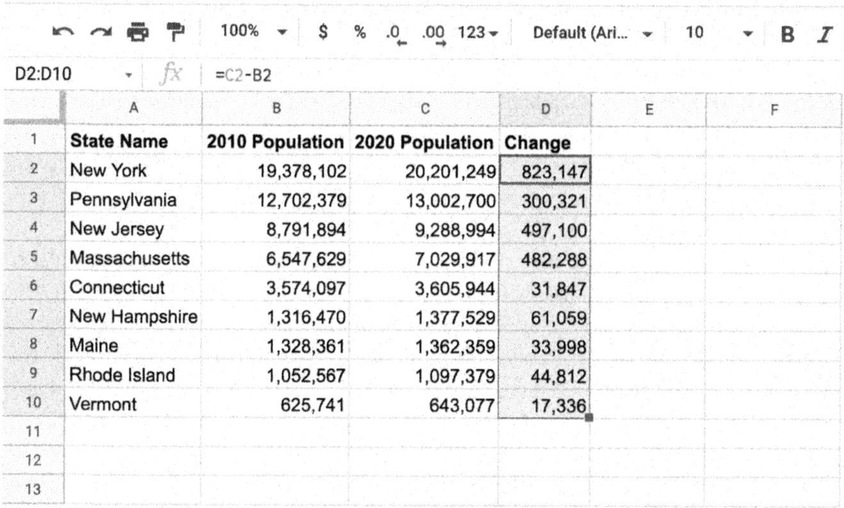

	A	B	C	D	E	F
	State Name	**2010 Population**	**2020 Population**	**Change**		
2	New York	19,378,102	20,201,249	823,147		
3	Pennsylvania	12,702,379	13,002,700	300,321		
4	New Jersey	8,791,894	9,288,994	497,100		
5	Massachusetts	6,547,629	7,029,917	482,288		
6	Connecticut	3,574,097	3,605,944	31,847		
7	New Hampshire	1,316,470	1,377,529	61,059		
8	Maine	1,328,361	1,362,359	33,998		
9	Rhode Island	1,052,567	1,097,379	44,812		
10	Vermont	625,741	643,077	17,336		
11						
12						
13						

Figure 4.5 After autofilling all the population differences in column D.

black plus (+). When that happens, clicking and dragging downward from cell D3 will draw a dashed outline around the cells below. If you let go in cell D10, the formula typed in cell D3 will have autofilled in the same fashion.

If dragging the cursor to autofill is problematic—say this isn't a small data table with 10 rows but instead has 10,000 rows—double-clicking on the square will cause it to autofill down the column, only stopping when it reaches the bottom of the table or a gap of blank rows.

Alternatively, the formula in cell D3 can be copied. Highlighting the range D4:D10 and then pasting will also autofill the formula.

We can see from the results now in column D that New York had the largest increase in population, growing by more than 800,000 residents between 2010 and 2020. New Jersey is a distant second, not quite breaking half a million new residents during the same time frame; at the other end, Vermont barely added enough people to fill a modestly sized sports stadium.

The answer to the question we've asked seems obvious: In the Northeast, New York grew more than any of its neighboring states since 2010. This is true—you've uncovered a fact from the data that can be clearly encapsulated in a single sentence.

But is it the whole story here? New York is a big state, with a population of over 20 million. For every Vermonter, there are roughly 30 New Yorkers. It would make sense that larger states with significant population centers would experience a bigger net inflow of people over time.

What you're comparing among these states in column D is the raw difference or **absolute change** in population. These values don't account for how large or small a state may be to begin with.

So, you probably want to examine these changes in population in **relative** terms as well to see them in proportion to the size of the state; that can be done by calculating the **percentage change**.

There are a few different ways to determine a percentage change, but one common method: first finding the difference between the two values by subtracting the older, or base, value from the more recent, or new, value and then dividing the result of that calculation by the base value: (new - base) / base. Note the parenthesis here—the order of operations needs to be preserved so that the subtraction happens first.

We happen to have that part of the formula completed already in column D to examine the raw population change.

In column E, we can again create a value in the header row to describe the column's contents, and then enter =D2/B2 in cell E2. If you wanted, the formula could also be repeated without referencing any cells from column D at all: =(C2-B2)/B2. Using the autofill feature will replicate the formula for all states.

Here's where controlling the formatting of cell values can be helpful. By default, Google Sheets will express these percentages as decimal values that are a fraction of 1 (which corresponds to 100%) with many significant digits—far more than necessary.

Highlighting column E and clicking on the percent icon (%) in the toolbar will format all the numerical values as percentages, rounded to the nearest hundredth. This can also be handled through the "Format" menu and choosing "Number": Google Sheets has different formatting presets to display numerical values as percentages, currency, and dates.

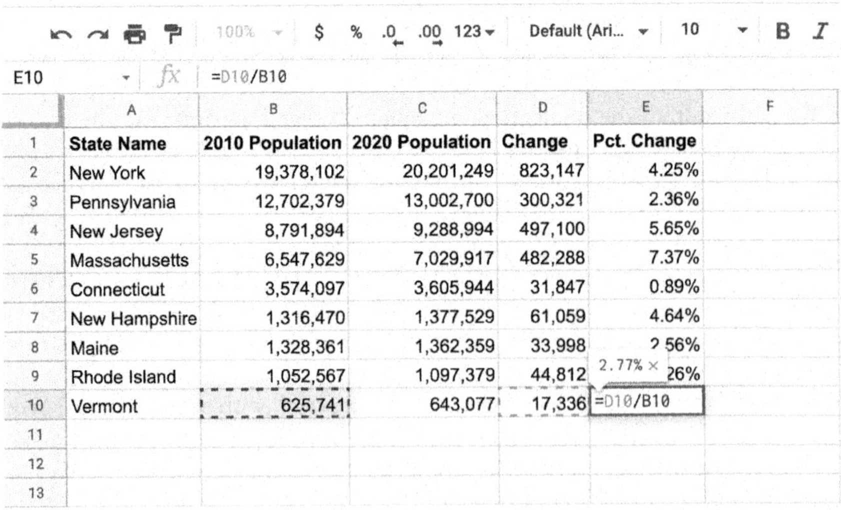

	A	B	C	D	E	F
1	State Name	2010 Population	2020 Population	Change	Pct. Change	
2	New York	19,378,102	20,201,249	823,147	4.25%	
3	Pennsylvania	12,702,379	13,002,700	300,321	2.36%	
4	New Jersey	8,791,894	9,288,994	497,100	5.65%	
5	Massachusetts	6,547,629	7,029,917	482,288	7.37%	
6	Connecticut	3,574,097	3,605,944	31,847	0.89%	
7	New Hampshire	1,316,470	1,377,529	61,059	4.64%	
8	Maine	1,328,361	1,362,359	33,998	2 56%	
9	Rhode Island	1,052,567	1,097,379	44,812	2.77% × 26%	
10	Vermont	625,741	643,077	17,336	=D10/B10	
11						
12						
13						

(Toolbar: 100% $ % .0 .00 123 ▾ Default (Ari... ▾ 10 ▾ **B** *I*)
(E10   *fx* =D10/B10)

Figure 4.6 Calculating a percentage change in population for Northeastern states by taking the population change in column D and dividing it by the base population value in column B.

The picture becomes a bit clearer with this new column of information. In relative terms, Massachusetts had the largest percentage increase in its population, growing by 7.4%. That 17,000-person increase in Vermont may have seemed anemic, but the state actually experienced a larger increase for its size than Connecticut, which had a net growth of less than 1%.

Let's say we also want to know what's happened to the region overall—it may add further context to these comparisons, allowing us to see a sort of baseline figure for the region.

While the quicksum menu can generate temporary totals for these states together in 2010 and 2020, something more permanent may be in order. And to help, we can use a **function** called SUM().

Functions are designed to perform specific tasks within a spreadsheet that would be unrealistic or impossible to accomplish with different math operators alone. While you could add the 2010 populations for these nine states together using a formula that begins =B2+B3+B4... , it's much easier to just use SUM() instead, one of the dozens of functions built into Google Sheets.

The parentheses next to the function's name are a place to hold the function's **arguments**, which are usually values or groups of values the function should do something with. SUM() exists for one specialized purpose: to calculate the sum for a range (or list of values) in the spreadsheet in one fell swoop.

Instead of having to add numbers individually, =SUM(B2:B10) will add the whole range of 2010 values.

Note: If you're ever stumped by the syntax of a function, selecting the question mark icon that appears to the left of the cell as you're typing a function's name will call up a brief overview of how it works, along with an example and a link to a full webpage with details.

The autofill capability we've used previously also works horizontally along rows, so the function doesn't have to be re-entered to see the sum of the 2020 populations in column C. That very same autofill feature can then extend the raw difference and percentage change down to row 11 for columns C and D, respectively, providing the same summary metrics that we have for states to the entire Northeast.

The only remaining step is to add an appropriate value to cell A11, which could be something like "Total."

By applying a few fundamental formulas to a small data table, a picture begins to emerge, and it acts as a springboard for potential stories. What, exactly, has driven the rush to states like Massachusetts and New Jersey? Why has there been relative stagnation in Connecticut over this most recent ten-year span? When growth is significant (or modest), what's the impact on public services, infrastructure, housing, or the tax base?

Maybe much of that growth was centered in suburban Boston or the towns along the Jersey Shore—it's hard to say from the macroscopic perch of state-level data. A deeper dive may be warranted, examining more granular population figures among counties and municipalities across the Northeast to sharpen these ideas. Further analysis will likely help you refine who to talk to and what to ask.

	A	B	C	D	E	F
1	State Name	2010 Population	2020 Population	Change	Pct. Change	
2	New York	19,378,102	20,201,249	823,147	4.25%	
3	Pennsylvania	12,702,379	13,002,700	300,321	2.36%	
4	New Jersey	8,791,894	9,288,994	497,100	5.65%	
5	Massachusetts	6,547,629	7,029,917	482,288	7.37%	
6	Connecticut	3,574,097	3,605,944	31,847	0.89%	
7	New Hampshire	1,316,470	1,377,529	61,059	4.64%	
8	Maine	1,328,361	1,362,359	33,998	2.56%	
9	Rhode Island	1,052,567	1,097,379	44,812	4.26%	
10	Vermont	625,741	57,609,148 × 77	17,336	2.77%	
11	Total	55,317,240	=SUM(C2:C10)	2,291,908	4.14%	
12						
13						

Figure 4.7 Using the SUM() function to find total population figures for all Northeastern states in 2010 and 2020, as well as autofilling the raw population difference and the population percentage change for these new values in cells D11 and E11.

Or perhaps the story is that the 2020 headcount for some of these states actually defied earlier predictions. This is what happened in New York, where the U.S. Census Bureau estimated the state began to contract in the 2010s, losing 40,000 people by 2020 rather than gaining more than 800,000.[6]

With the data you're able to say "this is what happened"; only through reporting—finding expert voices and doing research—are you able to also say "this is why it happened." But it doesn't take much work to get off to a strong start.

Notes

1 Karaian, J. (2015, December 22). This Is the Man Who Invented the Spreadsheet. But Don't Hold that against Him. *Quartz.* qz.com/578661/dan-bricklin-invented-the-spreadsheet-but-dont-hold-that-against-him.
2 ProPublica. (2019, April 9). IRS Audit Rates by County. *Github.* https://github.com/propublica/auditData.
3 BuzzFeed News. (2016, January 17). Methodology and Code: Detecting Match-Fixing Patterns in Tennis. *Github.* https://github.com/BuzzFeedNews/2016-01-tennis-betting-analysis.
4 Eadicicco, L. (2020, March 12). Google Quietly Reached a Major Milestone in Its Battle with Microsoft to Rule the Workplace. *Business Insider.* https://www.businessinsider.com/google-g-suite-gmail-2-billion-vs-microsoft-office-2020-3.
5 Google. (n.d.). Files You Can Store in Google Drive. *Google Drive Help.* Retrieved September 4, 2021, from https://support.google.com/drive/answer/37603.
6 Gebeloff, R. (2021, May 4). Why New York State's Population Growth Surprised Experts. *The New York Times.* https://www.nytimes.com/2021/05/04/upshot/census-new-york-surprise.html.

5   Sort, filter, pivot

The building blocks of data analysis

* * *

You never know in which order your data will arrive. It could be alphabetical by names in a column, have the more recent data first, or be completely haphazard. You don't want to be at the mercy of whatever default ordering has—or hasn't—been done within your data set because that would lock you into one specific way of looking at the table.

It may contain records you don't particularly care about for your story, or it could be enormous, running into thousands of rows and dozens of columns. Journalists regularly need to interpret data that's impossible to eyeball, extending far beyond what can fit on a laptop screen or desktop monitor.

That's why sorting, filtering, and pivot tables comprise the core of the data analysis process, unlocking the potential for spreadsheets to shed light on your data.

Reordering your data table with sorting

One of the fastest methods you have at your disposal to make sense of data is by **sorting** it; this is a quick way for journalists to see the maximum and minimum values that appear. And the mechanism is exactly as it sounds: Google Sheets will move each row of a data table so that it's in order, from the top of the sheet down or vice-versa, based on the values it finds in a column of your choosing.

Journalists frequently care about who or what is high or low in data because it can sharpen questions or lead to new story ideas. Sorting can also help identify **outliers**—values that deviate so far from the others contained in the same column that they deserve extra scrutiny and attention. They may ultimately be accurate data elements you can feel confident in, or they could point to troubling signs in the data. You won't know until you investigate further, and you may not even identify them at all unless you're sorting your data.

Let's return to an example like the one from the last chapter: states, their populations in 2010 and 2020, as well as how they changed over the ten-year span. Instead of focusing on just the handful of states in the Northeast, we have information for every state, along with their census-designated regions (like Northeast and South) and the geographic divisions within those regions (like Pacific and Middle Atlantic).

DOI: 10.4324/9781003182238-5

The first thing to do when sorting data is to ensure that you have the full range of cells you want to sort highlighted. This can be accomplished in a few different ways:

1　Typing the desired range into the name box near the top left of the screen.

2　Clicking on any cell within the data table, then using the keyboard shortcut command-A on macOS or control-A on Windows.

3　Manually highlighting the range of the full data table by clicking and dragging your cursor from the upper-left cell to the bottom-right cell.

We've talked a little about how Google Sheets can make certain choices for you automatically. Sometimes its algorithmic guesses are solid. In other situations, it can make assumptions that put your analysis in peril.

Selecting the range on your own and verifying that the extent of the data table is selected are necessary steps to make sure that you're not inadvertently only sorting part of your data—you don't want to exclude any rows or columns. If you sort some columns in the table and not others, you're creating a permanent split in your data that will impact the accuracy of any work that you do with the data from that point onward.

The next step, once the data table is fully highlighted, is to go to the "Data" menu and choose "Sort range," followed by "Advanced range sorting options." From here, a dialogue box should appear in the center of your screen, showing the range that Google Sheets will be sorting, from cell A1 to G52.

	State Name	Region	Division	2010 Pop.	2020 Pop.	Change	Pct. Change
1	State Name	Region	Division	2010 Pop.	2020 Pop.	Change	Pct. Change
2	Alabama	South	East South Central	4,779,736	5,024,279	244,543	5.1%
3	Alaska	West	Pacific	710,231	733,391	23,160	3.3%
4	Arizona	West	Mountain	6,392,017	7,151,502	759,485	11.9%
5	Arkansas	South	West South Central	2,915,918	3,011,524	95,606	3.3%
6	California	West	Pacific	37,253,956	39,538,223	2,284,267	6.1%
7	Colorado	West	Mountain	5,029,196	5,773,714	744,518	14.8%
8	Connecticut	Northeast	New England	3,574,097	3,605,944	31,847	0.9%
9	Delaware	South	South Atlantic	897,934	989,948	92,014	10.2%
10	District of Columbia	South	South Atlantic	601,723	689,545	87,822	14.6%
11	Florida	South	South Atlantic	18,801,310	21,538,187	2,736,877	14.6%
12	Georgia	South	South Atlantic	9,687,653	10,711,908	1,024,255	10.6%
13	Hawaii	West	Pacific	1,360,301	1,455,271	94,970	7.0%
14	Idaho	West	Mountain	1,567,582	1,839,106	271,524	17.3%
15	Illinois	Midwest	East North Central	12,830,632	12,812,508	-18,124	-0.1%
16	Indiana	Midwest	East North Central	6,483,802	6,785,528	301,726	4.7%
17	Iowa	Midwest	West North Central	3,046,355	3,190,369	144,014	4.7%
18	Kansas	Midwest	West North Central	2,853,118	2,937,880	84,762	3.0%
19	Kentucky	South	East South Central	4,339,367	4,505,836	166,469	3.8%
20	Louisiana	South	West South Central	4,533,372	4,657,757	124,385	2.7%
21	Maine	Northeast	New England	1,328,361	1,362,359	33,998	2.6%
22	Maryland	South	South Atlantic	5,773,552	6,177,224	403,672	7.0%
23	Massachusetts	Northeast	New England	6,547,629	7,029,917	482,288	7.4%

Figure 5.1 Ensuring the correct range (A1:G52) has been selected prior to any sorting.

Underneath that, you're given a checkbox option about whether your data table has a header row. Remember, most data sets you will work with will have a header row containing short descriptions of the values in the columns below. Selecting this option is important because that's the one row we want to remain stationary and not have sorted along with the others—it needs to remain at the top of our data table.

The next choice to make is how Sheets should reorder the table: It will appear as a drop-down menu that will list all the columns in the table individually by the value contained in the header row. (If you see items like "Column A" and "Column B," in the menu instead, the header row option hasn't been selected.)

To begin with, the census data was sorted by state name alphabetically, so let's try reordering the table based on the states' change in resident population by selecting "Change" from the menu.

Finally, you can decide which "direction" the sorting should take. By default, the order will be low to high, placing the smallest numerical value at the top of the table and the largest at the bottom. For a column containing text values, it would rearrange things alphabetically. This is called **ascending** order, represented in Google Sheets as "A → Z." The inverse is **descending** order ("Z → A"), which we'll select to see the states with the largest shifts in the number of residents first.

After clicking the green "Sort" button, the table should be fully reordered, with Texas now appearing at the top in row 2 because of the roughly 4 million people it added between 2010 and 2020. And while some of the largest states in the U.S. grew

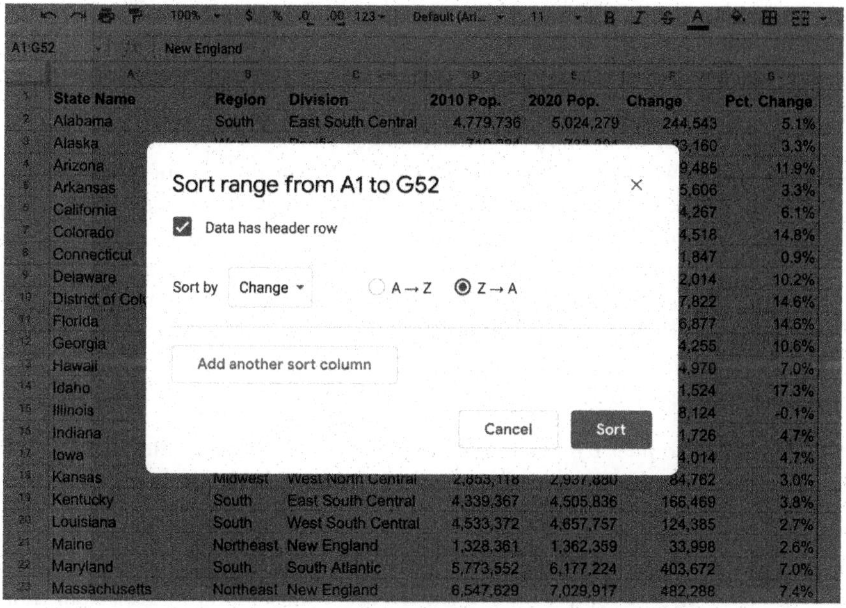

Figure 5.2 The dialogue box with options for controlling a sort. The population data has a header row, so that option has been checked, and the sort will occur in descending order (Z → A) based on the values in the "Change" column.

by millions of residents, repeating the process to sort instead by "Pct. Change" would reveal that places like Utah and Idaho saw their populations increase substantially relative to their size over that ten-year period—even more than Texas did.

Focusing on the most relevant information with filter

Another important tool in Google Sheets is the ability to add **filters** so you're only seeing certain records. This can help you count the number of items that meet specific criteria—like the number of states that experienced double-digit percentage growth between 2010 and 2020—or simply reduce the number of rows shown by temporarily hiding sections of the data that aren't relevant.

Filtering data can aid in cleaning up dirty data issues as well—but more on that later.

Just like with sorting, making sure that the full range of your data table is selected is important, especially all the rows—these are what you'll be showing or hiding from view, rather than the table's columns. A partial filter will end up leaving rows visible that you did not intend, potentially screwing up a count for your story. Google Sheets will try to identify the range for you automatically, but it's better not to leave anything up to chance.

In the "Data" menu, there's an option to "Create a filter." The funnel icon for filtering here is appropriate: We're effectively narrowing down our table.

After selecting that, the look of our spreadsheet grid changes. Google Sheets provides visual cues to let you know that your data is either set up to be filtered or actively being filtered. One of the first things you may notice: The row and column references just outside the spreadsheet grid change from light gray to a pale green for the full range of the data table, which also gains a dark green border line.

Aside from these temporary cosmetic changes, in the header row, each cell also now has a downward-facing triangle icon—like a striped chevron—on the right side. Clicking those brings up a **filter menu** with three major options:

- *The ability to sort the full range by that column in either ascending or descending order.* Like many tasks in Google Sheets, you're presented with a few ways to accomplish the same thing. This can serve as a shortcut to that ability without having to back up and repeat the whole process again. (At the top of the menu, represented as "Sort A → Z" and "Sort Z → A".)

- *The ability to filter by a condition.* Here you're able to set different kinds of criteria that values in the column either match or don't match; only the rows with matches will be shown.

- *The ability to filter by values.* This part of the menu gives you manual control over filtering and shows all the unique values found in cells from that column. Each has a checkmark next to it by default, which can be removed (or added back) to either hide (or show) rows with those corresponding values.

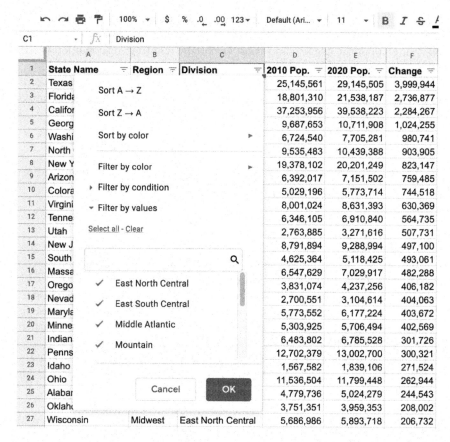

Figure 5.3 Filtering enabled on the state population table, along with the dropdown filter menu on the "Division" column.

Filtering by values

What appears in the list below "Filter by values" is every distinct value Google Sheets finds in that column's cells. (The list is expanded from the start; note the very small triangle icon facing downward next to "Filter by values." This can be clicked to show or hide that section of the filter menu.)

So, for example, in the filter menu for Column B, the four unique region values present are shown for U.S. states: Midwest, Northeast, South, and West. In addition to narrowing a data set, for **categorical data**, examining this option can provide insights about how many different values you're working within a column, as well as whether you have any missing values, which are shown in the list as "(Blanks)" at the very top.

By default, no records are hidden, and every value is shown; each unique value will have a checkmark along the left side, which will control whether rows with that value appear in the spreadsheet grid. The underlined "Clear" option above the list will remove all the check marks—clicking the "OK" button at the bottom of the menu after that would result in no rows being shown at all—while "Select all" brings all of the check marks back, essentially resetting the condition of the table to an "unfiltered" state.

Filtering by values is ideal when you have relatively few distinct values connected to the records you want to show. If you wanted to isolate and examine population changes only in western states, for example, you would:

1   Click the filter menu icon next to "Region" in the header row (cell B1).

2   Click the check marks next to "Midwest," "Northeast," and "South" to remove them.

3   Click "OK" at the bottom of the menu.

This manual selection process isn't the most efficient method of filtering for columns that hold many different values. In column G, for example, the filter menu shows every distinct percentage change in population between 2010 and 2020. Even for a relatively small data table like this, it's still a list of several dozen figures. To look only at the highest-growth states—those at or above a 10% increase in residents—filtering by values would involve clearing all the check marks and then manually selecting nearly a dozen numbers from the list.

In cases like these, where you want to show records that fall above or below a threshold (like states that had 10% growth or higher) or that contain a particular word, it's much easier to filter by condition.

Filtering by condition

These options start hidden from view within the filter menu; they can be expanded by clicking the right-facing triangle icon next to "Filter by condition." The drop-down menu of conditions defaults to "None," but below that are different types of selectable criteria that can be used to capture multiple unique values from the column at once.

One kind is text selections, which are not case sensitive, and can match against different portions of text values in a column. The options here do what they describe: To drill down to just the Carolinas, for example, choosing "Text ends with" or "Text contains" and then entering "Carolina" in the box underneath would remove anything but North Carolina and South Carolina data from view.

There are also numerical sections, where everything above, below, or between values of your choosing can be matched. To filter the data table so it only shows high-growth states:

1   Click the filter menu next to "Pct. Change" in the header row (cell G1).

2   Expand the "Filter by condition" option by clicking the icon next to it.

3   Choose "Greater than or equal to" from the drop-down options.

4   Enter "10%" in the text-entry box where it says "Value or formula."

5   Click "OK" at the bottom of the menu.

Make sure "10%" has been input rather than "10." Remember, seeing percentages in column G is a trick of cell formatting, making it easier for us to read, even though the true value there is a fraction of one with many significant digits behind the decimal.

Working with filtered data

When data has been filtered, you're presented with a new visual indicator: the filter menu icon in the header row changes into a solid-green funnel. Scanning the header row can be a quick way to see if you have any active filters in place on your data table.

Unlike other data manipulations we've undertaken, filter changes are temporary—they're just visual changes that don't actually modify your data in any way. Specific rows are only being temporarily removed from view. This fact is apparent from looking at the row numbers outside of the spreadsheet grid—if the data table was still sorted alphabetically by state name, there would be gaps. Idaho on row 14 is directly above Nevada on row 28, and so on.

Where this can be deceptive is when you're employing some kind of summary function on values in your data table, like SUM(). You may expect it to only add together the visible values in that range; in reality, the range you place into that function will likely include the hidden values that aren't included in your filter. Here, SUM(F2:F52) has the same result—calculating the total population change for all states, together—even with a filter in place.

For counts and summary statistics of filtered data, it's best to make use of the quicksum menu in the lower right corner of the interface; upon highlighting an entire column, you'll only see a summary of visible cells, rather than including values hidden by the filter.

So how should we interpret the outcome of this filter? Highlighting any column and then viewing the quicksum menu shows that 14 states experienced double-digit growth over the past decade, largely split among the West and South. While Texas is a clear stand-out in both absolute and relative terms, with 4 million additional residents, significant increases also occurred among the South Atlantic states—especially Florida.

And only one place in the Midwest, North Dakota, had a comparable increase, likely driven by an oil industry expansion, as new workers (some with families in tow) arrived to extract petroleum from the Bakken formation.[1]

What's also telling is what's missing from the filtered data. We know that the country is split into four major regions, and states from the Northeast are entirely absent.

Each one of these findings from the data could be a line in a story or a topic for further reporting on the dynamics that shape the characteristics of a state. Some will likely be similar, like Utah and Idaho, which are geographic neighbors. But the reasons for growth could diverge significantly between that part of the country and a place like Washington, D.C.

Other things to know about filtering

When filtering by more than a single column at once, fewer rows of data will be shown as fewer records match the criteria you set. As filters are added, the connection between the different criteria will always be "and": We can limit the visible results to states with double-digit growth *and* where the population increased by more than 1 million people, but we can't see that level of growth *or* states that grew beyond that million-person threshold together by filtering alone.

As helpful as filters can be, a data table may need to be rolled back to its original state, or you may want to remove a filter from a column.

Any filters can be turned off entirely by clicking the funnel icon on the toolbar above the spreadsheet grid or by going to the "Data" menu and then selecting "Turn off filter." This shows all rows and removes the filter menu icons from the cells in the header row.

Alternatively, filters can be removed from individual columns without turning them off completely:

- If selections have been made manually through "Filter by value," clicking "Select all" in the filter menu followed by the "OK" button will remove any filtering from that column.

- For "Filter by condition," returning the drop-down within the filter menu to "None," and then selecting the "OK" button will remove the filter.

Whenever filters are removed from a column, the filter menu icon in the header row cells will return to its original state as well.

Summarizing data sets with pivot tables

Much of journalism involves summarizing and synthesizing complex information for an audience—data journalism is no different. Sometimes there's too much data to digest at once, so the job of a journalist turns to figuring out how to look across a data set at a high level. There are times where it makes more sense to know how things look for a group rather than about what's happening at the individual level.

Take the census data we've used, for instance: With the SUM() function to add all populations together, and through the autofilling of some other formulas in

Chapter 4, we were able to treat states in the Northeast as members of one large group, effectively creating this kind of summary in the form of a total population figures in 2010 and 2020, as well as the absolute and relative change in the region's resident population.

In theory, even though it would be inefficient, this process could be repeated for each region or division—filter by values in those columns, add populations together as well as population change to figure out those summary values for each one.

But there's a faster way to establish groups and summarize them using **pivot tables**, a spreadsheet tool specifically designed for **aggregation**.

Finding meaningful groups in your data

Think of a roster for a professional sports association like the National Football League, where each row represents a player this season. What are some of the key groups that would exist among them?

One of the first that comes to mind is the team that they play for, like the Houston Texans or the Las Vegas Raiders. Another way to group players together would be by their primary position on the field, like quarterback or wide receiver. If we were considering how groups of players were performing on game days or how much they were getting paid, these would be some important ways to categorize them and then compare.

Groups can be made from any common elements shared within your data set's columns. We've relied on some of them already to sort and filter the census data, like a state's region or division.

Creating a pivot table

Let's say we're trying to summarize data about college costs in the United States, and we have information for all degree-granting institutions, including what they charged full-time students for tuition and fees, as well as their room and board costs in 2018 and 2019.

Individually, we can see which schools charged the most or had the largest swings in costs from year to year, which are certainly newsworthy findings. But we might also want to step back a bit, too, to better understand some of the largest trends taking place with the sticker price of college.

Treating all schools the same won't necessarily make sense here, either—they have different ownership structures, where some are public universities that receive funding from the state, while others are nonprofits. Some are four-year institutions, but others are community colleges that only offer associate degrees. The data contains large colleges with robust student-life hubs, housing and feeding thousands, as well as commuter campuses with limited dorm space.

Establishing important groups in this data keeps the apples separated from the oranges, so to speak, but it also lets us examine differences between groups. By summarizing the data this way, we can compare tuition changes at private schools versus public ones, among other things.

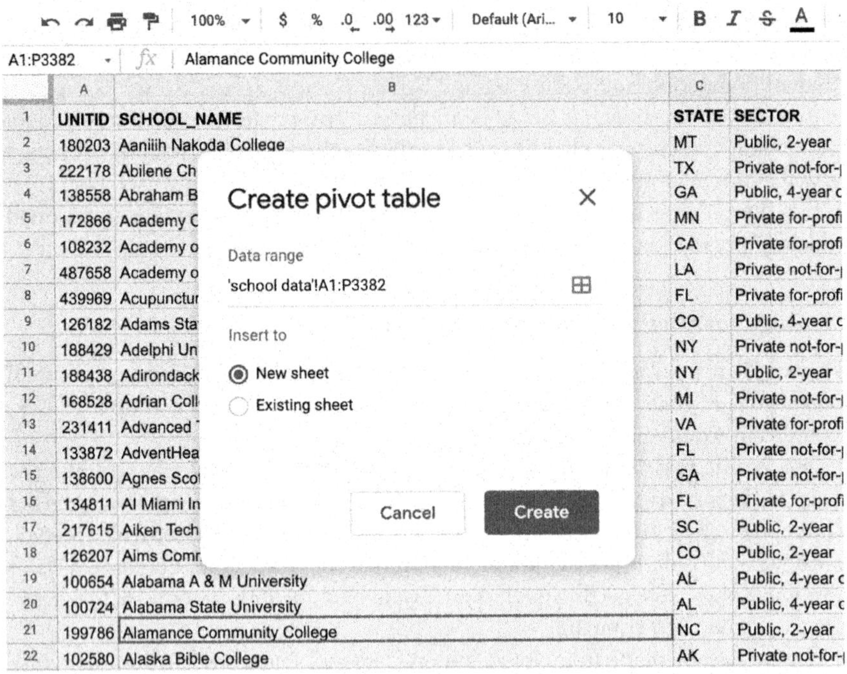

Figure 5.4 Creating a new pivot table. The full extent of the data table is selected, so the range for the pivot table is already completed.

This should begin to give a sense of some of the groups present in the data.

After going through the process of sorting and filtering, you can likely predict what's coming here. One of the first things we want to do is make sure the full range of data is highlighted so that all columns are rows are available to us within a pivot table.

Once the full table is highlighted, select "Pivot table" from the "Insert" menu. A new dialog box will open over the spreadsheet grid.

Because we've already highlighted the data for the pivot table, the "Data range" is filled in. The notation may seem a little odd, but all Google Sheets is doing is describing the range with an extra bit of information tacked onto the beginning to correctly denote the specific sheet where the data table is located. The format is always: *'sheet name'!first cell in the range:last cell in the range*. For this particular table, it would be: `'school data'!A1:P3382`.

You also need to choose where the new pivot table is created. It's generally easiest to place it in its own sheet; there's organizational value in keeping the original data table separate from this kind of summary analysis.

After clicking the "Create" button, you'll automatically be shown the new sheet, which will be named `"Pivot Table 1"` by default.

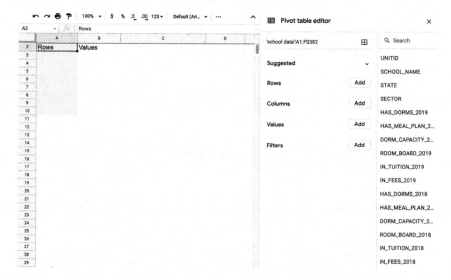

Figure 5.5 The pivot table editor on the right side of the window has two sections: a list of all column headers in the selected data table, and four pivot table elements where those columns can be added. When changes are made here, they are reflected in the pivot table itself on the left side of the window.

Within this new sheet, the spot where we would typically see a new spreadsheet grid is significantly altered. The interface is essentially split into two halves: You make changes within the **Pivot Table Editor** on the right and then see those changes reflected in the **pivot table** itself on the left.

On the far right of the Pivot Table Editor, underneath the search box with a magnifying glass icon, you'll see a listing of every column name in the data set, taken directly from the table's header row.

Immediately to the left of that, the Pivot Table Editor displays the range of data within the pivot table—which should mirror the range you selected when creating the pivot table—and then a list of four **pivot table elements** underneath: "Rows," "Columns," "Values," and "Filters." We'll get to the specifics of how each of these works in a moment.

Building a simple pivot table from a question

The key elements for any pivot table are the "Rows" and "Values." It may be helpful at the outset to think of them as "Groups" and "Summary" instead because that is very much how they function together.

As mentioned previously, journalists regularly come to a data set with at least one specific question in mind. With the higher education data example, we might be curious to see what undergraduate student fees looked like in 2019 across the different sectors (e.g., public, two-year schools or private, nonprofit four-year institutions) and which was the highest. Maybe even compare those to the previous year to see if there were significant differences that would warrant a story or be worth mentioning in a larger piece.

So, let's break the first overarching question into its component parts to get some clues about how we might analyze the data. A better, more direct way to phrase what we want to know could be: "Which <u>sector</u> had the <u>highest student fees in 2019</u>?"

The way we open this question tells us how we'll probably want to group the data: by the higher education <u>sector</u>.

For the purposes of our analysis, the "Rows" pivot table element will be used to hold our groups. Click the "Add" button next to "Rows" and then select Sector.

With "Rows," for any column added here, Google Sheets will pluck out the distinct values and establish them as separate groupings for the pivot table. Each group appears on its own row in the pivot table, hence the name.

Now, in the pivot table half of the interface, a set of values appears in column A where there had previously been nothing: each unique sector value.

It's worth noting that nothing done with a pivot table is set in stone—where Sector now appears as its own box underneath the "Rows" element in the Pivot Table Editor, it can just as easily be removed by selecting the "X" icon in its top right corner, returning the interface to its original state. Any changes you've made by adding different columns to the pivot table elements can be easily reset with a click.

We're not quite ready to sort anything to find what's high or low—we've established our groups, but we haven't actually analyzed anything yet. So, let's move on

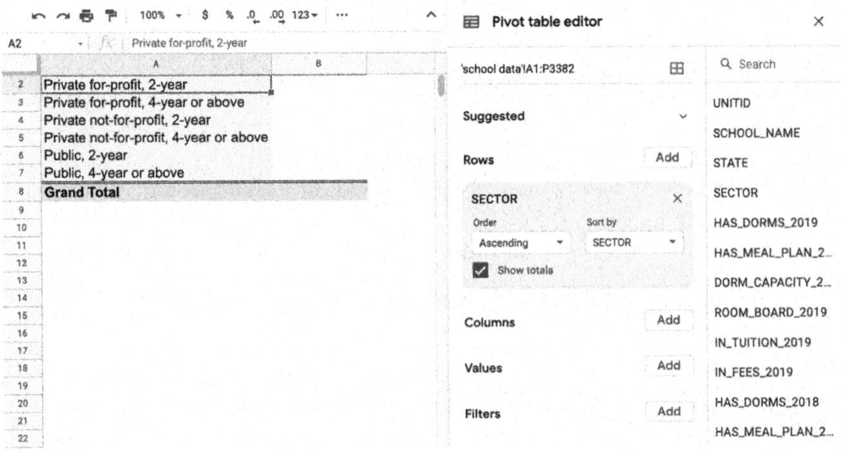

Figure 5.6 The "Sector" column added to "Rows." All unique values found in that column appear on their own row in the pivot table.

to the last part of our question: <u>student fees in 2019</u>. This is the column with the values that we'll want to examine.

And because we're interested in generating a meaningful summary for the group, we need to choose one that makes sense in this context. A sum or total won't do it—each institution is its own row, and the student fee listed for each is what the typical undergraduate pays.

In this case, a measure of central tendency, like an average or mean, will probably be among the best summaries for all of these fee values within each group—one number that provides a strong sense of what's typical.

Again, "Values" is where we summarize a column within the data table. Just as with the institution sector in "Rows," the 2019 fees column can be added to "Values."

With "Values," any column added here will be summarized in some fashion; that summary will be repeated for each group established through the "Rows" pivot table element. Google Sheets provides a range of summary options for each column—even the ability to create your own using formulas and built-in functions.

As usual, Google Sheets makes some default guesses on how to summarize this data based on what the program sees in the column. It will usually try to total up numerical values; text values (or a mix of text and numbers) will be summarized by counting.

Pivot table summary types

Google Sheets offers more than a dozen types of summaries for data sets, which can be changed at will through the "Summarize by" dropdown menu once the column has been added to "Values."

Among them are some common summaries you can do that will perform different calculations on numerical values in a column:

- SUM: Adds the values up for each group.

- AVERAGE: Finds the average or mean for each group: the sum of values divided by the number of values. Note that blanks are not considered values and will be excluded from the calculation.

- MEDIAN: Finds the median for each group: a midpoint figure where half the group's values are higher and half the values are lower. Like with an average, blank cells are excluded. For Microsoft Excel users, there's currently no equivalent median feature in pivot tables.

- MAX: Returns the highest value found in each group.

- MIN: Same principle as MAX, but for the lowest value instead. Used in tandem with MAX, this can be useful for assessing the range of values in each group.

But we're obviously not only working with numeric values in a spreadsheet. Google Sheets can also count the values that are present in a column, which can be helpful to establish the size of different groups.

- COUNTA: Counts every value in each group, ignoring the cells that are blank. It may help to think of COUNTA as "count all."

- COUNTUNIQUE: Counts every distinct value in each group. Much like when looking at the list of column values in a filter menu, repeated values are only counted one time.

- COUNT: Counts only numerical values in each group, ignoring the cells that contain text, that are a mixture of text and numbers, or that are blank. It's very easy, unfortunately, to confuse COUNT and COUNTA because names for these summaries are so similar.

As said previously, an average is going to make the most sense to express fees for these different sectors. Selecting "AVERAGE" from the "Summarize by" drop-down menu within "IN_FEES_2019" causes that column of the pivot table to reflect that change almost instantly.

You'll note that Google Sheets assigns an automatic name to the summary column in the pivot table that describes the action it's performing. Right now, it says "AVERAGE of IN_FEES_2019," but that can be overwritten by clicking in cell B1 and editing the text to your satisfaction. Those modifications are then reflected in the Pivot Table Editor.

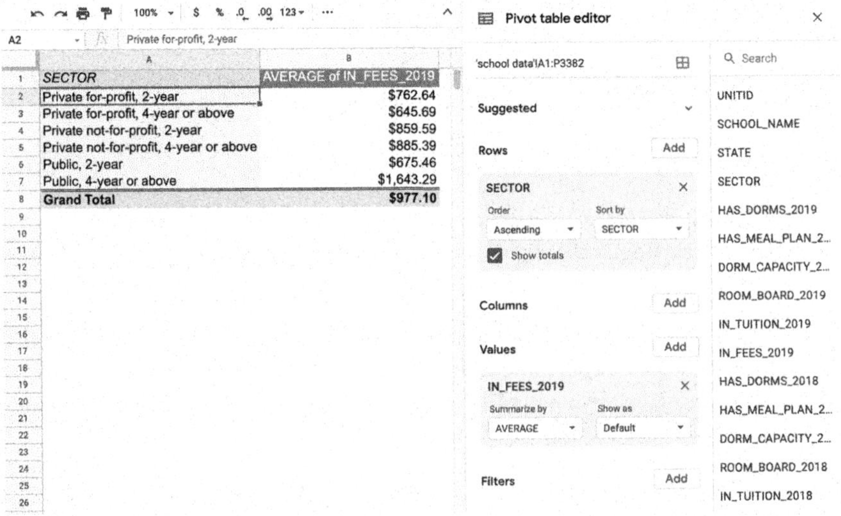

Figure 5.7 A pivot table grouping colleges based on their sector and showing the average student fees for each group in column B. The average values have been formatted as currency.

We probably also want these values to look more like currency as opposed to a random figure with many digits included after a decimal point. As discussed in previous chapters, that level of precision isn't particularly meaningful or necessary.

By highlighting column B in the pivot table, and then using the "Format" menu to select "Number" followed by "Currency," the values will be rounded to the nearest cent, gain a dollar sign, and add commas as a thousand-separator. This makes it a bit easier to read and digest. This modification does not actually impact the values underneath, only the way that they look within the pivot table.

Sorting a pivot table

Since there are only six different sectors to arrange into groups, sorting to see which one had the largest average fees isn't critical—we can just as easily look across the six summary figures to see that at more than $1,600, 4-year public colleges are considerably higher than the others. But groupings won't always be so manageable or easy to interpret.

The sorting process works differently in a pivot table than it does on the typical spreadsheet grid. In fact, if you try to reorder the rows through "Sort range," you'll end up with data that is briefly sorted but then snaps right back into its original state.

To control the sort, look back to the column you've assigned for grouping under "Rows" in the Pivot Table Editor. For "Sector," there are two dropdown menus: one for "Order" (either "Ascending" or "Descending"), and another called "Sort By," which lists each column currently displayed in the pivot table—not in the original data set.

Selecting the average student fees column in "Sort By" and then changing "Order" to descending order will move that $1,600 figure and the associated 4-year public university group to the top, followed by the other sectors from high to low.

You may have noticed the "Grand Total" at the bottom of the pivot table. Think of this like a summary across all the values in the entire column if there were no groups present. What we're seeing here is not a total, as in the sum of these various averages—that would be a nonsensical figure. Instead, it's the average of student fees in 2019 for all institutions in the data table, regardless of group. If having that overarching summary isn't important, unchecking the box next to "Show totals" for "Sector" will hide it.

Leaning into the flexibility of pivot tables

With this straightforward summary of average student fees by school sector, we've not yet run into the limits of what can be done with a pivot table. Not even close.

Pivot tables have the same flexibility as spreadsheets themselves, allowing you to expand the number of things you summarize about different groups in data, as well as provide ways to readjust those groups or drill down, focusing on more specific information.

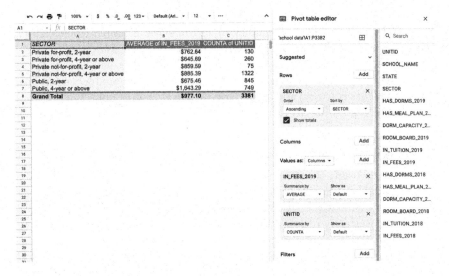

Figure 5.8 Adding another summary column to the pivot table.

While we consider the averages for each sector, we may also want to see just how many schools are included in each group to give a sense of how many student fee figures are a part of the calculation.

To do this, leave "IN_FEES_2019" in "Values." We will add another one of the data table's columns to "Values" instead. Any one of the columns will work as long as it has values present in every cell—there can't be blanks.

In this case, you can add the "UNITID" column to "Values," then change the summary type to "COUNTA." Every school in this data set has a UNITID—a unique identifier used by the Department of Education to distinguish between different campuses. Counting them up within each group yields a count of institutions. Cross-checking it with the original data set in the other sheet, you can see that all 3,381 schools (excluding that top header row) are represented in the pivot table through this new summary column.

Part of the flexibility is that you can keep adding different columns under "Values" in the Pivot Table Editor to summarize, thereby expanding the number of columns in your pivot table—even duplicates of the same column from the original data set, summarized in new ways. Removing them is as simple as clicking on the "X" icon next to the column name.

Similarly, a data set summarized within a pivot table can be regrouped at will—you don't have to start over with a new pivot table to do this.

For example, you may be curious about how student fees vary by state. Now, every state is going to have its own mix of schools that occupy different sectors, but it might be worth checking on any interesting regional variation.

Under "Rows," clicking the "X" icon for "Sector" causes those groups to disappear from column A, leaving behind only the selected summaries under

"Values" for the full data set on row 2. (Because the groups disappear from column A, everything shifts to the left—you may notice that column formatting, like currency, stays in the columns where you first assigned it.)

Adding "State" to "Rows" immediately regroups the data with each state abbreviation in column A. But it also keeps the earlier summary calculations from "Values"—the average for student fees in 2019 and the count of institutions—intact, now performing them for each state instead.

Filtering a pivot table

There are times when you may not want to include the entire table that you have at your disposal in summary form within a pivot table. For example, limiting the data you summarize can help in a situation like this: You want to see the average room and board in each sector for 2019, but recognize that not all institutions offer students housing or meal programs. Tossing all the schools together for an average wouldn't necessarily make sense because the presence (or lack thereof) of either type of student service will significantly impact the cost.

The "Filters" option in the Pivot Table Editor gives you the ability to remove data from consideration. In this data set, we have two columns that can help limit the scope for a more accurate average amount: One that's a simple yes/no value about whether the institution offers housing (HAS_DORMS_2019) and another for meal plans (HAS_MEAL_PLAN_2019).

To do this, we want to first take our pivot table back to its original state by clicking the "X" icon next to any columns added to the Pivot Table Editor.

From there, two changes set up the summary you want:

1   Add the "SECTOR" column to "Rows."

2   Add the "ROOM_BOARD_2019" column to "Values" and summarize by "AVERAGE."

Now, within the Pivot Table Editor, "HAS_DORMS_2019" and "HAS_MEAL_PLAN_2019" can be added to "Filters." As we haven't actually engaged any filters yet, each one currently says "Showing all items." But the dropdown menu for each should be familiar from earlier in the chapter; you're presented with a similar set of choices, allowing you to filter the data displayed either by conditions or specific values.

In this case, you want to do it by values. Deselecting the checkmark next to "N" from each dropdown menu omits schools that state they do not offer meal plans or campus housing from the analysis, ensuring that the average for each group—the sector—is generated from more comparable student situations.

Note that this impacts not only your group summaries, but any "totals" in the bottom row of the pivot table. You only see overarching figures for the data that passes through the filter.

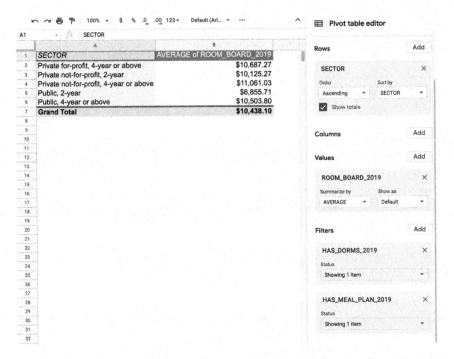

Figure 5.9 A pivot table showing the average cost of room and board at different types of institutions, using the "Filter" option to remove schools that don't offer meal plans or housing from the summary.

And if you add a count to the summary by adding "UNITID" to "Values" and summarizing by "COUNTA," you see a reduced number of institutions: only 1,820 schools in the data table, or a little more than half, have both offerings.

More than one way to group data

You may have noticed that a lot of attention has been lavished on grouping, summarizing, and filtering data in a pivot table with the aid of "Rows," "Values," and "Filters." So far, we've ignored the fourth major facet of the Pivot Table Editor: "Columns."

This feature functions exactly like "Rows," but for any data column added here, the distinct values representing different groups appear horizontally across the top of the pivot table, left to right, instead of vertically (top to bottom).

Going back to the higher education example: Rockford University is a four-year private nonprofit institution, like more than 1,300 others in this data table, but it's also located in the state of Illinois, which is home to over 130 institutions. Those groups intersect—there are only three dozen schools in the data that fit in both of those groups simultaneously.

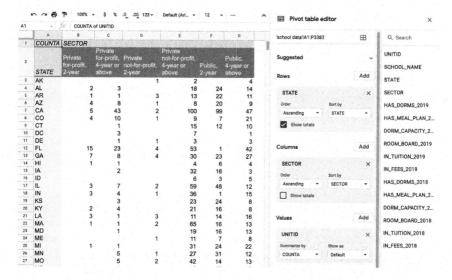

Figure 5.10 A crosstabulation using "Rows" and "Columns" together to group the data by state and sector at the same time, showing a count for each.

Adding columns to "Rows" and "Columns" in tandem lets you see summaries for these more granular groups; it's a form of cross-tabulation, showing how the summary values for each group changes as they become more specific.

Similarly, multiple groups can be created within "Rows," "Columns," or both, simply by adding more than one column to them from the data table.

The principle here is like sorting by more than one column, in that the order in which you assign columns to either "Rows" or "Columns" determines the order of grouping. For example, if sector is added first, appearing before (or above) state in "Rows," then sector will comprise that first level of grouping in column A, with breakouts for each individual state in column B.

Ultimately, what you're doing here is gaining control over the "shape" of your data, restructuring how the information is presented so that it's easier to understand, interpret, and communicate. This control goes beyond simple analysis for a story—these are also the very necessary ways journalists identify potential weak points in a data set, as well as the methods to restructure and prepare data for display in visual form.

Note

1 https://www.minotdailynews.com/news/local-news/2021/08/oil-counties-lead-in-percent-of-population-increase/.

6 Clean and repair

Techniques for more advanced analysis

* * *

If one of the early steps in data analysis is identifying problems and inconsistencies, the next is crafting a plan of action to solve them and get things on track.

In this way, a constant part of data journalism is playing a diagnostician of sorts. You're prodding different aspects of a data set, looking for issues that could undermine the reporting while smoothing them out as best you can. A couple of different methods will familiarize you quickly with the contents of each column in your data set: looking at the filter menu and creating frequency tables.

The filter menu and frequency tables

Using the filter menu is probably the most straightforward way with the fewest steps to see the contents of a column without having to scroll through the whole spreadsheet. Setting a filter for a column or columns, and then clicking on the arrow icon next to the column header, allows you to view the distinct values that occur in the column in alphabetical order under "Filter by values."

While it won't tell you anything about how often these different values are present, this arrangement makes blanks and values that have been spelled in various ways much more apparent.

To get a more expansive view, a specific kind of pivot table is the other tool at your disposal—one that counts the presence of values based on their frequency, hence the name "frequency table."

Once you've decided which column to examine, it's a simple counting summary.

Follow the steps you normally would to create a new pivot table; in "Rows," add the column header for the column that you want to summarize by its frequency.

But what you add to the "Values" section of the pivot table creator is a little different than you might expect because of the built-in summary functions devoted to counting cells.

As previously mentioned, Google Sheets has a few different count-related functions under the "Summarize by" dropdown menu for any column added to "Values"; the one to use here is COUNTA. (As a reminder, COUNTA is the equivalent

DOI: 10.4324/9781003182238-6

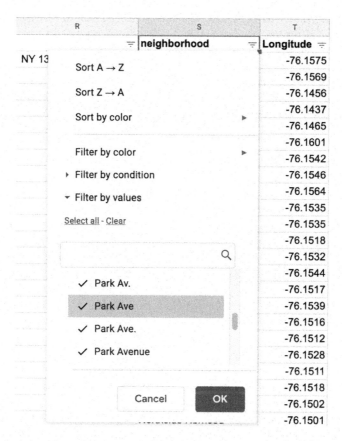

Figure 6.1 The unique values present in a column can be seen using the filter menu; here, there are multiple spellings of "Park Ave." that may need to be fixed.

of "count all"—when it finds a value in a column's cell, that value gets tallied up regardless of what kind of value it is. COUNTA does not discriminate between numbers and text.)

But the key here is that the COUNTA function will only count cells in a column that have a value. Be sure whichever column you place in "Values" counting has no blanks at all.

This should be repeated for most of the data table's columns to gain a better understanding of what's there.

Follow the recommendations from the previous chapter's checklist, using the "Order" and "Sort by" options for the column in "Rows" to reorder the frequency table by both the unique values from the column and their corresponding counts. What's the range of values, and which ones occur the most frequently? Do they align with your expectations based on research, reporting, or what you already know?

For example, if you expect each value should be unique in the original data and not appear in more than one row, like employees in a state personnel database, each full name in your frequency table should have a count of 1.

Or, when working with data that has a column that contains calendar years, what's the most recent year represented? How far back does the data go? If the most recent year appears much less frequently in the data set than others, it could be a sign that only a partial year is recorded. As always, don't make assumptions; make note of it and figure out who you could ask about the discrepancy.

Adding columns for cleaned values

Having nonstandardized values in a column can fracture the groups you establish for analysis—items with different spelling, capitalization, or even spacing can cause rows to be assigned to a different group. This can damage summaries by leaving out items you may assume were included in a certain group.

Let's say you're ranking films based on their 2021 domestic box office revenues, trying to figure out which one was the highest. Based on the data you've gathered, it's neck-and-neck between the top two films of the year, which both happen to be Marvel movies—*Spider-Man: No Way Home* and *Shang-Chi and the Legend of the Ten Rings*—which are only separated by a few thousand dollars. And yet, only one can have been the top money-maker in the U.S. market; it appears to be *Shang-Chi*, and you point it out in your piece.

But there's a problem: in the data set that you analyzed, *Spider-Man* is recorded three different ways. It also appears without the colon in the title (:), and in other instances, it's missing the hyphen between "spider" and "man." As it turns out, had those film titles been standardized and expressed in precisely the same way, this movie that seemed like a runner-up was, in fact, the one that had the largest box office take by a long shot.

Because this is a frequent occurrence in data, especially for digital records that have values that are entered freely by hand, by many different people, or that are collected over a long span of time, you need a method to be able to standardize those values without overwriting the original values.

Why should you care about leaving the original values intact if they aren't standardized? You always want to retain the starting place in case you make a mistake or change your mind about what the standard value should be. Once you overwrite the original, there's no point of reference to go back to. As time passes, you may not even be able to recall if you made a change at all or left the original value intact.

We need what's known as a **cleaning column** that we can modify freely. One good approach is to duplicate the column that has the non-standardized values, placing the copy immediately to the right of the original and changing the column header so that you know it's the one you've modified. Append a word like "clean" or "fixed" to make it very clear, even if it's a data set you put down for a while and come back to later.

To create a cleaning column:

1 Make room for the cleaning column in the existing data table: Highlight the column you'll be cleaning by clicking on its column reference, then going to the "Insert" menu, selecting "Columns" and "Insert 1 column right." This pushes the remaining columns in the data set to the right and creates an empty column in your spreadsheet.

2 Duplicate the column's contents: Click on the column reference of the column to be cleaned once more to highlight its contents; copy it all by using the appropriate keyboard shortcut or choosing "Copy" from the "Edit" menu; click the cell reference of the empty column that you just created; and, finally, paste those values into that space.

3 Change the column header to make it clear it's a column for cleaning or correction.

Now we need an efficient way to make changes to the cleaning column, one that's better than just scrolling through the data table and typing one-off tweaks as you see them.

Here, using the filter can be helpful not only to identify values that need to be corrected but to narrow your view to only those values, making them easier to correct all at once instead of bit by bit.

In the filter menu below "Filter by values," select "clear" to remove all check marks. Then, only reapply the check marks to the values that need to be standardized. After clicking the OK button, only those rows in the data table will be visible.

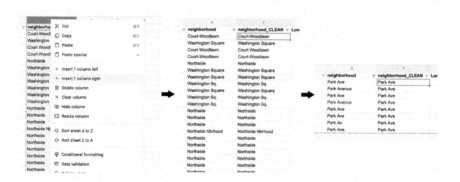

Figure 6.2 The process for creating a cleaning column: First, add a new blank column next to the one you're trying to clean. Then, duplicate the values from the original column and give it an appropriate column header. Finally, target values that need to be standardized using filter and correct them in the cleaning column.

Once you've figured out what the standard value should be, you can apply it to all the existing values in the cleaning column:

1   Enter the standard value in the cleaning column in the cell directly below the one that contains the column header—here it's fine to overwrite and replace whatever value is already present.

2   Copy the cell where you entered the standard value, using the "Copy" command from the "Edit" menu or the control/command-C keyboard shortcut.

3   Highlight the remaining visible cells in the cleaning column.

4   Paste the standard value into those selected cells, using the "Paste" command from the "Edit" menu or the control/command-V keyboard shortcut. Even though you've only copied the contents of a single cell, it will paste those same contents more than once across anything you've selected.

Repeat this process of selecting these close-but-not-quite values through the filter menu and making them the same in the cleaning column as many times as necessary until it only has standardized contents. Any column suffering from the same issues will also need a cleaning counterpart.

Functions to help you clean text

While this manual correction method to standardize values works best for issues like multiple spellings, it won't help as much when the inconsistencies are more widespread, like columns with cells that contain extra white space or have irregular capitalization. Data cleaning should make targeted fixes to a column rather than force you to go through each and every cell to correct the same sort of issue.

There is a range of functions devoted to working with text rather than numbers that can reduce the tedium of issues that crop up repeatedly.

Among the most helpful are:

- TRIM, which removes unnecessary whitespace from in and around text values. If spaces precede or follow text, they are removed. If the text in a cell has more than one space between different words, those are reduced to a single space.

  `=TRIM("Jane   R.M.  Smith")` → `Jane R.M. Smith`

- UPPER, which converts any letters to their uppercase versions.

  `=UPPER("Jane r.m. Smith")` → `JANE R.M. SMITH`

- LOWER, which does the same thing, except changing each letter to lowercase instead.

  `=LOWER("Jane R.M. Smith")` → `jane r.m. smith`

- PROPER, which changes the first letter of any word in a cell to uppercase and any that follows to lowercase.

`=PROPER("jAnE r.m. SmitH")` → `Jane R.M. Smith`

Using functions in a cleaning column

To make the best use of functions for cleaning and standardizing data, begin the same way as before: create a space for the cleaning column by inserting a new column to the right of the one that you want to standardize.

But instead of copying the contents of the original column, leave it blank; you're going to be referencing the cells in the original column while also applying one (or more) of the above functions.

	A	B
1	Name	Name Clean
2	jAnE r.m. SmitH	=PROPER(A2)
3	robert d. JONES	

After applying the function to the first value, Google Sheets will prompt you to autofill the remainder of the column with the same function, referencing each cell from the original column in order. Alternatively, you can manually fill the column by double-clicking in the bottom right corner of the cell or clicking and dragging from that same position down to the bottom of the column.

Getting your changes to stick with "Paste Special"

In spreadsheet grid cells that hold a formula, you generally see the end result of some calculation or behind-the-scenes processing. It's only when you double-click in the cell or check the formula bar while the cell is highlighted that you'll see the specific formula instead of the resulting value.

When using functions that alter text, it's possible that other modifications will need to be made even after whitespace is removed or capitalization is changed. Sometimes cleaning is a multistep process—widespread fixes are made first by using a function, and then more specific issues are addressed with the manual process of selecting certain distinct values via a filter and correcting them in the cleaning column.

But you can't make manual tweaks to cells in a cleaning column where formulas are still present.

To solve this, the "Paste special" ability can quickly wipe away a cell's underlying formula, replacing it with its visible value instead.

"Paste special" is accessed through the "Edit" menu, or through the contextual pop-up menu that appears on the spreadsheet grid by right- or command-clicking. Choosing "Values only" removes the formula in favor of the formula's result, placing that inside the cell instead. This can be done on a whole column as well as a single cell.

By copying and then using "Paste special" in the same column, any formulas are overwritten; it's best to store a copy of the formula elsewhere in the spreadsheet or your notes somehow for fact-checking purposes.

Using more than one function at the same time

When using functions to clean data, there may be more than one issue to address across all the cells in a column. Instead of tackling this as a series of steps in more than one column, like using `TRIM` in one cleaning column to get rid of excess whitespace, then referencing those trimmed values using `UPPER` in a new column to make them all uppercase as well, those steps can be combined by nesting those functions.

Nesting is exactly how it sounds—placing functions inside of one another. The innermost function is processed first, followed by whatever function immediately surrounds it. If there are others enclosing those, like a series of Matryoshka dolls, those are handled in the same order, from the inside to the outside.

To use `TRIM` and `UPPER` together, the format would look like this:

```
=TRIM(UPPER(" Jane   R.M. Smith     ")) → JANE R.M. SMITH
```

Note that the equals sign (=) is only used once; remember, it's the opening signifier in Google Sheets that the cell contents need to be handled by the software as a formula.

It's powerful to be able to use multiple functions at once, but a downside is that as more functions are layered atop one another, the series of actions taking place can become hard to follow. We're accustomed to reading a written line left-to-right (or right-to-left, depending on the language); these formulas are often interpreted in more of a "middle-out" fashion.

To keep it all straight, it can be helpful to conceptualize more complicated formulas as more of a series of steps rather than trying to enter them perfectly into a cell all at once.

So for the above, you could begin with the first step, which is converting the text string to uppercase letters:

```
=UPPER(" Jane   R.M. Smith     ")
```

Then build upon what you have with the next step—removing unneeded spaces— by enclosing it with the `TRIM` formula:

```
=TRIM(UPPER(" Jane   R.M. Smith     "))
```

Combining and separating cell contents

Ideally, data columns are going to hold one type of value rather than many different values sandwiched together. In data from the U.S. Census, we expect elements like places and population estimates to occupy their own columns; it wouldn't make much sense to have them blended together, like: `"Essex County New Jersey 863,728."`

You may also encounter data sets with values that are spread across multiple columns, even though these values could be combined to create one complete data element—think about how a month, day, and year form a full date when together. These may need to be assembled into a single column for sorting or filtering.

Using "Split text to columns"

Google Sheets' primary method of separating one column's contents in a way that works very much like the import process for a data format like comma-separated values (CSV): "Split text to columns."

With it, you identify a character that can serve as the delimiter, like a comma or a space. Each time Google Sheets encounters the delimiter, the cell contents are divided—or split—into a new column.

For example, a standard home or business address is made up of different components, generally including elements like a street number, city, and postal code. If all those elements occupy a cell together, it will be more difficult to group and summarize the data because each unique address would show up in a pivot table as its own group. That isn't particularly helpful if you're trying to summarize a data set by state or city—you need those parts of the location to be separated into their own columns.

Even though there are some obvious standardization issues that jump out just by scanning through some of the addresses—like the punctuation, spelling, and

	case_status	property_id	vacant_property	property_owner_name	property_owner_address	neighborhood
1	Open	003.-07-04.0	N	Michael Lembo	106 Sherwood lane, North Syracuse, NY 13212	Court-Woodlawn
2	Open	003.-23-14.0	N	Pothwei Bangoshoth	707 Turtle St, Syracuse, NY 13208	Washington Square
3	Open	005.-01-36.0	N	CNY Asset Management LLC	1900 West Genesee Street, SYR, NY 13204	Court Woodlawn
4	Open	005.-05-27.0	N	Peak Property Mgmnt Corp	PO BOX 5335, Syracuse, NY 13220	Court-Woodlawn
5	Open	006.-12-47.0	N	Inva Holding Company, LLC	7271 Roumare Road, East Syracuse, NY 13057	Northside
6	Open	007.-03-16.0	No	Brian Fitzgibbons	127 Maplehurst Ave, Syracuse, NY 13208	Washington Square
7	Open	007.-09-13.0	N	Bob Myers		Washington Square
8	Open	007.-09-17.0	N	Stickle & Gillen Entrprs LLC	5038 Yellow Wood Pkwy, Jamesville, NY 13078	Washington Sq.
9	Open	007.-10-18.0		O'Hanks Trust	4407 Cutting Blvd, Richmond, CA 94804	Washington Square
10	Open	007.-23-23.0		Mohammad Khan	392 Main St, Beacon, NY 12580	Washington Sq.
11	Needs Review	007.-23-23.0	N	Mohammad Khan	392 Main St, Beacon, NY 12580	Washington Sq.
12	Open	007.-24-47.0	N	Olga Aviles	138 Lawrence St, Syracuse, NY 13208	Northside
13	Open	007.-29-36.0	N	Hassan Muse	1224 Park St, Syracuse, NY 13208	Northside
14	Open	007.-32-12.0	No	Rosario DeCarciofolo	114 Mary Street, Sacramento, CA 13208	Northside
15	Open	008.-04-06.0	No	Delahoz Properties LLC	2263 W New Haven Ave, West Melbourne, FL 32904-3805	Northside Nbrhood
16	Open	008.-10-22.0	No	Sagacious Holding Group LLC	122 Edgehill Rd, Syr., NY 13224	Northside
17	Open	008.-11-07.0	N	Duyen Trang	173 Oswego River Rd, Phoenix, NY 13135	Northside
18	Open	008.-12-03.0	N	Kpaw Say	1029 Danforth St, Syracuse, NY 13208	Northside
19	Open	009.-01-06.0	N	Pro Home Group CNY LLC	74 Cherry Tree Cir, Liverpool, NY 13090	Northside
20	Open	009.-01-17.0	N	Alexom Productions LLC	323 E Water St, Syrcause, NY 13202	Northside
21	Open	009.-02-07.0	N	PATRIDAI INVEST NY LLC	2300 Milton Ave, Syacuse, NY 13209	Northside
22	Open	009.-02-19.0		Hinuera Properties LLC	48 Bright St, Jersey City, NJ 7302	Northside
23	Needs Review	009.-03-13.0	N	Phyllip Martin	1621 Midland Ave, Syracuse, NY 13205	Northside Nbrhood
24	Open	009.-06-11.0	N	Sang Nguyen	1801 Grant Blvd, Syracuse, NY 13208	Northside Nbrhood
25	Open	009.-10-02.0	N	EndZone Properties Inc	PO BOX 11506, Syracuse, NY 13218	Northside Nbrhood
26	Open	009.-17-12.0	N	Yohandra Marrero Mir	624 East Division Street, SYR, NY 13208	Northside Nbrhood

Figure 6.3 Rather than having different parts of a mailing address appear in separate columns, this data table keeps them together, making it difficult to group them by city or state.

capitalization for city names—they take a regular format. An address like "707 Turtle St, Syracuse, NY 13208" can be thought about as a pattern of components:

Components	[street number] [street name] [street suffix], [city name], [state abbreviation] [U.S. postal code]
Example	707 Turtle St, Syracuse, NY 13208

The pattern here has two strong breakpoints to separate some of these elements into their own columns in the form of commas, which can serve as the first delimiter: One comma sits between the street suffix and the city name, and another follows the city name, dividing it from the state abbreviation and postal code.

At the end of the process, one column should become three:

Components	[street number] [street name] [street suffix]	[city name]	[state abbreviation] [U.S. postal code]
Example	707 Turtle St	Syracuse	NY 13208

Once the delimiter character has been identified, the first step in this process is to make room for the portions of the cell contents that will end up in new columns.

property_owner_address			neighborhood	Longitude	L
106 Sherwood lane, North Syracuse, NY 13212			Court-Woodlawn	-76.1575	
707 Turtle St, Syracuse, NY 13208			Washington Square	-76.1569	
1900 West Genesee Street, SYR, NY 13204			Court Woodlawn	-76.1456	
PO BOX 5335, Syracuse, NY 13220			Court-Woodlawn	-76.1437	
7271 Roumare Road, East Syracuse, NY 13057			Northside	-76.1465	
127 Maplehurst Ave, Syracuse, NY 13208			Washington Square	-76.1601	
			Washington Square	-76.1542	
5038 Yellow Wood Pkwy, Jamesville, NY 13078			Washington Sq.	-76.1546	
4407 Cutting Blvd, Richmond, CA 94804			Washington Square	-76.1564	
392 Main St, Beacon, NY 12580			Washington Sq.	-76.1535	
392 Main St, Beacon, NY 12580			Washington Sq.	-76.1535	
138 Lawrence St, Syracuse, NY 13208			Northside	-76.1518	
1224 Park St, Syracuse, NY 13208			Northside	-76.1532	
114 Mary Street, Sacramento, CA 13208			Northside	-76.1544	
2263 W New Haven Ave, West Melbourne, FL 32904-3805			Northside Nbrhood	-76.1517	
122 Edgehill Rd, Syr., NY 13224			Northside	-76.1539	
173 Oswego River Rd, Phoenix, NY 13135			Northside	-76.1516	
1029 Danforth St, Syracuse, NY 13208			Northside	-76.1512	
74 Cherry Tree Cir, Liverpool, NY 13090			Northside	-76.1528	
323 E Water St, Syrcause, NY 13202			Northside	-76.1511	
2300 Milton Ave, Syacuse, NY 13209			Northside	-76.1518	
48 Bright St, Jersey City, NJ 7302			Northside	-76.1502	

Figure 6.4 Adding blank columns to the right of Column L provides open space for the values impacted by "Split text to columns" so that you won't overwrite existing data.

This is important: If you don't create new blank columns to the right of the column being split apart, you'll overwrite the contents of any existing columns; this will happen without a warning.

Here, as the values of one column are split into three separate columns, you'll need to insert two blank columns to the right of the existing property owner address column—any of the cell contents that comes before the first comma will just remain in the original column.

Highlight the property address column and then choose "Split text to columns" from the data menu. The address values should automatically split apart, with cities now occupying the column immediately to the right, and the state and postal code appearing together in the next rightmost column. Note, too, that the comma characters disappear after marking the breakpoint where cell contents should flow into a new column.

You didn't choose a delimiter, so how did this happen without any input on your part? Google Sheets examined the column and made an educated guess, essentially. And it's possible that the guess it made was incorrect.

Toward the bottom of the spreadsheet grid, there is a very small dialogue box that is not always easy to distinguish from the background: it's a selector where

	property_owner_address			neighbc
	106 Sherwood lane	North Syracuse	NY 13212	Court-W
	707 Turtle St	Syracuse	NY 13208	Washin;
LLC	1900 West Genesee Street	SYR	NY 13204	Court W
rp	PO BOX 5335	Syracuse	NY 13220	Court-W
LC	7271 Roumare Road	East Syracuse	NY 13057	Northsic
	127 Maplehurst Ave	Syracuse	NY 13208	Washin;
				Washin;
LC	5038 Yellow Wood Pkwy	Jamesville	NY 13078	Washin;
	4407 Cutting Blvd	Richmond	CA 94804	Washin;
	392 Main St	Beacon	NY 12580	Washin;
	392 Main St	Beacon	NY 12580	Washin;
	138 Lawrence St	Syracuse	NY 13208	Northsic
	1224 Park St	Syracuse	NY 13208	Northsic
	114 Mary Street	Sacramento	CA 13208	Northsic
	2263 W New Haven Ave	West Melbourne	FL 32904-3805	Northsic
) LLC	122 Edgehill Rd	Syr.	NY 13224	Northsic
	173 Oswego River Rd	Phoenix	NY 13135	Northsic
	1029 Danforth St	Syracuse	NY 13208	Northsic
.C	74 Cherry Tree Cir	Liverpool	NY 13090	Northsic
	323 E Water St	Syrcause	NY 13202	Northsic
.C	2300 Milton Ave	Syacuse	NY 13209	Northsic
	48 Bright St	Jersey City	NJ 7302	Northsic
	1621 Midland Ave	Syracuse	NY 13205	Northsic
	1801 Grant Blvd	Syracuse	NY 13208	Northsic
	Separator: Detect automatically ⬦	Syracuse	NY 13218	Northsic
		SYR	NY 13208	Northsic
	1610 Lodi St	Syracuse	NY 13208	Northsic

Figure 6.5 The "Separator" dropdown is how you control where Google Sheets creates a split in the values. Here, it's detecting the comma character automatically.

L	M	N		O
property_owner_address	owner_city	owner_st_zip		neighborh
106 Sherwood lane	North Syracuse	NY	13212	Court-Woo
707 Turtle St	Syracuse	NY	13208	Washingtor
1900 West Genesee Street	SYR	NY	13204	Court Woo
PO BOX 5335	Syracuse	NY	13220	Court-Woo
7271 Roumare Road	East Syracuse	NY	13057	Northside
127 Maplehurst Ave	Syracuse	NY	13208	Washingtor
				Washingtor
5038 Yellow Wood Pkwy	Jamesville	NY	13078	Washingtor
4407 Cutting Blvd	Richmond	CA	94804	Washingtor
392 Main St	Beacon	NY	12580	Washingtor
392 Main St	Beacon	NY	12580	Washingtor
138 Lawrence St	Syracuse	NY	13208	Northside
1224 Park St	Syracuse	NY	13208	Northside
114 Mary Street	Sacramento	CA	13208	Northside
2263 W New Haven Ave	West Melbourne	FL	32904-3805	Northside M
122 Edgehill Rd	Syr.	NY	13224	Northside
173 Oswego River Rd	Phoenix	NY	13135	Northside
1029 Danforth St	Syracuse	NY	13208	Northside
74 Cherry Tree Cir	Liverpool	NY	13090	Northside

Figure 6.6 The "Split text to columns" process is repeated on Column N, using a space character, separating state and postal zip code.

you can choose the delimiting character, which it calls a "separator." Just note that the presence of this selector box is fleeting—if you click anywhere on the spreadsheet grid, the toolbar, or the software menus, the selector disappears.

By default, this selector is set to "Detect automatically." Click on that, and it will reveal a short list of other common delimiters, like semicolons and space characters. There's also a "Custom" option where you can input a different character—or series of characters—to denote where the split should happen.

From here, revise the column headers so that they reflect the split. They will be blank for the two newly created columns.

Splitting up a column can be a multistep process with more than one "pass" that involves finding new breakpoints.

In the third column of the split, which holds the state abbreviation and postal code, "Split text to columns" would need to be repeated with a space character as a delimiter instead of a comma.

Merging values

Just like values in a cell can be split apart at predetermined points, they can be combined. In a spreadsheet, there's both a specific function meant to connect multiple values together in the same cell: the CONCATENATE function.

It takes what amounts to a list of separate values and brings them together. When used in a formula, the CONCATENATE function takes values as a list separated by commas:

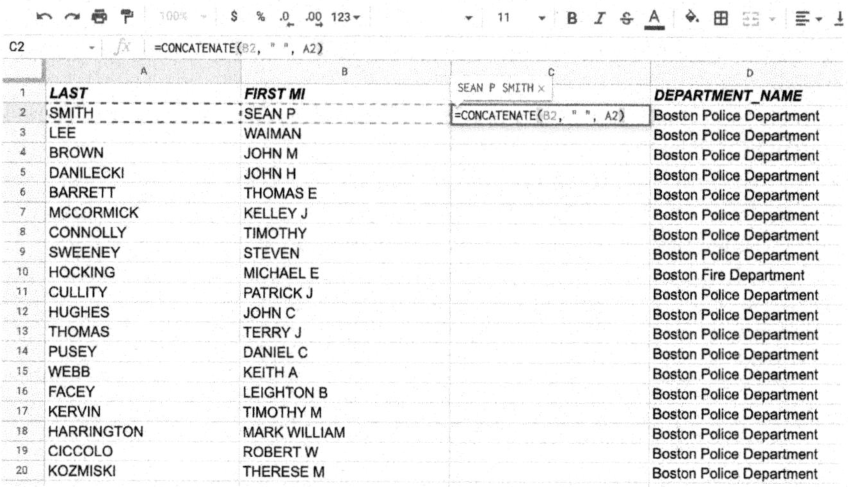

C2 =CONCATENATE(B2, " ", A2)

	A	B	C	D
1	LAST	FIRST MI		DEPARTMENT_NAME
2	SMITH	SEAN P	=CONCATENATE(B2, " ", A2)	Boston Police Department
3	LEE	WAIMAN		Boston Police Department
4	BROWN	JOHN M		Boston Police Department
5	DANILECKI	JOHN H		Boston Police Department
6	BARRETT	THOMAS E		Boston Police Department
7	MCCORMICK	KELLEY J		Boston Police Department
8	CONNOLLY	TIMOTHY		Boston Police Department
9	SWEENEY	STEVEN		Boston Police Department
10	HOCKING	MICHAEL E		Boston Fire Department
11	CULLITY	PATRICK J		Boston Police Department
12	HUGHES	JOHN C		Boston Police Department
13	THOMAS	TERRY J		Boston Police Department
14	PUSEY	DANIEL C		Boston Police Department
15	WEBB	KEITH A		Boston Police Department
16	FACEY	LEIGHTON B		Boston Police Department
17	KERVIN	TIMOTHY M		Boston Police Department
18	HARRINGTON	MARK WILLIAM		Boston Police Department
19	CICCOLO	ROBERT W		Boston Police Department
20	KOZMISKI	THERESE M		Boston Police Department

Figure 6.7 The CONCATENATE function is combining three things together into one value: The first name and middle initials in Column B; a space character to separate the values contained in Columns B and A; and the last name in Column A.

```
=CONCATENATE("Jane", " ", "Smith") → Jane Smith
```

In this case, two text strings containing a first and last name are being joined together with a space character between them; otherwise, you'd end up with "`JaneSmith`."

Splitting cells at specific positions: focus on dates

There are times when an obvious delimiter character isn't going to be present in a column. Regardless, there may be patterns embedded in the column's cells that you can use to your advantage, like how many individual characters make up a specific value.

An example of this would be a calendar date in a numeric format. For a date like "`2019-07-20`," there's an obvious format: four characters for the year, a date separator character, two characters for the month, and another separator character, followed by two characters for the day. The whole thing is ten characters long.

Now, spreadsheets are generally good at recognizing date formats and automatically turning them into a usable value. If you type the date "`2019-07-20`" into a cell, then reformat it as a whole number, you would see "`43666`"—that's the number of days that elapsed between January 1, 1900 and July 20, 2019, and how Google Sheets keeps track of this kind of chronological information. And functions like `MONTH`, `DAY`, and `YEAR` are specifically designed to extract and return those respective date components.

But the software can't parse less conventional date formats like "23/11/2016/09:18:00.00" or "050322" and correctly recognize them, leaving you to deconstruct the components of the date and rebuild them into something usable.

One way to manage this is with a set of functions that grab portions of cell contents based on the position of the characters.

You can think of the contents of a cell as a list of characters that go in a sequence. Each character occupies a position in order, beginning at 1. Take the name "Jane Smith," which is nine alphabetical characters and a space:

Character	J	a	n	e		S	m	i	t	h
Position	1	2	3	4	5	6	7	8	9	10

This value starts with "J" in the first position and ends with the letter "h" in the tenth position.

Segments of this name can be sliced out with the LEFT, MID, and RIGHT functions:

- LEFT, which starts at the left side of the cell (the first position), and takes a specified number of characters to the right. To get the first three characters of the name:

  =LEFT("Jane Smith", 3) → Jan

- MID, which takes a specific number of characters to the right after starting from a position that you designate. For example, starting at the letter "n" in position 3 and then taking a total of five characters (the letters found in positions 3, 4, 5, 6, and 7):

  =MID("Jane Smith", 3, 5) → ne Sm

  RIGHT does the exact opposite of LEFT, beginning at the last position in the cell and working backward to take a specific number of characters to the left. To get the last four characters of the name:

  =RIGHT("Jane Smith", 4) → mith

Apply this to the first date example, "23/11/2016/09:18:00.00," which is a combination of a date in the "day-month-year" format, followed by a 24-hour time value:

Character	2	3	/	1	1	/	2	0	1	6	/09:18:00.00
Position	1	2	3	4	5	6	7	8	9	10	11–22

The day portion of the date occupies the first two characters; the month is found in the fourth and fifth position; and the characters making up the year are in positions seven through ten.

C	D	E	F	G	H	
property_zip	case_number	case_open_date	day	month	2014 ×	nature_of_complaint
13208	L00035	04/06/2014/00:00:00.00	04	06	=MID(E2, 7, 4)	Lead Paint Violations/He
13208	L00130	31/12/2014/00:00:00.00	31	12	2014	Lead Paint Violations/He
13208	L00609	31/01/2019/00:00:00.00	31	01	2019	Lead Paint Inspection
13208	L00518	26/09/2018/00:00:00.00	26	09	2018	Lead paint inspection/He
13208	L00015	23/11/2016/00:00:00.00	23	11	2016	Lead Paint Violations/He
13208	L00748	06/12/2019/00:00:00.00	06	12	2019	Lead Paint Inspection/He
13208	L00543	22/10/2018/00:00:00.00	22	10	2018	Lead Paint Inspection/He
13208	L00647	05/06/2019/00:00:00.00	05	06	2019	Lead Paint Inspection
13208	L00225	30/03/2015/00:00:00.00	30	03	2015	Lead Paint Violations/He
13208	L00693	19/07/2019/00:00:00.00	19	07	2019	Lead Paint Inspection/He
13208	L00727	23/09/2019/00:00:00.00	23	09	2019	Uncorrected lead paint h
13208	L00571	28/12/2018/00:00:00.00	28	12	2018	Lead Paint Inspection/He
13208	L00752	01/11/2019/00:00:00.00	01	11	2019	Lead Paint Inspection/He
13208	L00132	04/01/2013/00:00:00.00	04	01	2013	Lead Paint Violations/He
13208	L00184	27/03/2014/00:00:00.00	27	03	2014	Lead Paint Violations/He
13208	L00290	31/08/2017/00:00:00.00	31	08	2017	Lead Paint Violation/Hea
13208	L00749	12/11/2019/00:00:00.00	12	11	2019	Lead Paiint Inspection/H
13208	L00773	24/10/2019/00:00:00.00	24	10	2019	Lead Paint Inspection/He

Figure 6.8 Taking different date components from the value in Column E; with the MID function, the extraction is beginning with the seventh character present in the cell and moving forward four characters to capture the year.

With this pattern, `LEFT` and `MID` can be used to extract these portions of the date into three new columns. If the value occupied cell `A1`, the resulting formula would look like this:

- `=LEFT(A1, 2)` → `23`

- `=MID(A1, 4, 2)` → `11`

- `=MID(A1, 7, 4)` → `2016`

From here, the next step is to reassemble the fragments that have been split apart and set them up so that Google Sheets recognizes these components together as a valid date. This can be accomplished with the `DATE` function, which will take a year, month, and day value—in that order—and return them as a complete date:

`=DATE(2016, 11, 23)` → `11/23/2016`

Adding new categories based on a condition

Overtime hours and other compensation can dramatically boost the paychecks for first responders, like police officers and firefighters. At times, some employees may earn more from this "extra" compensation from overtime or paid detail work than they do from their regular salaries. In a city payroll data set, you may want to perform an analysis to see which employees fit into this category.

DEPARTMENT NAME	TITLE	REGULAR	RETRO	OTHER	OVERTIME	INJURED	DETAIL	EDUCATION INCENTIVE	TOTAL
Boston Police Department	Police Officer	$96,890.67		$850.00	$16,595.52			$24,222.83	$138,559.02
Boston Fire Department	Fire Fighter	$127,532.31		$2,665.34	$21,638.82		$6,380.00		$158,216.47
Boston Police Department	Police Officer			$9,924.38					$9,924.38
Boston Police Department	Cadet (Police)	$15,599.70							$15,599.70
Boston Police Department	Police Officer	$79,021.12		$800.00	$12,940.29	$16,568.94			$109,330.35
Boston Police Department	Jr Building Custodian	$38,733.42		$250.00	$15,676.01				$54,659.43
Boston Police Department	Police Sergeant	$119,678.12		$800.00	$43,322.09	$2,402.50			$166,202.71
Boston Police Department	Police Officer	$84,380.75		$800.00	$32,298.83		$26,542.00		$144,021.58
Boston Police Department	Police Officer	$97,337.78		$800.00	$20,042.67		$49,082.00		$167,262.45
Boston Fire Department	Fire Fighter	$122,741.61		$2,729.36	$11,021.12				$136,492.09
Boston Police Department	Police Officer	$101,622.31		$800.00	$7,281.42		$53,912.00	$20,324.25	$183,939.98
Boston Police Department	School Traffic Supv	$10,169.11	$460.93	$520.00					$11,150.04
Boston Police Department	Police Officer	$101,649.97		$800.00	$28,955.54		$10,856.00		$142,261.51
Boston Fire Department	Fire Fighter	$62,232.91		$550.00	$7,345.37		$1,676.00		$71,804.28
Boston Police Department	Police Detective	$117,457.28		$9,152.54	$59,937.85		$2,300.00		$188,847.67
Boston Police Department	Police Officer	$110,587.17		$10,665.06	$152,318.86		$10,672.00		$284,243.09
Boston Police Department	Police Clerk And Typist	$39,343.01		$935.14	$528.52				$40,806.67
Boston Police Department	Police Officer	$91,259.61		$800.00	$47,661.04		$14,168.00	$8,525.50	$162,404.15
Boston Police Department	Police Officer	$8,694.29		$40,958.87			$5,750.00	$1,907.96	$57,311.12
Boston Police Department	Police Detective	$108,803.25		$10,471.42	$73,844.61		$46,782.00	$27,200.78	$267,102.06
Boston Fire Department	Fire Fighter	$118,266.43		$9,859.04	$25,074.28	$10,064.23			$163,263.98
Boston Fire Department	Fire Fighter	$126,542.03		$550.00	$33,811.80		$4,829.50		$165,533.13

Figure 6.9 An example of different compensation components for Boston Police and Fire Department employees.

The first inclination may be to filter the table. But what would you filter here? If the payroll table has each employee's compensation information on its own row, with the different components of pay shown across columns, there's no real way to do this. While filters allow you to narrow the visible scope of a data table based on selected criteria, they don't allow for comparisons across cells within the same row. You could, for example, winnow the list to every employee who made more than $100,000 in overtime pay, but there's no way to see if that overtime exceeded their base salary.

That's a new detail for us to add to the data set—a column that shows the result of this comparison. And employees can fall into one of two categories: Either their regular salary (in column D) was higher, or the combined compensation from overtime (column G) and detail work (column I) was.

These sorts of comparisons are based on logic, and they involve comparison operators like "greater than" (>), "less than or equal to" (<=), and "not equal" (<>). Earlier, we talked about Boolean values in a spreadsheet, where something can either be true or false. Using a formula, any comparative statement you make will result in a true/false value. The statement "2 > 3" would return a value of FALSE, because two is not greater than three; "40 = 40" would return TRUE because 40 is, in fact, equal to itself; and so on.

In a new column (column L), you can create this comparison between components of pay, starting with the employee in row 2. To figure out whether the base salary was smaller than the combination of overtime and detail pay, the comparison statement would look like this: =D2 < (G2 + I2).

Copying that formula down the column creates two new possible groups in the data set: one where the result of this comparison is TRUE, and the employee did make the majority of their income from these two pay types, and another where it's FALSE.

For situations where having a Boolean value isn't going to be descriptive enough, there's also a function IF that acts in a similar way: it takes a logical statement that would result in a Boolean value, allowing you to choose what values are returned (or other actions are taken) if the statement is true or false:

```
=IF([logical statement], [what to do if true], [what to do if false])
```

To set up the same comparison about employee pay using the IF function, it should return a different text string depending on which pay source was greater:

```
=IF(D2 < (G2 + I2), "More from Overtime/Detail", "More from Regular Salary")
```

Finally, there's actually a third possible outcome here that we haven't talked about yet: An employee may have gotten exactly the same dollar amount for the types of compensation being examined here.

This comparison isn't set up to handle this possibility—it would evaluate something like "$100,000 < $100,000" as FALSE.

In situations like these, the IF function can handle logical evaluations that may go beyond a simple true and false by adding another IF function within the section of the function that deals with a false outcome.

One way to think of it is by building a short series of steps out of the IF functions; one logical statement is evaluated, and if it's true, everything stops. But if it's false, another IF function is there, with a new logical statement to evaluate.

```
=IF(D2 < (G2 + I2), "More from overtime/detail", IF(D2 > (G2 + I2), "More from regular salary", "Amounts are equal"))
```

7 Simple tools for everyday data visualization

* * *

Once you're deeply familiar with a dataset for a story, the results of your analysis may seem obvious to you. But keep in mind that your audience won't be as familiar with the information you're sharing. Nor will they necessarily hang on your every word or idea—they may just skim the top of a piece or watch its beginning.

Visualizing your data in a graphical form can be a helpful way to capture attention and explain a key point or different important parts of a story. The audience may also need some additional visual cues to best understand the data, its scope, and what it shows. There may be more information buried in your data than you can include in a story or talk about during a news segment—charts and graphs can be a good outlet for that.

And that's where thinking visually comes into play. The very nature of data analysis is quantification, and visualization is about attaching those quantities to aspects like width, hue, and size.

Common types of visualizations and when to use them

If you go back to the first chapter of this book, it touched on the different types of questions journalists frequently ask of data. Among them:

- How much, or how often?

- Who or what is affected the most—or the least?

- How has it changed over time?

- How does it compare with other situations or places?

Common chart types are often linked to these lines of questioning, and journalists try to use the best graphic form to show them clearly.

Graphic designers, researchers, journalists, and others have classified different schemes for data visualization based on the nature of the information being

DOI: 10.4324/9781003182238-7

displayed. Publications like Jon Schwabish's *"The Graphic Continuum,*[1]*"* itself a synthesis of many different past works on information visualization and design, is one example. Meant to streamline this process,[2] it led to projects like the one the Financial Times created for its newsroom, the "Visual Vocabulary,[3]" which further refines some of the categories and purposes based on what the different graphic forms are attempting to convey.

There are certain chart types that lend themselves well to direct comparison. Or ranking different categories. Showing the individual components that comprise a larger whole. Data that shows clear longitudinal trends as part of a time series.

The nice part is because of constant exposure, we have a shared understanding of what many of these different basic forms are trying to say or show. This dates back to the introduction of personal computers, desktop publishing, the burgeoning field of business intelligence, and the use of graphics in news.

If you show someone a basic column chart, chances are that they are going to understand what they're looking at. They'll look at the height of the various columns, extending upwards along the graph's vertical dimension (or y-axis), and recognize that those distances correspond with numerical values. The columns themselves may represent different categories or linear time series consisting of months or years—they will probably begin making comparisons between the heights of the columns before they even realize it's happening, looking for spikes, dips, an overall rising or falling trend, or how the categories rank. The point is: There's generally been enough exposure, consumption, and acculturation that they get it.

This text is not meant to be an exhaustive exploration of all the different graphic forms available, including every possible use case. Look at it as a starting point: Chances are, The endpoint of your analysis could likely fit into one of these categories or data visualization types.

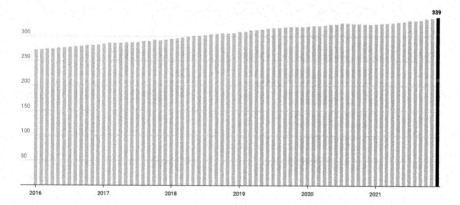

Figure 7.1 A column chart showing the monthly Consumer Price Index for housing costs in the Los Angeles metropolitan area through the end of 2021; data from the Bureau of Labor Statistics.

Bar and column charts

These are among the most commonly used kinds of visualizations. Bars are horizontal, usually extending to the right for positive values, while columns are vertical (like the example above).

These types of charts are good for illustrating comparisons between different groups in your data, especially when it's ranked or ordered in some fashion. Columns, in particular, can be used when grouping around periods of time, like months or years, to show a trend from left to right. Simple columns or bars are good for representing a single value across groups or time periods.

But there are two other major ways they can also appear.

One is as a **stacked bar** or **stacked column** chart. This is a way that the composition of a value can also be represented—the tinier pieces that make up the larger whole.

Another way to represent information this way is by using **paired** or **clustered columns** (or bars) for easier comparison. This tends to work best when there are only a few items—too many, and it's probably better to rely on another format that excels at displaying many values at once that are going to compete for attention.

Line charts

These are also sometimes called "fever charts" and are good for time series, especially when you're trying to represent many different time periods in one

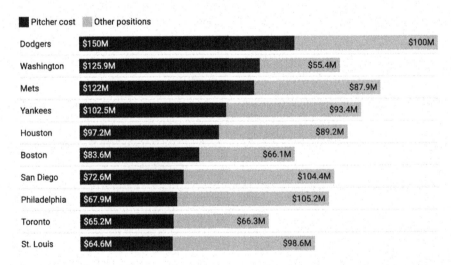

Figure 7.2 A stacked bar chart showing total baseball player salaries for the ten teams that spent the most on pitchers in 2021. The fall length of the bar represents their salary roster for the year, while the components of the bar divide the players into two overall groups: pitching positions and all others. Data from Major League Baseball and USA Today.

Natural gas costs skyrocket in 2021

National Grid's effective price per therm for residential natural gas customers in upstate New York.

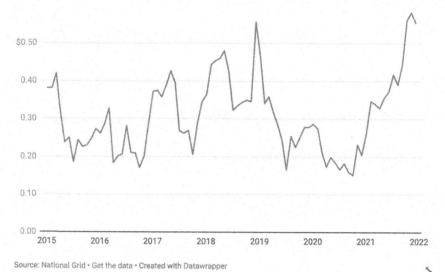

Source: National Grid · Get the data · Created with Datawrapper

Figure 7.3 A time series line chart showing monthly natural gas prices to residential consumers in New York; data from National Grid.

visualization (i.e., lots of days, weeks, months, or years all together), or when the time periods shown are very granular, so much so that it makes sense to have them all connected with a line.

That connection is key—the audience is going to visually follow that line, so it needs to make sense to sit in between each individual data point.

Like column and bar charts, these are among the most common types of data visualizations used by journalists in various ways.

Area charts

You might think of these like line charts with a little bit extra; like stacked bar and column charts, these can be a great way to show changing composition over time—whether as absolute values or as a percentage of a whole. They act like a line or fever chart, but with some additional details.

These do have a downside, though: It may be easy to look at the "first" component and clearly see the quantity that it represents, but other components under the line get pushed upward by the components underneath, making it harder to track them as cleanly over time.

Power generation sources in the United States

In kilowatt hours

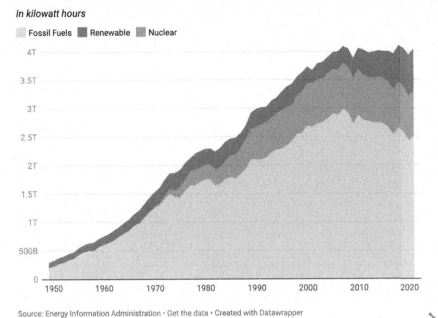

Source: Energy Information Administration · Get the data · Created with Datawrapper

Figure 7.4 An area chart showing seven decades of electricity generation in the U.S., split into three primary modes of creation; data from the Energy Information Administration.

Scatter charts

Where some of the previous chart types can show one value for different groups or time periods (or the things that make up that value), scatter charts are good for showing how two different values for the same item or group are connected to one another. One gets represented across the horizontal dimension; the other, in the vertical. And it can potentially show a lot of information at once.

For example, taking a look at the 2010 median household income and male life expectancy in U.S. counties—more than 3,000 of them—we can see a "shape" to all of these discrete points together that would have potentially been difficult to comprehend in some other format. It's not true in every single case, but generally speaking, annual household income and life expectancy track together—one increases with the other.

In the far upper-right quadrant of the chart, you've got a handful of counties in Northern Virginia near Washington, D.C., where the median household makes six figures and the men can expect to live past 80. Compare that with counties at the other end, in Kentucky, West Virginia, and Mississippi, where life expectancy is in the mid to low 60s, with incomes under $25,000.

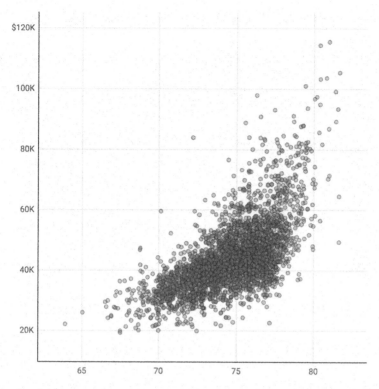

Figure 7.5 A scatter chart where each point represents a U.S. county in 2010. The vertical axis, or height of the point, corresponds with the median household income in that county. The horizontal axis shows the life expectancy for men in years. Shown together, you can see how they're related to each other. Data from the U.S. Census Bureau and the Institute for Health Metrics and Evaluation.

And remember: Just because there's a correlation between two data points in the same record does not mean that one necessarily causes the other; correlation does not equal causation. Think about all the other socioeconomic and demographic factors at play here that we're *not* considering, the ones that influence prosperity, well-being, and health. It's the job of the reporting to begin unraveling the reasons behind the connection.

Geospatial charts

You probably know these by their more common name: Maps. Unsurprisingly, these are often used when data has some geographic information attached to it, but they're best used when visualizing geographic patterns and specific locations are critical to explaining a story.

The major types of maps include **choropleth maps**, a type of thematic map, which use different color shades and saturation in geographic areas—like whole countries or states—to convey the magnitude of values.

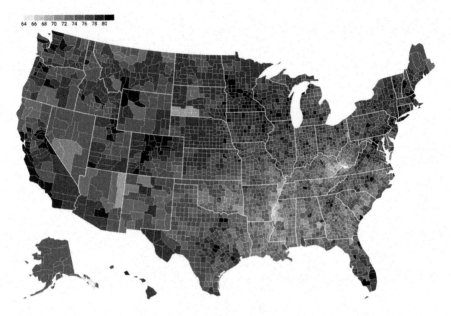

64 66 68 70 72 74 76 78 80

Figure 7.6 The same life expectancy data shown in geospatial form.

Another common type is a **symbol map**, in which a shape, like a circle, is anchored to a specific geographic point on a map, and their different sizes are used to represent values.

In these forms, maps are generally good at showing one value really well. For example, in a U.S. state map, it would be challenging to show a percentage breakdown of different ethnicities in each state within a single map. But it could show the share of a specific race or ethnicity in each state or a combination of them, as long as each state had a single value being shown in some fashion.

So, when might a map be unnecessary, even when a set of coordinates or a county name is available to you? One thing to consider: Does your data just end up showing you spots where many people live, with the greatest intensity around urban areas that have a high density of people? If so, think about some other ways to show the information, or whether it needs to be represented in some relative manner instead.

The process of creating a data visualization

Tools like Datawrapper, Flourish, and Infogram make it easy to move from a concept for a graphic or chart to a publishable form very swiftly. Instead of giving users a blank canvas where they can do absolutely anything—more akin to software like Adobe Illustrator—they provide them with an array of visual options and customizations, reducing the need to spend a lot of time on bespoke or freeform graphic design. These platforms aren't meant to be used in every situation or to fit every need, but they are used by major news organizations[4] to produce common types of data visualizations on deadline.

First, get your data in shape

While Datawrapper has some ability to calculate new data columns or group data on the fly after an import, it's not meant to be full-on data analysis software.

This means that you're going to have to be at or near the endpoint of your data analysis process before moving on to the data visualization—you're going to be working with the summary rather than the original data.

What groups, categories, times periods, and values do you want to represent in the chart? At this point, extraneous information can be left out.

After choosing to create a new data visualization in Datawrapper, you can use your computer's clipboard, copying and pasting a data table from another program, like Google Sheets; import a delimited text file, like a CSV; or connect an existing Google Sheets file, though it must have its sharing settings changed so that its content is at least viewable for those with a hyperlink. Also, Datawrapper will look for data in the first sheet in the file. Clicking "Proceed" moves you through the different stages of the process.

You'll also need to ensure that Datawrapper is recognizing the different types of data that you have (like text and numbers) in the data table correctly. Much of this happens automatically, but in the "Check & Describe" portion of the import process, you have the opportunity to make changes. The software will allow you to examine your imported data through an interface similar to what you would find in a spreadsheet—clicking on a column reference letter gives you the ability to change the data type, control the number of significant digits in a number, etc.

Sometimes, the formatting you use for numbers in Google Sheets, like currency symbols or thousands separator characters, can cause numbers to be identified as text. When this happens, go back to the originating software and get rid of them—Datawrapper provides plenty of ways[5] to format the look of numerical values for publication.

Choosing the right form

At this point, you should have a rough idea of which visualization form could fit the data. For example, if you're working with inflation data from the Bureau of Labor Statistics, it's likely grouped into a time series and broken up into separate values that correspond with months or years, which might lend itself well to a line chart or a column chart.

Even if you don't know exactly which chart type would express the data the most clearly, there's room in Datawrapper for experimentation—you're not locked into anything.

Datawrapper's "Visualize" section is where you're going to spend quite a bit of time, even after making a selection from the "Chart type" tab.

One more thing to note: If you've formatted the data correctly, but it's not showing up in chart form the way you think that it should, try transposing the data (essentially swapping its rows for columns and vice-versa, sort of like turning the data table on its side). These issues tend to arise with data sets that show a parts-to-whole relationship, which you might put into a form like a stacked bar

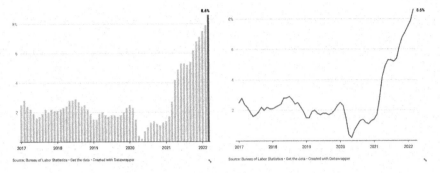

Figure 7.7 Year-over-year monthly inflation data shown in two different ways: as a column chart and as a line chart. Data from the Bureau of Labor Statistics.

or column chart—the program may not always be clear on whether the values in rows or columns are meant to be shown as parts of the larger whole or are supposed to be the different groups. A swap can fix that.

Thinking through the details

Under the "Refine" tab, you have the most control over the appearance of the data visualization. What you're able to change is going to be dependent on which graphic form you choose, to a certain extent.

Go through each section to fine-tune what's being shown on the horizontal and vertical axes, how it's all labeled, and the visual characteristics of the shapes being drawn in the visualization.

Several overarching tips as you move through this process:

- For numerical labels, make sure you choose an appropriate format; if it's a percentage or currency, format them that way.

- Don't overdo it with grid lines across the visualization. Not everything needs a precise, dense grid across the chart—you're generally OK with a set of grid lines, either horizontal or vertical, that align with the numerical value you're trying to show. Ask yourself, too: Will you label every bar, column, or other representation of a value with the value itself? Then you might not also need to double up the information with grid lines and axis labels.

- For line charts, you have more visual options at your disposal than just changing the color of the line (and more on color choice in a moment)—weight and style of line can help distinguish an important part of a time series.

- While Datawrapper will automatically choose a complimentary color palette for you, "customize colors…" gives you fine control over specific groups in your data. By selecting "all," you can make wholesale changes to every group, or multiple elements by holding shift while you select them.

Extra explanatory information for clarity and context

Datawrapper provides two different methods for going beyond the chart's form, its axes, and labels: The ability to add **annotations** to the graphic that highlight and explain different components, and **tooltips** that provide light interactivity to the data visualization, extending the level of detail shown. Both are under the "Annotate" tab.

- Annotations: You can add specific text annotations to the graphic, including a line or arrow to point to a specific element. For example, in a chart documenting annual inflation rates for U.S. consumers, you'd likely want to point out abrupt drops or increases that coincided with a connected event for additional context.

  You're also able to highlight different ranges in the data, which can be especially useful when working with time series. Going back to the previous example, inflation collapsed in the United States at the outset of the global COVID-19 pandemic in early 2020, falling to near zero before rebounding as lockdowns eased. Once vaccines were widely available and demand came back faster than the supply chains could handle (among other causes), an annual inflation rate that hovered in the vicinity of 2% or 3% in recent years skyrocketed. Highlighting ranges can be used to denote these kinds of shifts.

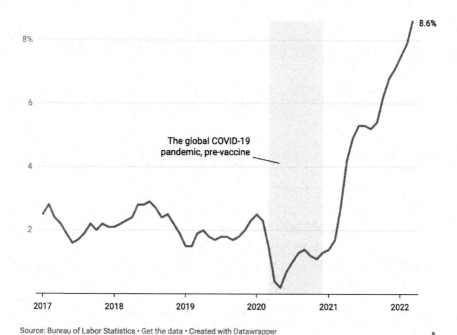

Source: Bureau of Labor Statistics • Get the data • Created with Datawrapper

Figure 7.8 A line chart using (1) a highlighted range to show the period during the coronavirus pandemic before vaccines were widely available in the U.S. and (2) a text annotation with a line to describe what the audience is seeing.

- Tooltips: These are pop-ups with additional information that appear when the audience clicks or touches a part of the graphic.

    In the scatter plot mentioned above, the audience certainly gets a sense of the "shape" of the data, and how median household income and life expectancy are correlated. There are more than 3,000 different points representing counties, though, so it would be impossible to label them all directly—that would completely overwhelm the graphic.

    Enter tooltips, which can show this information for one element at a time. In a situation like this, users would probably want to be able to learn more about outliers and counties on the edges of this relationship (like those with exceedingly low life expectancy and household incomes compared to the rest of the nation).

    Through "Customize tooltips," you are able to pull values from different columns in a data set out and arrange them in a fill-in-the-blank format.

Median household income and life expectancy in 2010

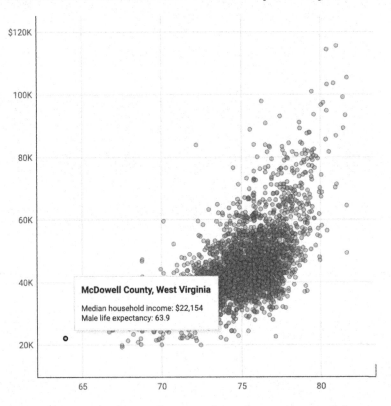

Figure 7.9 Tooltips can show more information about a data visualization. Life expectancy and median household income are the values being visualized using the scatter chart, but a pop-up for each point shows more specifics for each county.

Publishing your graphic and getting it online

"Embed code" presents the chart as an iframe HTML element that can be used on a web page. An iframe, short for "inline frame," creates a kind of window in a web page that allows content from another location on the internet to appear. When the embed code is placed in an HTML file and then subsequently rendered in a web browser, the data visualization is loaded from the Datawrapper site and shown as if all the code and styling to generate it were right there.

You'll likely want the responsive version of the embed code: It includes additional information that allows the data visualization to conform to whatever HTML element it's enclosed by, like a content division. Otherwise, the embedded data visualization will remain at its preset height and width dimensions, which may be problematic on smaller screens.

Beyond the data visualization: other critical things to consider

A lot of time and energy goes into the visual representation of data and figuring out which form best fits the story you're trying to tell or point that you're trying to make. But these aren't the only things that express necessary information, and without thinking them through as well, the end product could easily suffer.

Headlines and chatter

Much like the role of headlines for news articles, this is a short method for telling the audience what they're looking at. And the chatter is usually a sentence or two telling the audience what they're looking at and what their overall takeaway should be from the data presented. What do they do for data visualization? Well, they're more than just a title and description.

Are these two elements necessary all the time? No. In digital presentation, there are examples where data visualizations, often multiple charts and graphs, are intermixed directly in a written piece, and the intention is that the audience moves back and forth and consumes them together, whereas a good headline and a well-composed piece of chatter set a data visualization up to stand on its own, even if it gets separated somehow from the larger piece of journalism that it's accompanying.

Going back to the idea of takeaways and explaining to an audience what they're examining, this pair generally falls into one of two categories:

1   The **literal**, which describes exactly what the data is. This is easier to write, but that probably means you're putting the burden on your audience to figure out what the data analysis means. For example, if your chart headline were "Multiracial Population Changes In Metro Area," you're leaving it up to your reader to draw conclusions based on what they're seeing and how it's represented in the graphic, rather than summing it up for them. Did the population grow? Shrink? By how much? And where? This type of headline needs

additional description in the text of the visualization to ensure the audience isn't confused.

2   The **conclusion**, which tells the audience what they should see in the data visualization. For example, that same headline about population changes might instead read "More People Identify As Multiracial In Metro Area." With a conclusion headline, your audience may more easily grasp what you're trying to show. But since you're likely working with limited space, you may not be able to say everything you want to say in this type of headline, still necessitating more description in the data visualization's chatter.

Because headlines and chatter work together, if you use a literal headline, you probably want to have a conclusion, or takeaway, in the chatter—and vice versa. Avoid being very literal for both. You want to help the audience understand why you're showing data in a visual format and why they should care.

Source

Where is this data from? Your audience needs to know where you got the information you're presenting so they can be confident that the source is reliable. But you're not putting together footnotes for a research paper here with a complete citation—stick to the name of the entity that created or maintains the data.

Credit

The audience also deserves to know who created the data visualization. Think of this in the same vein as byline or credit that goes on any journalistic work that you create. It's an important part of accountability in reporting.

Notes

Consider this the only optional component listed here; a line for notes at the bottom of a chart can be used to help explain any nuances that didn't fit well into the chatter. Here, think about anything in the data visualization that could potentially confuse or mislead. For example, are you missing data from a certain year? Does the data only include a specific category of people? Explain to your reader in a bit more detail what they should know in order to increase their understanding of the information you were able to present.

Using color in data visualizations

It may seem obvious for a visual element that getting the colors right is important.

In data visualizations, journalists generally use colors to create visual contrast between different groups within the data and to separate different value ranges as a part of a scale. But the colors you choose can give other visual cues

Power generation sources in the United States

Fossil fuels remain the nation's largest electricity source, but renewables like solar and wind make up a fast-growing share — one that was roughly on par with nuclear power in 2021.

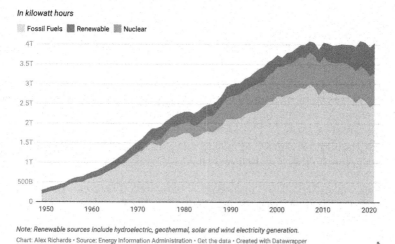

In kilowatt hours

Fossil Fuels ▮ Renewable ▮ Nuclear

Note: Renewable sources include hydroelectric, geothermal, solar and wind electricity generation.
Chart: Alex Richards · Source: Energy Information Administration · Get the data · Created with Datawrapper

Figure 7.10 A data visualization complete with a headline, chatter, notes, credit, and source. Note the difference in the headline, which is a more literal description of the chart, and the chatter, which helps the viewer understand the point being made; they complement one another. The note here gives more detail about which electricity sources are considered renewable, something that might not be immediately apparent.

to your audience as well. Different data visualization platforms—Datawrapper included—typically provide you with an array of options or the ability to precisely target desired colors by controlling variables like the hue, saturation, and value or inputting a hex color code, like #0B6E4F.

You can create a color palette – the scheme of colors you'll use in your data visualization – using online tools like Learn UI Design's Data Color Picker[6] or Adobe Color.[7] These programs automatically generate complementary colors so you can be sure the colors in your visualization don't clash.

A few tips for using colors in your data visualizations:

• When an individual color represents a group, avoid using too many colors. The audience can only mentally juggle the meaning of so many different colors in their heads at once—and think of how distracting it is to have to look back and forth between a color key or legend and the data visualization itself multiple times. This can also lead to a problem where there isn't enough contrast between colors, so it becomes hard to tell what's what. When representing many groups, more than a half-dozen or so, differentiating by color might not be the best way to go.

- Don't contradict strong, everyday color associations. Don't use blue shades to represent the Republican Party (which is historically represented by red, with the Democratic Party represented as blue). Don't use green shades to represent areas where forest fires are burning.[8]

- Approach the use of color with sensitivity when using it to signify marginalized or underrepresented groups of people. On one level, this means not using colors that reinforce stereotypes, like pink against blue to show a contrast between men and women, or using flesh-tone colors to denote different racial and ethnic groups.[9] Another aspect to consider is how color could evoke specific emotions or thoughts when used. If using deepening shades of red, for example, to mark high concentrations of poverty, it might appear as an infestation or blight.[10] The Urban Institute's guide on equity awareness in data visualization sums it up nicely with this question: "If I were one of the data points on this visualization, would I feel offended?"

- Don't make the colors too intense or saturated. These can be distracting, overpowering, and unpleasant to look at[11]. Take it easy on your audience's eyes by adjusting how light or dark the colors are and how intensely they're presented in your data visualization.

- Use gray (or a fainter, more neutral tone) to your advantage. A data visualization that makes liberal use of gray can make an important data point stand out with just a pop of color.[12]

- As mentioned earlier, a data visualization creator like Datawrapper will offer a set of default color schemes that are useful in choosing how you want your visualization to look. But remember: You can't always count on the defaults.

What can go wrong?

The short answer: A lot. While online data visualization platforms and even the built-in charting functions of software like Google Sheets streamline the process enough to help you avoid some potential problems, it's worth keeping an eye on common pitfalls:

- Skipping important components: Your data visualization is only as useful as its parts. Don't forget to include a headline, chatter, and the other components necessary to inform your audience. Ask yourself whether the audience would still be able to understand what they're looking at and the point it's trying to express if faced with the data visualization in isolation.

- Confusing or problematic colors: This can stem from using too many colors and overwhelming the audience, or using colors that don't offer enough contrast between groups or along scales. Similarly, keep background colors neutral so that the visualization stands out—using background colors that obscure the chart will greatly decrease readability for your audience.

- Clutter: Don't use clip art or photos to stand in for standard shapes (i.e., bars or columns) or in the background of your data visualization, unless you have a very good reason for doing so. It can be distracting and peel attention away from the point you're trying to make. The more cluttered your visualization, the less readable it will be.

- Odd bar/column heights: When dimensions like height and width are used to express a quantity, the audience expects those distances to be proportional. If one column represents 50 and another is 100, the latter should be twice as high as the former. Data visualization platforms usually help you keep this kind of thing from happening, but it can quickly turn a simple chart into a confusing disaster. And it can occur sometimes when axes don't begin at zero.

- Starting the vertical axis in a spot other than zero: There are exceptions to every rule, and sometimes it makes sense to truncate the vertical scale, beginning it at a higher number.[13] But you have to ask yourself if that kind of change is going to mislead the audience or inform them more clearly because it has the potential to make relatively small differences seem much more significant. In some cases, it's completely appropriate.

- Upside down or inverted scales: Remember, people think of the bottom as zero and the top as the highest number. Flipping that on its head may seem creative, but it's actually just confusing. Same goes for the left-to-right relationship. When the audience looks at a data visualization, it generally goes in with the expectation that bars will grow longer to the right, representing larger positive values, or that columns will rise from the horizontal axis to show the same thing.

- Unclear scales: Tell your audience what the numbers in your data visualization represent. Is this scale showing temperatures? Numbers of people? Numbers of people per 100,000? Without clearly labeling your scale, you're relying on the audience to guess or intuit too much information about the visualization.

- Over-labeling: At the same time, if you're pinning labels directly on bars, columns, or points along a line that show their numerical value, then having a scale off to the side might not be necessary—the audience probably doesn't need to see this information in two different places.

- Inappropriate line usage: Going back to the tenets of line chart usage above, lines should not be used to connect different groups or categories in your data. They really only work when your visualization represents a time series.

- Not respecting the part-to-whole relationship: For stacked bar and column charts, area charts, and pie or donut charts, the subdivisions rely on the fact that each chunk is a component of the larger whole. When put together, they add up to a complete absolute value or 100% of the total.

It can be tempting to try to represent change over time this way. If you knew that city budget revenues grew by $4 million this year, you might want to look at the different components of city income and how each contributed to this sizable jump in funds. But what about revenue sources that actually declined between years, that were just offset by growth elsewhere? You'd want something that could represent this divergence instead.

* * *

Aaron Williams knows what you're streaming on Netflix

Not every data journalist works at a news outlet. Aaron Williams applies his data storytelling skills to his work as a Senior Visualization Engineer at Netflix.

Instead of informing a large general-interest news audience, he's sifting through internal data that the streaming platform stores about how users interact with content, trying to give executives and managers a clearer view of performance—and maybe what they should do next.

"It's very similar to journalism—you have a data set, you want to tell a story around that data," he said. "Can we build something that helps people make actionable decisions off of that?"

Williams said he works with data scientists and other "brilliant mathematical minds," but that his time in newsrooms and journalism skills transferred well to a tech company.

"Getting super smart, super quick on the topic, with very little notice, and with very tight deadlines—knowing how to move in that kind of environment actually makes you really good at all kinds of [stuff]," Williams said.

After picking up some web skills in college while redeveloping a college publication website, Williams said he still planned to be a writing-focused reporter. But he learned to code, building small apps, and realized he could use them to inform his stories. These skills opened new professional doors for Williams, giving him the opportunity to learn more from colleagues and expand his versatility.

"One of the powerful things we can do as data journalists is by publishing that data and hopefully building it in a way where people can explore it," he said. "Ideally, they're not just reading your story—they can place themselves directly in it. And then maybe that can lead to some impactful action afterward."

Notes

1 PolicyViz. (2014, October 6). *Inspiration for the Graphic Continuum*. https://policyviz. com/2014/10/06/graphic_continuum_inspiration/.

2 Smith, A. (2016, August 17). Simple Techniques for Bridging the Graphics Language Gap. *The Financial Times Limited*. https://libezproxy.syr.edu/login?url=https:// www.proquest.com/trade-journals/simple-techniques-bridging-graphics-language-gap/ docview/1820116835/se-2?accountid=14214.

3 Smith, A. (2021, February 9). Chart-Doctor/Visual-Vocabulary. *Financial Times*. https://github.com/Financial-Times/chart-doctor/tree/main/visual-vocabulary.

4 Welsh, B. [@palewire]. (2019, November 28). *Today's @latimes Features the First Web Charts Shipped to Print with No Extra Production. No Adobe Illustrator. No CMYK Conversion* [Tweet]. Twitter. https://twitter.com/palewire/status/1200086925140316160? lang=en.

5 Rost, L.C. (2021, September 21). Number Formats You Can Display in Datawrapper. *Datawrapper.* https://academy.datawrapper.de/article/207-custom-number-formats-that-you-can-display-in-datawrapper.

6 Learn UI Design. (2022). Palette Generator. *Data Color Picker Powered by Learn UI Design.* https://learnui.design/tools/data-color-picker.html.

7 Adobe. (n.d.). *Adobe Color Wheel.* Retrieved March 8, 2022, from https://color.adobe.com/create/color-wheel.

8 Muth, L.C. (2018, May 29). What to Consider When Choosing Colors for Data Visualization. *Datawrapper.* https://blog.datawrapper.de/colors/.

9 Schwabish, J., & Feng, A. (2021, June 9). Do No Harm Guide: Applying Equity Awareness in Data Visualization. *Urban Institute.* https://www.urban.org/sites/default/files/publication/104296/do-no-harm-guide.pdf.

10 Evergreen Data. (n.d.). *How Data Visualization Can Unintentionally Perpetuate Inequality.* Retrieved March 8, 2022, from https://stephanieevergreen.com/dataviz-inequality_pt1/.

11 Wang, L., Giesen, J., McDonnell, K. T., Zolliker, P., & Mueller, K. (2008). Color Design for Illustrative Visualization. *IEEE Transactions on Visualization and Computer Graphics, 14* (6), 1739–1754. https://doi.org/10.1109/TVCG.2008.118

12 Kirk, A. (2015, January 21). Make Grey Your Best Friend. *Visualising Data.* https://www.visualisingdata.com/2015/01/make-grey-best-friend/.

13 Yanofsky, D. (2015, June 8). It's OK Not to Start Your Y-axis at Zero. *Quartz.* https://qz.com/418083/its-ok-not-to-start-your-y-axis-at-zero/.

8 Introduction to R and the tidyverse

* * *

Spreadsheet programs are incredibly functional pieces of software and can do a lot, but they have a little bit of an efficiency problem. That's not meant to be any kind of dig on what they allow you to do; it's more of a comment on the fact that it can be challenging to show your work—the whole process you went through to analyze a data set and arrive at different findings.

If the data you're working with gets updated at some point, and you need to include the fresh records as part of your reporting, you'll likely be left going through the same analysis or cleaning process again that you went through previously.

There's a certain amount of repetition here—think about the actions you take when using a spreadsheet to sort data. Previous chapters have broken it down as a series of steps to follow: First, you select the full extent of the data table; then you visit the "Data" menu to select "Advanced range sorting options"; then you determine whether your table has a header row in place; etc.

Common programming or scripting languages are exactly that: You're writing a script for software to follow, step by step. But instead of driving this process manually with a mouse or trackpad, it largely happens through the keyboard by issuing a series of written commands for an **interpreter** to execute.

Among the languages that many journalism professionals have embraced for data reporting in recent years is **R**, a free, statistics-focused tool with strong roots in the academic world. Reporters use it because of its ability to save time and enhance the transparency of their reporting: When you're writing a script in R, it means that anyone with the same original data set that you have can follow along by running it on their own machine—as long as they also have R installed—seeing each step executed along the way. There's no question about what transformations (like grouping for summarization) were done, how a data set was altered to make it more standardized, or what the outcome was—from the script and the output, it's plain to see.

As mentioned earlier, this is an ability where spreadsheets generally fall flat. Even with a platform like Google Sheets, which takes advantage of online storage to keep a series of file snapshot "steps" by saving a new version with nearly every substantive change as you go, for an outside observer, it can still be tough to piece together how the original user worked with a data set to get their results.

DOI: 10.4324/9781003182238-8

By recording all your work as part of a script, it's also possible to more easily reproduce complicated analyses and even data visualizations that were originally created in R as a data set receives updates, all with minimal effort.

The best way to work with R

Working with R is a bit different than firing up Google Sheets through a web browser or using some other local software on your computer. For one, you need to download and install the base R software,[1] which gives you access to the R language itself, as well as a command-line **environment** where you can write R commands and have them interpreted and carried out—the R Console.

The environment in R is a bit more complicated than this, but a way to think of it is like an active workspace for whatever you're doing. As you bring in data to analyze, clean, or visualize, both the data and the changes you make to it generally end up stored there.

While the plain R console is OK for executing a few quick statements in the R language, even without knowing much about the syntax or how it all works yet, you can likely see how entering R code and executing one piece at a time—even though it keeps a history log—could start to cause confusion.

So, in addition to the main R software, you also want to install an IDE (integrated development environment) called **RStudio.**[2] It's a limited interface that sits atop R, offering a single place to compose R scripts, as well as run commands through the console. It ties a lot of different things journalists (and other R users) would want to do with R together.

It brings in some graphical interface elements into R, making certain aspects a bit more point-and-click, and RStudio also makes it easier to view data in the same fashion that you can in a spreadsheet. (A big difference, though, is what occurs in the program depends on the code you write.) Among its significant advantages are that it gives you a place to compose and carry out R scripts that you write; allows you to see what variables have been defined, which can hold entire data sets inside of them (more on these in a moment); and easy access to the installation of outside packages that extend what the base version of R can do.

Overview of the RStudio interface for R

RStudio's interface is split into three "panes" when it's first run:

1   One for the R console, which by default takes up the left half of the RStudio window. RStudio should automatically find the computer's main R installation and have it running and accessible upon launch.

2   Another in the top right that shows anything defined within the current R **environment**. (To start, this should be empty.)

3   One in the bottom right that shows a listing of files and folders in the folder R has automatically been chosen as the active "working directory" on your

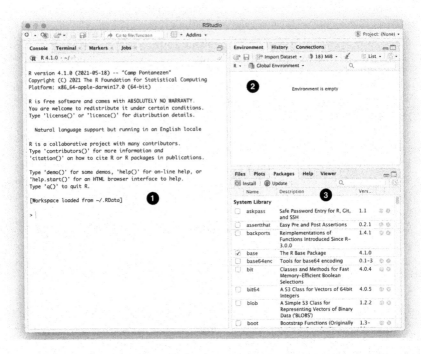

Figure 8.1 The Rstudio interface on initial startup. (1) The Console pane, where you can enter R code. (2) The Environment pane, where defined variables—like imported data sets — will appear. (3) This pane allows you to see your present working directory and navigate the filesystem on your computer, as well as access installed packages that extend what base R can do.

computer (this can be a different folder depending on your computer's operating system, but you have the ability to change it). This pane also has options spread out as different tabs across the top, like **packages** and **help**.

As it stands, the interface is missing one key component discussed above: An R script file to compose, edit, and execute your R code in. A fresh one can be generated in a couple of ways, but using the "File" menu and choosing "New File" and then "R Script" will do it.

This opens up a fourth pane in the top left portion of the RStudio interface, pushing the pane that holds the R console pane downward into the bottom left of the window and reducing its size.

Much of what you write in R will be done in these left-hand panes. The R script file, which is empty by default, serves as a repository for the different steps. You have the power to run through all of them, start to finish, by clicking "Source" at the top of the script file pane, or you can highlight individual portions of your code and "Run" them separately.

We'll start, though, with some basics in the R console.

Using R: understanding variables

In any scripting or programming language, an important concept is the **variable**. The name is apt because its contents can vary—you can think of variables as containers that you define at will. You assign variables a name that can be referenced later on; you also choose what the variable is meant to represent.

In a way, this idea isn't dissimilar from how you've been using cell references in spreadsheets. You might think of the spreadsheet grid as a bunch of different variables with names assigned to them based on their position in the rows and columns, like `A1` or `E18`.

When you needed to access the cell contents of, say, `E18` for use in a formula or function, you didn't have to reenter everything that was inside of cell `E18`. You were able to use the cell reference as a stand-in—Google Sheets knew to take the value or formula sitting within that cell and use it elsewhere as if it had been written in manually.

The analogy isn't perfect, but something similar was taking place: The name is a shortcut or a storage point for other information. The R language relies on variables to store all kinds of things.

An incredibly simple example might be creating a variable named `"x"` that holds the number 2. In the R console, it would look like this:

```
x <- 2
```

The angle bracket and hyphen characters together (`<-`) form a sort of arrow icon in the code—whatever is on the right side of the arrow (what the arrow is pointing at) is going to be stored inside of that variable, which will be named what's on the left side of the arrow. (If you've ever seen any code from languages like Python or JavaScript, these variable definitions are handled with an equals sign (`=`) instead.)

In the RStudio interface, once `"x"` is defined, it pops up in the environment pane under "Values," showing that `"x"` now contains the number 2.

So, in the console, if you want to add 2 and 2 together, `"x"` is going to be treated the same way as the content it contains—as a value of 2:

```
> 2 + 2
[1]  4
> x + 2
[1]  4
> x + x
[1]  4
```

(The `[1]` here can be ignored; it's just a prefix for the output of your command in the R console. It's meant to help you keep track of longer outputs that require more than one line in the console to display.)

A variable can hold a single number. It can contain one word. It can call up an entire text string that makes up a whole chapter of a book. But more importantly, for us, it can also be a sequence of individual values:

```
states <- c("New York", "California", "Illinois", "Texas")
```

The c() function here is just R's way of combining a set of separate things into something the program can recognize as a single list of component elements, called a **vector**, with commas as a separator.

And in R, functions play a similar role as ones introduced for spreadsheet software like Google Sheets—they're specialized, they take different arguments inside of a set of parentheses, and they are meant to do something specific with those arguments. And much like Google Sheets, text values need to be wrapped in quotation marks, while numerical ones don't.

Inputting a line like this into the R console will show this newly stored variable "states" in the environment pane as well, along with some additional information about the vector: chr [1:4] "New York" "California" "Illinois" "Texas". The values here are being treated as text characters (chr), and there are four of them, hence the [1:4], starting at position 1 with "New York," ending with "Texas" in position 4.

Putting "states" in the R console will recall everything stored in that variable for use:

```
> states
[1] "New York"    "California" "Illinois"    "Texas"
```

Or, using square brackets ([ ]) in combination with the variable name, you can subset the variable and access different values within the vector based on their position. Inside states, "New York" is in position 1; "Illinois" is in the third position; and if we wanted to start with the second position and fetch everything in states through the third position, we'd end up with a new vector with just two the two "middle" items:

```
> states[1]
[1] "New York"
> states[3]
[1] "Illinois"
> states[2:3]
[1] "California" "Illinois"
```

Ultimately, using variables is critical for working with data sets in R because they also serve as a spot to store the data that you've imported. Once complete data tables are moved into R, they can be integrated and referenced within the script you write without having to redefine what's stored in the variable again.

Expanding base R with outside packages

Dedicated researchers, data scientists, and others are regularly extending and augmenting what R can do by creating new packages that can be downloaded and installed through RStudio.

The idea behind bringing other packages into your R environment is that it's like expanding the number of different tools in your R toolbox. These packages usually hold a specialized suite of new functions that can enable new capabilities and streamline your use of the software; people have created brand-new abilities that anyone can access very simply in R and reuse without writing out a lot of detailed code themselves.

One group we'll make use of here is a set of complementary packages that comprise what's called the **tidyverse**. The core tidyverse packages contain functions that help with importing data into R, restructuring it as necessary, and taking other steps to get the desired output—even creating data visualizations with it directly through writing code. Some of these capabilities are meant to be improvements on the base R program that make it easier to use with data; others are newly created functions that bridge what its creators perceive as gaps in R's standard abilities.[3]

Like the other software platforms discussed in this book, R and the tidyverse itself has a dramatically larger user base than news gatherers. That's a good thing—it means the software is constantly being improved and the scope of what it can do is generally growing rather than stagnating.

One way we'll use it here is to bring R very close to functioning like a traditional **database manager**, which journalists have used for decades[4] to tackle large and complex data sets, at times stored across multiple tables. The way in which you interact with imported data is similar, and aspects of the tidyverse syntax—how you summarize and analyze data—is in line with **SQL**, a data querying language used by databases. A foundational understanding of how to manipulate data in this way opens a wide range of abilities, from simple to complex.

Journalists have used the capabilities of R and the tidyverse packages together to handle advanced statistics for stories. For example, ProPublica used R to examine the pronounced racial disparities in how vehicle insurance companies set premiums by zip codes in several states,[5] finding that the difference between minority areas and majority-white areas was larger than risk alone could explain. The news organization also made some of its data and the analysis in R publicly available[6] to download.

Installing and loading packages within RStudio

There are a couple of ways to load these outside packages in RStudio so that you can access their abilities within the environment. The first thing to do is make sure they are installed. Clicking on the "Packages" tab in the lower right pane will reveal every installed package that R can access.

If the tidyverse isn't present in that list, click on the "Install" button within the "Packages" tab, which has an icon of a cube next to it that contains a downward-facing arrow. You'll be presented with a dialog box that permits you to install one or more packages at a time. In that same dialog box, under "Packages (separate multiple with space or comma)," typing "tidyverse" should cause it to automatically appear. You shouldn't need to change where it downloads the outside packages; the default location is fine.

Be sure, though, that the box next to "Install dependencies" is checked. While the tidyverse uses a set of eight "core" packages that provide most of the

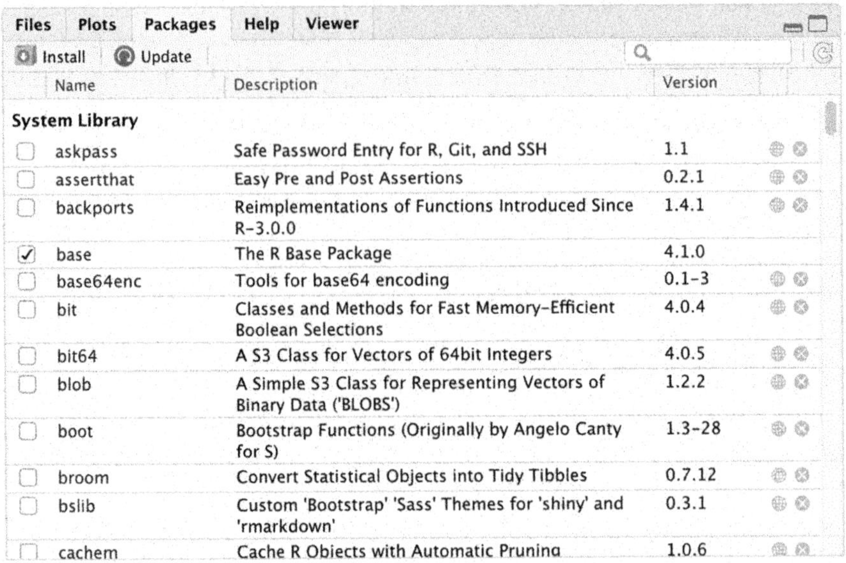

| Files | Plots | Packages | Help | Viewer | | | |

| ☉ Install | ⓦ Update | | | Q | | ⓖ |

	Name	Description	Version	
System Library				
☐	askpass	Safe Password Entry for R, Git, and SSH	1.1	⊕ ⊗
☐	assertthat	Easy Pre and Post Assertions	0.2.1	⊕ ⊗
☐	backports	Reimplementations of Functions Introduced Since R–3.0.0	1.4.1	⊕ ⊗
☑	base	The R Base Package	4.1.0	
☐	base64enc	Tools for base64 encoding	0.1–3	⊕ ⊗
☐	bit	Classes and Methods for Fast Memory–Efficient Boolean Selections	4.0.4	⊕ ⊗
☐	bit64	A S3 Class for Vectors of 64bit Integers	4.0.5	⊕ ⊗
☐	blob	A Simple S3 Class for Representing Vectors of Binary Data ('BLOBS')	1.2.2	⊕ ⊗
☐	boot	Bootstrap Functions (Originally by Angelo Canty for S)	1.3–28	⊕ ⊗
☐	broom	Convert Statistical Objects into Tidy Tibbles	0.7.12	⊕ ⊗
☐	bslib	Custom 'Bootstrap' 'Sass' Themes for 'shiny' and 'rmarkdown'	0.3.1	⊕ ⊗
☐	cachem	Cache R Objects with Automatic Pruning	1.0.6	⊕ ⊗

Figure 8.2 The Packages pane, which allows you to install, update, and activate outside packages through the RStudio GUI.

functionality, there are other packages it will install at the same time and play a supporting role. As such, you may end up with layers of different packages that "depend" on each other and work together.

After clicking the "Install" button on the dialogue box, you'll see `install.packages("tidyverse")` appear in the R console pane, followed by a flurry of text as RStudio downloads all of the packages connected to the tidyverse, along with these dependencies, and installs them. When it's finished, you should see "tidyverse" present in the "Packages" listing along with other new entries.

To activate a package within the R environment, all you need to do is click on the box next to it in the "Packages" pane. When you do that, you'll see `library(tidyverse)` in the R console followed by text that looks something like this, though it could vary a bit:

```
── Attaching packages ──────────── tidyverse 1.3.1 ──
✓ ggplot2 3.3.5     ✓ purrr   0.3.4
✓ tibble  3.1.6     ✓ dplyr   1.0.8
✓ tidyr   1.2.0     ✓ stringr 1.4.0
✓ readr   2.1.2     ✓ forcats 0.5.1
── Conflicts ──────────────── tidyverse_conflicts() ──
x dplyr::filter() masks stats::filter()
x dplyr::lag()    masks stats::lag()
```

A couple of things are happening here. First, your actions in RStudio's GUI correspond with actions in the R console. Instead of having to use the `install.packages` function, which will retrieve an outside package from CRAN and install it, and the `library` function, which loads a package (or in this case, a group of packages) into R, RStudio also provides a limited point-and-click route to handle some of these tasks and fills in the appropriate command for you.

Second, this output is notifying you that all the core packages that comprise the tidyverse are ready to be used. It's also making it clear whether any conflicts exist; there are a couple of functions within `dplyr`, a tidyverse package that helps group and summarize data sets, that clash with another package because the function names they use are the same. When this happens, you're being notified that the ones from `dplyr` are going to take precedence. For our purposes, this isn't any cause for concern.

It's possible, too, that warning messages will appear in the R console if there's some sort of problem upon load. A common one is that packages were "built" under a newer or different version of R than the one you're currently running, which could lead to compatibility issues if the gulf between them is wide. Generally, during these early steps in R, it's not going to derail anything. Going back and installing the most current version of R should make them disappear.

Importing a simple data table from CSV

With the tidyverse loaded into the R environment, we're ready to import an outside data table to analyze.

As discussed previously, delimited text files like CSVs are a popular format for storing tabular data because they can be parsed by many kinds of software. To import them, the `readr` package within the tidyverse has a function called `read_csv()`.

Before diving into any task, it can be helpful to look through RStudio's built-in documentation section. In the bottom right pane, clicking on the "Help" tab and then entering the name of a package, specific function, or term in the search bar (look for the magnifying glass icon) will bring up any available documentation or description about it.

Here, searching for `"readr"` provides a quick overview of the package and its purpose; looking up `"read_csv"` offers an overview of how the function works, what arguments it can take (and what they're intended to do), and different examples of its use.

You might notice from the documentation that `read_csv` can take a lot of different arguments between its parentheses—well over a dozen. Most of these have values already set by default, so you don't need to worry about them now; these will allow you to deal with other situations in the future, like text data sets with different delimiter characters or data without a header row.

For now, we're going to give this function one argument: The file name and where R can locate it: `read_csv([path to file and the file name])`

Where is R looking for files?

RStudio uses your operating system's "home" directory as the default **working directory**, which serves as the root folder from where you can describe the path to different file locations on your computer. For example, on macOS, this would likely be your main user folder (which holds other commonly used folders like "Downloads" and "Desktop"), while on Windows, it can be the "Documents" folder, which exists directly inside of your user folder.

Regardless of where it is by default, in the lower right pane, clicking the "Files" tab and then "Home" next to the house icon will display the contents of the current working directory.

So, if the working directory is your computer's user folder, and you're trying to point R toward a file (`test.csv`) inside of a folder called "Projects" that's located within the "Documents" folder, the path to that file would look like this: ~/Documents/Projects/test.csv

The tilde symbol (~) represents the current working directory; folder names inside that working directory are separated by slashes (/).

The current working directory can also be changed, and it may make sense to make it a folder that houses all your data and other materials for a specific project. This can be done by navigating to the appropriate folder through the "Files" pane, then clicking "More" next to the gear icon and choosing "Set As Working Directory."

An example with `read_csv()`

Let's start with the file `example1.csv`, located in whichever working directory is currently set.

We'll store this outside data in a variable called `"example."` In the R console, this CSV file can be imported and stored in the environment by entering the following:

```
example <- read_csv("example1.csv")
```

After pressing return or enter, this output will appear on the R console:

```
Rows: 4 Columns: 6

── Column specification ─────────────────────────
Delimiter: ","
chr (5): First Name, Last Name, DOB, State, Zip Code
dbl (1): Hourly Rate

i Use 'spec()' to retrieve the full column specification
for this data.
i Specify the column types or set 'show_col_types =
FALSE' to quiet this message.
```

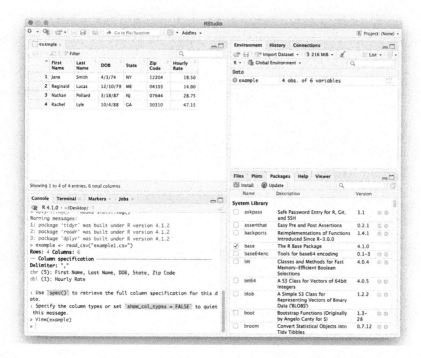

Figure 8.3 The imported data set, stored in the variable "example," open for view within RStudio.

What this means: The `readr` package looks through the various columns in this small CSV table, offering its best guess on which data type is present in each of the six columns. Based on what it sees, it's choosing either `"chr"` or a new data type `"dbl,"` short for "double," which is meant to hold numerical values that include a decimal. (Even for whole numbers, also known as integers, it's not uncommon for the data type to be "double" as well.)

Over in the "Environment" pane, under "Data," the data table is stored along with variables that were input previously.

Clicking on `"example"` in this pane allows you to view the contents of the table in a graphical format. (When you do this, `View(example)` appears in the R console—what it's actually doing here is using the `View()` function to open a data viewer.) While you can't make changes to the table as you would in a spreadsheet program, the RStudio GUI does give you some rudimentary ways to do a quick sort and filter of whatever table you're viewing.

Data tables, tibbles, and adjusting data types

Typing `example` into the console producing the following output:

```
# A tibble: 4 × 6
'First Name' 'Last Name' DOB       State 'Zip Code' 'Hourly Rate'
  <chr>        <chr>       <chr>     <chr> <chr>              <dbl>
1 Jane        Smith       4/3/74    NY    12204               18.5
2 Reginald    Lucas       12/10/79  ME    04103               14
3 Nathan      Pollard     3/18/87   NJ    07644               28.8
4 Rachel      Lyle        10/4/88   GA    30310               47.2
```

Importing data using `read_csv()` stores it in a type of "data frame" called a **tibble**. Data frames are a way in R to store a collection of values like an imported data table in an organized way. Tibbles have a tabular structure that you'll likely recognize from working with data tables in spreadsheets: they're composed of rows and columns, and columns have names, which becomes an important feature when you're interacting with the data.

Here, outside of the GUI, we're seeing R print out the `example` variable with some extra pieces of information:

- The dimensions of the data (4 × 6: four rows in six columns). Generally, looking at the data this way will permit you to see the first ten rows.

- The column names, with a backtick character (`) used to enclose any column names that include spaces.

- The data type for each column.

While the `read_csv()` import chose appropriate data types for this simple table, it struggled with the DOB column, which it's treating like any other text string. That could be a problem for trying to sort the data chronologically or performing any kind of analysis around a specific calendar date.

Any one of the columns in `example` can be accessed as a vector using the dollar sign character ($) between the variable name and the column name:

```
> example$State
[1] "NY" "ME" "NJ" "GA"
> example$'First Name'
[1] "Jane"      "Reginald" "Nathan"    "Rachel"
```

This is helpful because we can in effect pull all the values out of a column this way, modify them as necessary, and then place them back into the column. Here, we're going to want to convert these values that are obviously calendar dates into values that R can properly recognize as a calendar date.

The `readr` package also has a series of functions that can parse different kinds of values, setting a proper date type. They begin with `"parse_"` and can handle these conversions. The one to use here is `parse_date()`, and as discussed above, it's always good practice to run any new functions through the "Help" pane before using it.

It's especially helpful here because this function can't automatically recognize the order of the month, day, and year components, or even discern which one is which—you have to describe that using another argument beyond the specific date or vector of dates you're trying to convert. The documentation available via "Help" provides a list of different characters preceded by a percent sign (%), and how they can be used to represent standard date components, showing the function how the date should be interpreted:

```
> parse_date("5/19/07", format = "%m/%d/%y")
[1] "2007-05-19"
> parse_date("Apr. 3, 1986", format = "%b. %d, %Y")
[1] "1986-04-03"
```

The dates in the DOB column are all month, day, and two-digit year, using a forward slash character (/) as the date separator:

```
> example$DOB
[1] "4/3/74"   "12/10/79" "3/18/87"  "10/4/88"
> parse_date(example$DOB, format = "%m/%d/%y")
[1] "1974-04-03" "1979-12-10" "1987-03-18" "1988-10-04"
```

It's important to note, though, that no permanent changes are being made to the contents of the example when you do this. R is using the DOB column as input material and then only displaying the output. These alterations aren't being kept anywhere—yet.

To commit the correctly parsed dates to the DOB column, we're going to point to the DOB column in the same way as when defining different variables in the R environment:

```
example$DOB <- parse_date(example$DOB, format = "%m/%d/%y")
```

Putting it all together in an R script

Up until now, you've been executing different bits of code piecemeal in the R console. As previously mentioned, you can use an R script file to enshrine the steps that do exactly what you want for future use—and it's a script that anyone can run on their own if they also have the `example1.csv` file.

So far, we've actually only done three different things to get the example data set to where it is now: We loaded the tidyverse packages after installing them; we used `read_csv()` to import the data set; and we converted its dates to the correct data type.

In an R script file, it would look like this:

```
library(tidyverse)
example <- read_csv("example1.csv")
example$DOB <- parse_date(example$DOB, format = "%m/%d/%y")
```

To run this script, start to finish, click on "Source" within the R script window. To run one line at a time, you can position the cursor on the line you want to execute and click "Run"; if there's a larger section of the script that you want to run at once, you can highlight that portion and then hit "Run" as well.

Three commands are not much, but you might want to add some **comments** to the script to describe in plain language what's happening at each point. Comments in R are lines in the script that get completely ignored by the interpreter; any line that begins with a hashtag character (#) will be considered a comment. It's not a requirement, but adding comments can provide helpful documentation to your scripts that help others understand what each part is doing. It can even help you when coming back to a script after a long period of time, when the memory of writing it in the first place is not as fresh:

```
# load tidyverse packages
library(tidyverse)

# import the example data set
example <- read_csv("~/Desktop/example1.csv")

# convert DOB from text to date
example$DOB <- parse_date(example$DOB, format = "%m/%d/%y")
```

Notes

1 The Comprehensive R Archive Network. (n.d.). *Download and Install R.* The R Project. Retrieved December 4, 2021, from https://cran.r-project.org/index.html.
2 Posit. (n.d.). *Download the RStudio IDE.* Retrieved November 12, 2022, from https://posit.co/download/rstudio-desktop/.
3 Wickham, H., Averick, M., Bryan, J., Chang, W., D'Agostino McGowan, L., Francois, R., Grolemund, G., Hayes, A., Miller, E., Milton Bache, S., Muller, K., Ooms, J., Robinson, D., Seidel, D.P., Spinu, V., Takahashi, K., Vaughan, D., Wilke, C., Woo, K., & Yutani, H. (2019, November 19). Welcome to the Tidyverse. *Tidyverse 1.3.1.9000.* https://tidyverse.tidyverse.org/articles/paper.html.
4 Landau, G. (1992). Quantum Leaps: Computer Journalism Takes Off. *Columbia Journalism Review, 31* (1), 61+. https://link.gale.com/apps/doc/A12158400/AONE?u=nysl_oweb&sid=googleScholar&xid=dfc6f716.
5 Angwin, J., Larson, J., Kirchner, L., & Mattu, S. (2017, April 5). Minority Neighborhoods Pay Higher Car Insurance Premiums than White Areas with the Same Risk. *ProPublica.* https://www.propublica.org/article/minority-neighborhoods-higher-car-insurance-premiums-white-areas-same-risk.
6 Angwin, J., Larson, J., Kirchner, L., Mattu, S., Haner, D., Saccucci, M., Newsom-Stewart, K., Cohen, A., & Romm, M. (2017, April 5). How We Examined Racial Discrimination in Auto Insurance Prices. *ProPublica and Consumer Reports.* https://www.propublica.org/article/minority-neighborhoods-higher-car-insurance-premiums-methodology.

9 Using R for data analysis

* * *

In the last chapter, it might have seemed like there was a lot of setup to write a three-line R Script that activates the tidyverse within our R environment and imports a small data table. But ultimately we're not bringing data into R only to view it. We want to be able to do the same things that we could in a spreadsheet—and more.

For starters, let's import another data set using `read_csv()`, working with some of the same census data from earlier in a CSV format.

Before you do anything, it's a good idea to create a new folder on your computer for the project you're working on in R and set it as your working directory. (This way we can focus on the filenames rather than having to include the directory pathways so R can locate those files; if we export any of our analyzed data, it will show up in this same folder as well.)

As a reminder of how this works, in the lower right pane, click the "Files" tab, and then navigate to the folder that holds the data. Once you're there, click on "More" and choose "Set as Working Directory" from the menu.

Start a new R Script to preserve the code you're writing:

```
library(tidyverse)

state_pop <- read_csv("census_states.csv")
```

After clicking on "Source" in the R Script, which executes all the steps, you'll see "state_pop" appear under "Data" in the Environment pane.

Even though this CSV file stored the 2010 and 2020 population figures for U.S. states with a thousand separator, `read_csv()` is able to parse these two columns as numbers during the import process, stripping the comma characters from the values. `read_csv()` can also catch currency symbols that precede a figure and remove those too.

If it *hadn't* done this correctly for some reason, you could use a similar process to the one in the last chapter where you altered the column contents, changing a date from text, using the `parse_number()` function this time:

```
state_pop$'2010 Pop.' <- parse_number(state_pop$'2010
Pop.')
```

DOI: 10.4324/9781003182238-9

Note: If the population columns were parsed correctly, trying the above command would result in an error message on the R console. `parse_number()` *converts values that R treats as text to a number only—it can't parse a number that is already in numerical form.*

Changing the data's column headers

As mentioned previously, altering data imported into the R environment isn't as easy as typing over the top of existing cell values like it is in Google Sheets. The function `rename()`, which is in the tidyverse package `dplyr`, assigns a new column header to an existing column: `rename([data], [new header] = [current header], [new header] = [current header])`

To simplify some of the headers in this data table, dropping the spaces and removing the punctuation, we can use `rename()` change the column headers for three of the existing columns: `State Name`, `2010 Pop.`, and `2020 Pop.`:

```
state_pop <- rename(
  state_pop,
  state = 'State Name',
  pop2010 = '2010 Pop.',
  pop2020 = '2020 Pop.'
)
```

Note that the indentation here is purely to make the R code more readable in the R Script, especially if you are working with a longer series of arguments packed together inside of a function—so many that they can't all fit on a single line in the R Script file. The example above is generally going to be easier to read than this:

```
state_pop <- rename(
  state_pop,
  state = 'State Name',
  pop2010 = '2010 Pop.',
  pop2020 = '2020 Pop.'
)
```

Sorting and filtering data in RStudio and the tidyverse

As mentioned previously, RStudio gives you the ability to do some simple sorting and filtering directly in the GUI, not unlike what you can do in a spreadsheet. Clicking on any variable in the "Data" section of the Environment pane will open the data table in a more traditional "grid" view of the data in a new tab in the upper left pane, next to any R Script file you have open.

Clicking on any column header there will cause the table to reorder itself in ascending order, then descending order (indicated by the direction that the small blue arrow is pointing next to the column name).

There's also a filter button and search box immediately above the column headers. The filter button adds a text box immediately below the column names, allowing you to limit the visible records to columns that contain certain text or that fall into a range of numerical values. The search box will look for matching text across all the table's columns.

But to store some of these changes more permanently in the same variable or a new one, you can sort and filter data sets in R using a pair of functions in the dplyr package called arrange() and filter().

To start, sort the data by the newly renamed pop2020 column in ascending order using the R console. arrange() needs the name of the data set variable along with a column name (or a list of column names to sort by more than one):

```
arrange(state_pop, pop2020)
```

The output in the console should look like this:

```
# A tibble: 51 x 5
     state          Region     Division                 pop2010 pop2020
     <chr>          <chr>      <chr>                      <dbl>   <dbl>
  1 Wyoming        West       Mountain                   563626  576851
  2 Vermont        Northeast  New England                625741  643077
  3 District of
     Columbia       South      South Atlantic             601723  689545
  4 Alaska         West       Pacific                    710231  733391
  5 North Dakota   Midwest    West North Central         672591  779094
  6 South Dakota   Midwest    West North Central         814180  886667
  7 Delaware       South      South Atlantic             897934  989948
  8 Montana        West       Mountain                   989415 1084225
  9 hode Island    Northeast  New England               1052567 1097379
 10 Maine          Northeast  New England               1328361 1362359
# ... with 41 more rows
```

None of these changes have been committed to the state_pop variable yet, which holds our data set. Unlike earlier, when you used rename() to alter a few of the data's column headers, the result, or output, of this function isn't being stored anywhere. Appending state_pop <- would overwrite the existing variable with the sorted data:

```
state_pop <- arrange(state_pop, pop2020)
```

Now, any time you click on that variable in the Environment pane and view the table, it will appear sorted by the 2020 population rather than alphabetically by state name, which was its original condition.

To change the sort so that it's happening in descending order—high to low—add the desc() function *around* the name of the column that you want to use to sort the table. This still happens within arrange(), using the same syntax as before:

```
arrange(state_pop, desc(pop2020))
```

Finally, arrange can reorder a data set by multiple columns, much like a spreadsheet can. Add the columns to `arrange()` in the order that you want the table sorted; to see the state with the highest population in every region, for example, you first sort by the `Region` column and then by `pop2020` in descending order:

```
arrange(state_pop, Region, desc(pop2020))
```

Filtering the data table so that it returns a subset of the original rows is a bit more complex than the sorting process; the potential criteria involved are more complicated than simply choosing to see data arranged in ascending or descending order. With the `filter()` function, you can remove rows in multiple ways.

- **Filter for a value in one column**
  For text, this limits the returned rows to those that have an exact match in the specified column. For example, to only return rows where the state column contained "New York":

  ```
  filter(state_pop, state == "New York")
  ```

  For numerical values, you can use the two equals signs (==) for an exact match, or symbols like "greater than" (>) or "less than or equal to" (<=) to return all matching rows that meet the criteria:

  ```
  filter(state_pop, pop2010 == 897934)
  filter(state_pop, pop2020 > 15000000)
  ```

- **Filter for values in multiple columns**
  You can use logical operators in R, like "and," which is the ampersand character (&) and "or," which uses the pipe character (|), to string together a series of different columns to use in a filter.
  For example, to see only Midwestern states with a population over 10 million residents in 2020, you would filter by the `Region` column *and* by the `pop2020` column:

  ```
  filter(state_pop, Region == "Midwest" & pop2020 >
  10000000)
  ```

In a spreadsheet, we're usually relegated to this kind of additive filtering. When we employ filters on various columns, the visible subset becomes smaller and smaller. The relationship between the different filters is the same as the example above—always "and."

But here we can also employ "or" to broaden the records shown. Let's say you wanted to see all states in the Northeast along with Washington, D.C.

Filtering the `Region` column and the `state` column with "or" will return any row that matches either of these criteria rather than both:

```
filter(state_pop, Region == "Northeast" | state ==
"District of Columbia")
```

- **Filtering for a partial text value**

In the previous examples, filters for text have to be a precise match, and that includes the capitalization of those text values. Including `state == "new york"` in a filter will return an empty result, matching no rows.

Another function can help make some of these more imprecise connections: `str_detect()`, which looks for whether a portion of text is present inside another text value. It acts as a simple gatekeeper, blocking anything that comes back as false during a check of each value in a column.

To return any rows where the word "New" appears within the `state` column:

```
filter(state_pop, str_detect(state, "New"))
```

One remaining potential issue is that this partial matching setup still takes capitalization into account. "yo" wouldn't be found inside "New York," for example. There are many complex ways to match text patterns, including the use of **regular expressions,** but we can do something much simpler here with `toupper()` or `tolower()` functions, which work in an essentially identical manner to `UPPER()` and `LOWER()` in Google Sheets.

The contents of the `state` column are modified to be uppercase or lowercase on the fly, as its being examined—this case change isn't permanently made to the table—so that the case of the text you're searching matches the case of the text you're looking for:

```
filter(state_pop, str_detect(tolower(state), "new"))
```

For multiple partial text strings, you can list them out between the quotation marks with an "or" operator in between. Just note that any spaces or punctuation between those operators will be a part of what the function tries to detect:

```
filter(state_pop,  str_detect(tolower(state),
"new|dakota|virg"))
```

- **Filtering for a range of numeric values**

You can set up an upper and lower boundary for the search using two different filter criteria in combination with the "and" operator:

```
filter(state_pop, pop2020 >= 6000000 & pop2020 <= 8000000)
```

The between() function does something similar to the above, checking to see if a value falls between a smaller number and a larger number:

```
filter(state_pop, between(pop2020, 6000000, 8000000))
```

- **Filter for multiple exact values in a column**
  To do this, we'll use c() again to generate a vector of different values to find within a column. We'll also use an operator called %in% to check and see whether values in the selected column appear within this list of values that we want to find. To only show the rows for New York, New Jersey, and Pennsylvania:

```
filter(state_pop, state %in% c("New York", "New Jersey",
"Pennsylvania"))
```

Using "pipes" in the tidyverse to keep your data analysis straight

Up until now, the steps you've taken with data using R are more or less singular. We rely heavily on different functions to help analyze a data table, and those functions need specific arguments so that they know which variable actually holds the data (or columns in the data) and what you want to do with the data.

So, let's say we wanted to both filter and sort this census data, rather than just do one or the other, like see only Midwestern states with populations in 2020 that were over 6 million, all in descending order based on the population figures. The filtering portion of this analysis would be nested inside the arrange() function because first, we want to toss out the rows that don't meet this criteria and then rearrange what's left:

```
arrange(
  filter(state_pop, Region == "Midwest" & pop2020 > 6000000),
  desc(pop2020)
)
```

As you start adding more of these steps to an analysis, the deeper the nesting will go, and the tougher the R code will be to decipher.

This is where the concept of **pipes** comes in. Instead of dealing with this nesting or "inside-out" way of having to write what you want to do with a data set, pipes in the tidyverse make it possible to treat data analysis as more of a sequence of separate actions that follow one another.

Pipes are designated with a specific %>% operator. Using pipes, the earlier R code to filter and sort the data set would look like this:

```
state_pop %>%
  filter(Region == "Midwest" & pop2020 > 6000000) %>%
  arrange(desc(pop2020))
```

What's happening here:

1 We're starting with the `state_pop` variable that holds the census data.

2 The whole data set in the variable is "piped," or passed, to the `filter()` function with the specific criteria that we set (any non-Midwestern states with populations at or below 6 million are removed).

3 The resulting subset of data is then passed to the `arrange()` function, which reorders the data table's rows.

Another key difference also emerges when writing R code this way. In the earlier examples of `filter()` and `arrange()`, these functions needed a minimum of two arguments: one for the variable with the data, another for the desired transformation.

When using pipes, the incoming data that it will change is a given, so that first argument drops away. Instead of:

```
arrange(state_pop, desc(pop2020))
```

The same thing can be written as:

```
state_pop %>% arrange(desc(pop2020))
```

Expanding your analysis into new columns

You can generate new columns in the data set using a function called `mutate()`. To start, we'll do something we already did with this census data in a spreadsheet: Since we have populations for two different time periods that can be compared, we can create columns that calculate both the absolute and relative change in population for each state.

To add a column named `change` that contains the raw change in population between 2010 and 2020:

```
state_pop %>%
  mutate(change = pop2020 - pop2010)
```

The output of this command is a version of the `state_pop` table that has this new column added onto its right-hand side.

But you can also add more than one new column to a table at a time using a single `mutate()` function by separating the new columns you're creating with a comma:

```
# Version 1
state_pop %>%
  mutate(
      change = pop2020 - pop2010,
      pct_change = (pop2020 - pop2010) / pop2010
  )
```

The `mutate()` function can also reference these new columns as they're being created. In Version 1 above, the `pop2020 - pop2010` calculation is input twice—once for the new `change` column, and again as part of the equation to determine the percent change that will appear for each state in the `pct_change` column. But the new values in the `change` column can be referenced immediately in subsequent columns:

```
# Version 2
state_pop %>%
  mutate(
      change = pop2020 - pop2010,
      pct_change = change / pop2010
  )
```

We can also take advantage of the pipe operator to introduce other actions and changes to the resulting data in a single statement. For example, to generate these new calculated columns, sort by the percent change, filter for only states in the "Pacific" census division, and store the resulting table inside of a variable called `pacific`:

```
pacific <- state_pop %>%
  mutate(
      change = pop2020 - pop2010,
      pct_change = change / pop2010
  ) %>%
  arrange(desc(pct_change)) %>%
  filter(Division == "Pacific")
```

As you add new columns that analyze data row-wise, you may also want to simplify the data set by removing existing columns or rearranging the order in which they appear.

The `select()` function lets you choose which columns to preserve from a table and the order that they should be in, left to right. Dropping a column from a table can be as simple as not including it as an argument in the function:

```
pacific %>% select(Region, state, pct_change)

# A tibble: 5 x 3
  Region state       pct_change
  <chr>  <chr>            <dbl>
1 West   Washington      0.146
2 West   Oregon          0.106
3 West   Hawaii          0.0698
4 West   California      0.0613
5 West   Alaska          0.0326
```

Summarizing a data set by different groups

We can replicate the summary functionality of pivot tables from spreadsheets using different tidyverse functions—along with piping—to move a data set through a straightforward analysis process. In addition to preserving the analysis steps without having to redo them using the pivot table editor interface, R is also capable of handling much larger data sets without some of the sluggishness of Google Sheets, which is constantly transferring information via the internet.

To demonstrate some of these core abilities using the tidyverse, we'll work through some data analysis that could underlie a news story on vehicle crashes. While there are an estimated 6 million vehicle crashes in the U.S. each year, the National Highway Traffic Safety Administration (NHTSA) tracks and releases detailed data on the ones that result in any fatalities, including the location, circumstances of the crash, and the vehicles involved. In 2020, NHTSA had data covering more than 35,000 of these fatal accidents from that calendar year.

This data, which is part of the Fatal Accident Reporting System (FARS), is broken up into multiple CSV files. Each one is its own data table, and they all hold different pieces that together paint a nearly full portrait of an accident. We'll focus on the one where each row or record in the file corresponds with a single accident where there was a death.

Putting it into the working directory, we can use `read_csv()` again to bring it into the R environment:

```
fars20 <- read_csv("accidents.csv")
```

Right off the bat, we might want to understand a few things about the most recent year of data: How many crashes were there? How many people died in these accidents? How many people in total were involved in the crashes? Which states had the most fatal crashes?

The last question is a bit tricky to answer using only the data we have in hand, which can show crashes in raw numeric terms—you'd expect far more of them to happen in California than in Wyoming because those states have wildly different populations. But it's a necessary starting point.

Think back to making a pivot table. The process here in R isn't unlike that; you're generally going to ask yourself a similar series of questions. You can almost run through them as a list that will help you write the R code that will, in turn, summarize your data in different ways.

1   **What data am I using?**
The first thing you need is the name of the variable that holds the data table, followed by a pipe operator—you're going to be passing it all along to other functions.

```
fars20 %>%
```

2   **Which columns do I need for the summary?**
Key function: `select()`
    Just note that this step isn't strictly required—ultimately the output of this analysis will be determined by the groups you're using along with the summary or summaries you're generating for those groups. But it can be useful to only keep a subset of columns from the data set that you need to establish groups, that you want to summarize in some way, or that you need for filtering the data.
    As mentioned earlier, you can select the columns that you want with the aptly named `select()` function.
    Here, where we're going to look at fatalities (the `FATALS` column), the number of vehicles (the `VE_TOTAL` column) and people involved (the `PER-SONS` column), and the states where these accidents occurred (the `STATENAME` column, which will be the groups), we could pick those particular columns out, leaving us with a simplified and streamlined version of the original data table to analyze.

```
fars20 %>%
   select(STATENAME, VE_TOTAL, PERSONS, FATALS)
```

3   **What groups in the data do I want summaries for?**
Key function: `group_by()`
    The whole point of summarizing data is putting records in different groups based on a shared value. With the tidyverse, the function to use is `group_by()`, and it takes a column or a list of columns (if you're establishing multiple groups at once) that contain the distinct values that you want to use as the different groups in the data.
    The concept is similar to choosing the columns for "Rows" in a pivot table editor.
    At this point, we'll move the smaller selection of columns from the 2020 FARS accident data forward with another pipe operator, and we'll establish groups based on the state where the accident happened using the `STATENAME` column:

```
fars20 %>%
  select(STATENAME, VE_TOTAL, PERSONS, FATALS) %>%
  group_by(STATENAME)
```

4   **What kind of summary or summaries do I want to perform?**
Key function: `summarize()`
   This is the point at which you choose not only what types of summaries to perform for the different groups in the data—in our case, for states—but which columns to summarize.
   These summaries are not necessarily complicated—the `summarize()` function works in conjunction with a set of specific summary functions that can do things like adding a set of numbers together, calculating a median, or counting the number of records included in a group. Like above, the process is not all that different from choosing which data columns to put into the "Values" section of a pivot table editor.
   To see how these two functions work together, it's probably easiest to look at an example and dissect what it's doing. If we examine the following statement:

```
summarize(crashes = n())
```

   For the summary, we are creating a new column called `"crashes."` The `n()` function takes no argument—its job is to simply count up the number of records in each group.
   So, if we add that to the code so far, it would look like this:

```
fars20 %>%
  select(STATENAME, VE_TOTAL, PERSONS, FATALS) %>%
  group_by(STATENAME) %>%
  summarize(crashes = n())
```

```
# A tibble: 51 x 2
   STATENAME                crashes
   <chr>                    <int>
 1 Alabama                    852
 2 Alaska                      53
 3 Arizona                    967
 4 Arkansas                   585
 5 California                3558
 6 Colorado                   574
 7 Connecticut                279
 8 Delaware                   104
 9 District of Columbia        34
10 Florida                   3098
# ... with 41 more rows
```

Everything up to this point where we use `summarize()` has been a kind of setup—with the columns selected and groups chosen for analysis, the function essentially creates a whole new table that begins with the established group(s) as the leftmost columns, followed by the summary columns in the order in which they were generated. And in this case, we only have one summary column: The count of crashes in each state.

In addition to `n()`, some of the other summary functions from the tidyverse that can be used inside of `summarize()` are:

- `sum()`: Find the sum of all numeric values in a column for a group.

- `average()` and `median()`: Find these measures of central tendency for numeric values in a column for a group.

- `max()` and `min()`: Find the highest (or lowest) numeric values in a column for a group.

- `n_distinct ()`: Find the number of unique or distinct values in a column for a group.

A big difference, though, is that all of these summary functions need the name of a column as an argument, like:

```
summarize(deaths = sum(FATALS))
```

We can also summarize more than one column at a time for these groups. To see not only the number of crashes in each state that year, but also the total number of vehicles involved in these collisions, the total number of people involved (regardless of whether they were injured or killed), as well as the overall number of fatalities:

```
fars20%>%
   select(STATENAME, VE_TOTAL, PERSONS, FATALS) %>%
   group_by(STATENAME) %>%
   summarize(
       crashes = n(),
       vehicles = sum(VE_TOTAL),
       persons = sum(PERSONS),
       deaths = sum(FATALS)
   )
```

4 **How do I want the summarized data to be ordered?**
Key function: `arrange()`
   We can also add an optional `arrange()` function to any of these new summary columns. To reorder by the number of fatalities to see the states with the most at the top:

```
fars20 %>%
  select(STATENAME, VE_TOTAL, PERSONS, FATALS) %>%
  group_by(STATENAME) %>%
  summarize(
      crashes = n(),
      vehicles = sum(VE_TOTAL),
      persons = sum(PERSONS),
      deaths = sum(FATALS)
  ) %>%
  arrange(desc(deaths))
```

5   **Are there any other changes that I need to make?**

Using the five questions above to form the core of a summary analysis, you can plug in other actions at different points throughout the process where they make sense. This could be filtering for specific criteria in the data set before even getting to the grouping or summarizing; it could be using mutate() to create new columns from the summary, or focusing on a subset of your groups.

For example, you may want to limit this new summary table to only show states that had 1,000 or more vehicle deaths in 2020:

```
fars20 %>%
  select(STATENAME, VE_TOTAL, PERSONS, FATALS) %>%
  group_by(STATENAME) %>%
  summarize(
      crashes = n(),
      vehicles = sum(VE_TOTAL),
      persons = sum(PERSONS),
      deaths = sum(FATALS)
  ) %>%
  arrange(desc(deaths)) %>%
  filter(deaths >= 1000)
```

A tidyverse superpower: joining data sets using a column with shared values

One thing we haven't done yet, either in spreadsheet or in R, is combine two data sets into a single, consolidated table. The data tables you're merging need to have some sort of "key"—a column with shared values—so that R knows where to match the different rows so that they combine as a fuller set of details for a record.

This shared column could hold values like names or ID numbers. It's really going to depend on what kind of data you're dealing with—and what you're trying to do with it.

Take the FARS data, for example. As was mentioned earlier, it's chopped up into many different CSV files. That's because it exists as a **relational database**.

Instead of having one massive table with all the information on crashes, vehicles, people, and other critical elements, it's organized by keeping these things separate from one another to preserve a rational structure.

In the data table we've been dealing with, `fars20`, each accident is a single row. The second accident listed in the dataset, a crash that happened in Alabama with an identifier of `"01002"` in the `ST_CASE` column, had four vehicles involved. In a separate vehicles-only table, each of these involved vehicles occupies a separate row with specific details about each one—make, model, etc.—along with that same identifier: `01002`. This joining ability would allow you to merge the data sets around these identifiers based on what you're trying to learn.

Journalists sometimes also want to blend data together to see where overlap exists, if any. Imagine if you had a list of all the donors to a particular elected government official's campaign committee. Let's say you also had a data set with all the public employees who worked in the same segment of government as the official. A join here would be able to show at least a preliminary or rough version of which contributors work for or alongside that official.

Here, though, our summarized crash data is missing an important element that would be helpful: state populations. While it's true that the number of people who live in a state doesn't perfectly align with the miles of roadway present there or the estimated million vehicle-miles traveled each year, it's a way to level the playing field with a "per capita" rate and account for sizable differences in population that play a role in how many crashes occur.

State names from the accident data table can be aligned with the population table, allowing us to do this kind of analysis and figure out which states have the most (or least) crash fatalities per 10,000 residents.

The types of joins

Merging different data sets isn't one-size-fits-all; you have a level of control over what the output from the combination looks like. The tidyverse offers four important kinds of joins.

These join functions take arguments in a similar format and require four major components:

- The first table

- The second table

- The shared column in the first table

- The shared column in the second table

All together, it looks like this: `[join function]([first table], [second table], by = c("[shared column in first table]" = "[shared column in second table]"))`

The "by" portion of the syntax here is probably the trickiest to parse. We've previously used the c() function to combine a set of values into a vector, but those values have been separated by commas and have not included an equals sign.

Let's say our shared column—the one we want to use for a join—is called birthdate in one table and DOB in the other. The argument to show the desired connection between them would look like this:

```
by = c("birthdate" = "DOB")
```

If we were trying to make the matches more precise, only merging the tables in a situation where both a birthdate value and a name were matched (with a column appearing as name in the first table and fullname in the second):

```
by = c("birthdate" = "DOB", "name" = "fullname")
```

However, if the shared columns have the exact same name between the tables, you don't have to explicitly show that one column should be matched up with another—it will just look for a counterpart column with the same name:

```
by = c("birthdate") or by = "birthdate"
```

Left join

Let's say we have two simple tables where each row represents a person—besides an identifier like a name, one table (table1) has a column with age information and the other (table2) has a column with their city of residence:

Table 1

name	age
Jane	50
Reginald	28
Megan	35
Robert	19
Dane	27

Table 2

name	location
Reginald	Duluth
Jane	Orlando
Vera	Dallas
Madge	Reno
Megan	Milwaukee

Table 1 + 2 (left join)

name	age	location
Jane	50	Orlando
Reginald	28	Duluth
Megan	35	Milwaukee
Robert	19	
Dane	27	

Figure 9.1 In a left join, the contents of the first table remain, along with any matching records from a second table. Only Jane, Reginald, and Megan from Table 1 have a matching record in Table 2. The entirety of Table 1 appears after the join, along with new columns from Table 2. Vera and Madge aren't shown because they don't have a match in Table 1; Dane and Robert only appear because they were already present in Table 1.

```
table1 <- tibble(
  name = c("Jane", "Reginald", "Megan", "Robert", "Dane"),
  age = c(50, 28, 35, 19, 27)
)

table2 <- tibble(
  name = c("Reginald", "Jane", "Vera", "Madge", "Megan"),
  location = c("Duluth", "Orlando", "Dallas", "Reno", "Milwaukee")
)
```

The left_join() function preserves the data table on the "left" side—which is also the first table that you introduce into the function. Rows from the second table (a.k.a. the "right" side) will only appear if a match exists.

Robert and Dane don't have a counterpart in table2, therefore there's no match. Because this is a left join, they remain in the result but have "NA" values in the location column, which R uses to represent missing values—values that are "not available."

```
left_join(table1, table2, by = c("name"))

# A tibble: 5 × 3
  name        age    location
  <chr>      <dbl>     <chr>
1 Jane         50    Orlando
2 Reginald     28    Duluth
3 Megan        35    Milwaukee
4 Robert       19    NA
5 Dane         27    NA
```

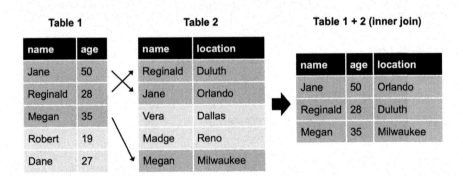

Figure 9.2 The primary difference for an inner join when compared to a left join is that only rows that have a match will appear in the result. Only Jane, Reginald, and Megan appear in both tables, therefore they're the only records that are present in the resulting join.

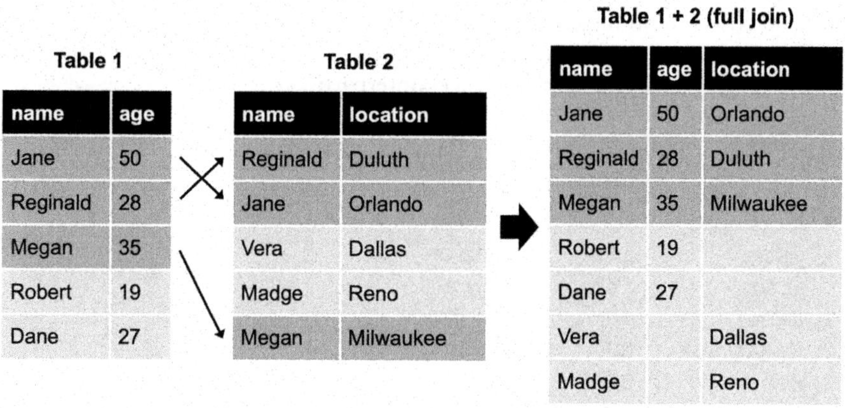

Table 1

name	age
Jane	50
Reginald	28
Megan	35
Robert	19
Dane	27

Table 2

name	location
Reginald	Duluth
Jane	Orlando
Vera	Dallas
Madge	Reno
Megan	Milwaukee

Table 1 + 2 (full join)

name	age	location
Jane	50	Orlando
Reginald	28	Duluth
Megan	35	Milwaukee
Robert	19	
Dane	27	
Vera		Dallas
Madge		Reno

Figure 9.3 In a full join, all records from Tables 1 and 2 appear, whether or not a match is present. In the resulting join, we see Dane, Robert, Vera, and Madge, along with the values that are present for them, even though they don't appear in both tables.

`left_join()` also has a counterpart `right_join()` function that mirrors the example above: Instead of preserving the contents of the first table, all rows from the second table are shown. Data from the first table only appears when a match is found.

Inner join

The inner join discards any records from either table if a match doesn't exist between them, effectively creating a combined subset of the data that only has matches.

Only three of the names—Jane, Reginald, and Megan—appear in both of the tables, so those are the only records that are shown as a result of using `inner_join()`.

```
inner_join(table1, table2, by = c("name"))

# A tibble: 3 x 3
  name       age   location
  <chr>     <dbl>    <chr>
1 Jane         50  Orlando
2 Reginald     28  Duluth
3 Megan        35  Milwaukee
```

Full join

Sometimes called an "outer" join, because it does not discriminate between records with a match and those that don't have one—it merges the tables. Though we have a set of five names in `table1` and another five in `table2`, only three of them exist in both tables.

The result of using the `full_join()` function is that we also see the two records on each side that don't have a counterpart:

```
full_join(table1, table2, by = c("name"))

# A tibble: 7 x 3
  name        age    location
  <chr>       <dbl>    <chr>
1 Jane        50     Orlando
2 Reginald    28     Duluth
3 Megan       35     Milwaukee
4 Robert      19     NA
5 Dane        27     NA
6 Vera        NA     Dallas
7 Madge       NA     Reno
```

The "anti" join: which records don't have a match?

The `anti_join()` function is handy when you're trying to figure out which rows in a particular table do not have a match in another. It's a little different than the examples above in that it does not return a merged table; you'll only see unmatched rows from the first table in the function.

If you were trying to figure out which records in `table2` didn't have a matching name in `table1`, you'd only see the rows for Vera and Madge, who do not appear in the first table:

```
anti_join(table2, table1, by = c("name"))

# A tibble: 2 x 2
  name     location
  <chr>     <chr>
1 Vera     Dallas
2 Madge    Reno
```

Returning to the crash data: merging it with populations

To start, you can simplify some of the summary work from above to create a table that shows three things: the name of the state where the crashes occurred; the number of separate vehicle accidents in each state; and the total number of deaths that resulted from those crashes. It's going to be helpful to store the resulting summary table in its own variable, separate from the original `fars20` data set:

```
crash_summary <- fars20 %>%
  group_by(STATENAME) %>%
  summarize(
      crashes = n(),
      deaths = sum(FATALS)
  )
```

In this case, it doesn't matter if you use `left_join()` or `inner_join()` to combine these tables. Each one of them has 51 unrepeated rows; every single state in `crash_summary`, along with Washington, D.C., has a counterpart record in `state_pop`.

```
left_join(crash_summary, state_pop, by = c("STATENAME"
= "state"))
```

The result is a full combination of these tables where only the column used for the join isn't duplicated (STATENAME is retained, but the `state` column from `state_pop` goes away). This means that we still have other columns in here that we don't necessarily need, like the geographic census division or the state population in 2010, which would be a bit dated for our purposes here. Moving the output from this join onward to the select() function allows you to pick and choose only the columns you want to keep:

```
left_join(crash_summary, state_pop, by = c("STATENAME"
= "state")) %>%
  select(STATENAME, crashes, deaths, pop2020)
```

Finally, we want to do some row-level analysis on the newly joined data to do two things: Generate a new column that calculates a "per capita" rate per 10,000 residents for vehicle deaths and reorder the data table so that the state with the highest number of fatalities per 10,000 residents appears at the top.

To find the rate, you divide the number of deaths in the state by the population, then multiply the result by 10,000. Preserve the correct order of operations by putting parentheses around the first part of the formula:

```
(deaths / pop2020) * 10000
```

This can be added as a new column through `mutate()`; finally, this new column can be used to sort the whole data table:

```
left_join(crash_summary, state_pop, by = c("STATENAME"
= "state")) %>%
  select(STATENAME, crashes, deaths, pop2020) %>%
  mutate(per10k = (deaths / pop2020) * 10000) %>%
  arrange(desc(per10k))
```

The new data table shows sizable differences in the number of fatal accidents when contrasted with the number of people who live in a state—Mississippi had roughly 2.5 deaths per 10,000 people, which is about five times the rate in Massachusetts. Illinois and Tennessee had about the same number of fatalities in 2020, even though Illinois has nearly twice the number of residents.

```
# A tibble: 51 × 5
   STATENAME       crashes deaths pop2020  per10k
   <chr>             <int>  <dbl>   <dbl>   <dbl>
 1 Mississippi         687    752 2961279    2.54
 2 Wyoming             114    127  576851    2.20
 3 Arkansas            585    638 3011524    2.12
 4 South Carolina      962   1064 5118425    2.08
 5 Montana             190    213 1084225    1.96
 6 New Mexico          365    398 2117522    1.88
 7 Alabama             852    934 5024279    1.86
 8 Louisiana           762    828 4657757    1.78
 9 Tennessee          1119   1217 6910840    1.76
10 Kentucky            709    780 4505836    1.73
# ... with 41 more rows
```

Before pushing ahead with this, we'd probably want to know more. Do some of these lower-population states have more miles of paved roadway? Do these differences hold up against government estimates for vehicle travel in these states, i.e., do Mississippians drive considerably more than New Yorkers, for example?

But of course, the overarching question to answer with reporting is going to be "why?" What's contributing to the seemingly outsized death rate in states like Mississippi, Wyoming, and Arkansas? Was 2020 an outlier for these states, influenced in some way by the onset of the COVID-19 pandemic? NHTSA has previously acknowledged that 2020 marked a significant uptick in vehicle deaths from the previous year,[1] and the highest number of deaths since 2007. There's unlikely to be a simple or black-and-white answer that sums it all up on a national scale.

Joining perils: ending up with duplicated data

Because of how data is matched up during the joining process, records can end up being inadvertently duplicated. It's not hard to avoid if you're mindful that it can happen; it's a problem because by expanding the number of rows or records in a table, this can throw off counts, totals, and other kinds of summaries, potentially skewing other analyses and leading you down the path to a fact error or other incorrect conclusion.

Going back to the earlier example with `table2`, let's say it had two more rows: Another location value for Jane and another for Megan.

If there's a one-to-many relationship between matches, duplicate rows will appear in the result of the join. So, what was once a three-row `inner_join()` between tables becomes five:

```
inner_join(table1, table2, by = "name")

# A tibble: 5 × 3
  name       age    location
  <chr>      <dbl>  <chr>
1 Jane       50     Orlando
2 Jane       50     Jacksonville
3 Reginald   28     Duluth
4 Megan      35     Milwaukee
5 Megan      35     Chicago
```

It's easy enough to see in a small example, but much harder to spot in a join that results in hundreds or even thousands of records.

An easy way to see if merging tables is creating extra rows: Using the `left_join()` function first. Ideally, you've looked over in the Environment pane to see how many "obs." or "observations" there are in the variable holding the data table—this is the number of rows or records that exist.

In a situation where the join results in a one-to-one connection between data tables, the number of rows should be exactly the same before the join as afterward. If the resulting table has grown, it's because it's finding multiple matches for shared values.

To zero in on the duplicates, group by the shared column, summarize by count, and filter to show only those that appear more than once:

```
left_join(table1, table2) %>%
  group_by(name) %>%
  summarise(count = n()) %>%
  filter(count > 1)

# A tibble: 2 × 2
  name     count
  <chr>    <int>
1 Jane     2
2 Megan    2
```

Next steps in R

These basics with R and the tidyverse quickly unlock other things you can do with the software. Using the tidyverse as a code-based version of a spreadsheet position you well to be able to visualize the data or apply other functions designed for more complex statistical analyses.

For example, the tidyverse also includes a data visualization package called ggplot2, which uses a "layered" approach to build charts and graphs from your data sets. You define which parts of a particular table should correspond with the horizontal and vertical axes of the graphic, as well as an overarching type of visualization that the package should generate.

Data visualization here can be used as an exploratory part of the analysis process, or a springboard into graphics that can be exported for use online.

For more direction about where to turn after this initial foray into R, see several of the recommended readings in Chapter 12, "Where to learn more."

* * *

Andrew Ba Tran uses R for fast analysis and investigations

Andrew Ba Tran first dove into data analysis several years into his journalism career. After working as a beat reporter in Florida and then taking a job as an online producer in Boston, he knew he wanted more. He met with some fellow journalists, and together, they taught themselves new skills, including data analysis.

Now a data reporter for the Washington Post's rapid-response investigative team, Tran spends much of his time on his own projects. And with his knowledge of R and his ability to dig into datasets, he's also become an asset to his Post colleagues.

Depending on the reporters' experience working with data, they sometimes want Tran to dig up data, analyze it and synthesize it into just a few sentences. Others get deeper into the process, even if they don't know how to use a language like R to do it on their own.

"Sometimes you're working with reporters who love getting into and looking through the data themselves, or have ideas on how to work with it," Tran said. "They kind of know where they want the data to fit in the story, and what they're hoping the data can say in the story, and so they can kind of guide the analysis in that way."

Some fellow reporters also look to Tran for updates to data for stories they wrote a year or more ago. Tran has been able to use his coding skills to automate those updates, allowing him to get his colleagues the information they need quickly "so that I'm not redoing it from scratch every time," he said.

Note

1 National Highway Traffic Safety Administration. (2022, March 2). NHTSA Releases 2020 Traffic Crash Data [Press Release]. https://www.nhtsa.gov/press-releases/2020-traffic-crash-data-fatalities.

10 Making the modern web with HTML and CSS

* * *

Like the purveyors of nearly every other modern website, journalism organizations have harnessed the power of webpages to act as multimedia platforms. Indeed, as many journalism organizations have shifted to a "web first" structure, more reporting is presented on the internet, which opens the range of possibilities for presentation and interaction with the audience.

So, why learn about HTML and CSS, two of the primary languages used to present content online? It's all about agency. As a journalist, you want to have a basic understanding of how some of these core internet technologies work so that you can collaborate more effectively with digital specialists, web producers, developers, and IT personnel. It helps to be able to do some of this on your own, and to speak at least a little of their language.

Note: This book isn't going to make you an expert web developer. It's just meant to give you the necessary grounding to create and lay out relatively simple responsive webpages. It's a good starting point if you want to learn more.

An HTML primer

HTML stands for "hypertext markup language." Devised in the early 1990s, it's an evolving system for displaying the digital content of the internet and a way to take advantage of a unique communications medium.

The *hypertext* part of the name describes individual online documents— webpages—threaded together through "hyperlinks"—though today, we'd be more inclined to simply call them "links" instead. Rather than having to thumb through an index to locate and then visit a separate piece of content, a one-way leap could be directly established, like a doorway linking one document to another.

Ultimately, these hyperlinks between webpages act as the individual connections that make up the World Wide Web, a major component of the internet. They're significant enough that the terms "web" and "internet" are used almost interchangeably today.

As a *markup language*, HTML defines the structure and holds the content of a document, which can include text and references to image files and other digital

DOI: 10.4324/9781003182238-10

media, as well as semantic information that gives important cues about what the content represents.

More importantly, though, a markup language like HTML works together with another language called CSS, which describes how all content should be displayed. These instructions include the visual flourishes—color, dimensions, size, position, and more.

The concept of a markup language isn't unique to the internet or the web, and you encounter them in more places than you might think. They keep your Microsoft Word files formatted properly and can feed content to the mobile apps on your phone.

HTML is no different; it's just meant to be interpreted and shown by a web browser, like Apple Safari or Google Chrome.

So, writing or revising an HTML document goes beyond just the content itself—you're also writing the instruction manual for the look, feel, and overall experience of a webpage.

Figure 10.1 The homepage of the Flatwater Free Press, a nonprofit newsroom based in Omaha, Nebraska.

What you need to create HTML

Before you do anything with HTML, you'll need the right setup. Just as you needed spreadsheet software like Google Sheets to rearrange and summarize data, you need a place not only to write HTML and CSS, but also to render that code and display it properly. That includes two non-negotiable elements: A **text editor** and a modern web browser.

You might think software like Microsoft Word or Google Docs would work as a text editor, but in this case, word processor programs designed for publishing just won't do—hence, the need for software that deals with **plain text**.

Options for text editors abound, like Microsoft's Visual Studio Code or Sublime Text. A good text editor gives us two things: syntax highlighting, which makes it easier to read HTML and CSS, and the ability to see (and control) where files are being saved.

You'll also need a browser on your computer to view the HTML. Many modern browsers (Google Chrome or Mozilla Firefox, for example) include what are known as "developer tools." This suite of functions allows people writing or modifying these fundamental internet technologies a way to peer behind the curtain, so to speak, to see the underlying HTML source and how the browser is communicating back and forth with a web server.

Let's start with a simple example webpage consisting of the most basic components to cover what each one does.

Write the following in the text editor and save this to a new folder on your computer. You can name the folder that holds the file whatever you want—something easy, like "test-website." To start, keep all the files for the webpage in that same folder or directory. HTML files use a suffix of .html or .htm—name this file "simple.html."

Within the text editor, make sure that you select the proper syntax for what you'll be writing; the way to set this can vary by program. When opening a file in a text editor, it can generally parse the file's suffix (e.g., .html or .css) to figure out which type of highlighting to use.

```
<!DOCTYPE html>
<html lang="en">
  <head>
    <meta charset="utf-8">
    <meta name="viewport" content="width=device-width,
initial-scale=1">
    <title></title>
  </head>
  <body>

  </body>
</html>
```

You'll also want to open the file you're working within a web browser of your choice at the same time to see your changes and additions. Getting to the file itself is a bit different than going to a specific website or running an internet search through the address bar—you will need to locate and open the HTML document as a file through the browser, which can be done through the "File" menu.

As you modify the HTML document in a text editor and save your changes, you will then refresh or reload the file in the browser to see the updates.

This may look like a foreign language to you—and that's because markup basically is a foreign language. For our purposes, you'll need to know some crucial parts of that language, but not everything. Knowing the fundamentals is fine and lays a solid foundation for expanding your knowledge where necessary.

The parts of an HTML element

HTML is built from a series of elements with opening and closing tags that enclose or wrap around the content. An HTML element's tags always include angle brackets (< >) around an element name, and closing tags include angle brackets and a forward slash (/) before an element name:

```
<element>Some content for the webpage goes here.</element>
```

Let's say you want to add some content to the sample webpage. Maybe you'll want to call it "Example Webpage." But how do you make that title show up, using HTML? Above, you'll see an empty `<title>` element meant specifically for this purpose. Right now, the full HTML element consists of the following parts:

- Opening tag: `<title>`

- Closing tag: `</title>`

Between the tags, add the text "Example webpage" so that the completed element looks like this:

```
<title>Example Webpage</title>
```

As you can see, the content you want to show goes between the opening tag and the closing tag. When you save the file in the text editor and then open it in a web browser, you should see the content you entered in the title element appear on the browser tab. Those tags won't actually show up on the website—they're just directions that go along with the content to help a browser display it correctly.

Some of the elements in our sample HTML document are ones you'd want to better understand if you were trying to be a web developer, rather than a journalist who understands the fundamentals of web design. Here, we're giving you a basic webpage structure in which to add the more basic elements.

Part of that structure is the first thing you see: `<!DOCTYPE html>`. That code just lets the web browser know HTML is inbound, so it should expect to parse and display HTML.

In keeping with what you already know about how HTML elements work, it will probably come as no surprise that the very first element you need is `<html>`.

```
<html>
Content you want to show up: All the HTML elements for a
webpage, including head and body elements.
</html>
```

Literally everything else you do will be added between that opening and closing `<html>` tag. All other elements will be nested within that.

You might have noticed in the example webpage that some of the HTML elements are inside of other elements. The `<head>` element, for example, is inside of the `<html>` element. And the `<title>` element is inside of that. As HTML elements are nested inside one another, you might have also noticed that they are indented.

In developer guidelines put out by companies like Google,[1] it's recommended that many elements go on a new line, and enclosed elements are indented by two spaces compared to the element that they're inside. Many text editors will automatically create these indentations as you write HTML.

A lot of these practices speak to making the HTML more readable. In theory, all your HTML elements could be squashed into a single line—as long as the HTML elements were in the proper order, a browser would still be able to properly render it. But, unfortunately, no one would be able to easily read the code.

Basic webpage structure and other common HTML elements

So, you've already told the browser that you'd be using HTML, and you know that other basic elements will be nested within your opening and closing `<html>` tags. But what are those other common elements?

A couple elements are related to the basic structure of every webpage:

`<head>`: This element tells the browser how to interpret the body and how to incorporate any outside resources, libraries, and more—items that won't appear on the webpage as content. One bit nested inside of `<head>` that you'll want to pay attention to is `<title>`, which we've already used to give your webpage its title in the browser tab.

The two `<meta>` elements you see nested inside keep the page contents, like text, from shrinking down too much on a mobile screen and ensure that special characters, like é and ö, will be displayed correctly.

`<body>`: This is where you build your page's content and structure. Anything you see on a webpage—including text, images, and other embedded multimedia content—all those elements are nested within the `<body>`.

This list is not exhaustive, but some of those primary elements include:

HTML text elements

`<h1>`: Turn the enclosed text into a header. It works to make regular body text stand out as a header or subheader—by default, the type is larger and has more vertical space above and below. There are six header sizes, `<h1>` through `<h6>`, which become progressively smaller.

`<p>`: Turn the enclosed text into its own separate paragraph. Without this, any text on a webpage just runs on and on without clear separations. No matter how many times you hit the return key, the webpage won't know that you're trying to start a new paragraph without this element.

`<ol>` or `<ul>`: Turn the enclosed text into a list, which can either be a numerically ordered list (ol) or a bulleted list (ul). Each list item exists as an `<li>` element within the `<ol>` or `<ul>` element:

```
<ol>
  <li>First list item.</li>
  <li>Second list item.</li>
  <li>Third list item.</li>
</ol>
```

`<hr>`: Add a horizontal rule text break (a physical horizontal line you can see that breaks the text into sections). This is an "empty" element[2] that can't hold content, so it has no closing tag.

`<br>`: Add a line break (like the equivalent of hitting return or enter). It also holds no content, so has no closing tag.

How several of these different elements might work together inside of the `<body>` element, using a version of this section's text as content:

```
...
<body>

    <h1>Basic webpage structure and other common HTML
elements</h1>

    <p>So, you've already told the browser that you'd be
using HTML, and you know that other basic elements will
be nested within your opening and closing html tags. But
what are those other common elements?</p>

    <p>A couple elements are related to the basic structure
of every webpage:</p>

    <ul>
        <li>
            <p>head: This element tells the browser how to
interpret the body and how to incorporate any outside
resources, libraries, and more.</p>
```

```
        </li>
        <li>
            <p>body: This is where you build your page's
content and structure. Anything you see on a webpage
-- including text, images, and other embedded multime-
dia content -- all those elements are nested here.</p>
        </li>
    </ul>
</body>
...
```

Hyperlinks and an introduction to attributes

<a>: An anchor element that embeds a working hyperlink in text or some other element. The opening and closing tags enclose whatever content will become the link.

The format here is a little different than the text elements above. An anchor element on its own won't do much—you need to specify a destination URL or pathway to another file within the same website.

To do that, you give the anchor element an attribute, "href," which is short for "hypertext reference." When HTML elements have attributes—and there may be more than one—they are placed inside of the element's opening tag. An attribute will also have a corresponding value. Together, the format looks like this:

```
<element attribute="value" attribute="value">Some content
here.</element>
```

So, let's say you wanted to have a segment of text within a paragraph element (<p>) function as a hyperlink to the Google Search homepage using an anchor element (<a>):

```
<p>Sed viverra ipsum <a href="https://www.google.com">
dignissim enim sit</a> amet venenatis urna nunc. Ae-
nean vel elit scelerisque mauris pellentesque pulvinar
pellentesque.</p>
```

In the browser, the placeholder text "dignissim enim sit" would be colored blue and underlined, and clicking on it would take you to the specified URL.

Another potential attribute for anchor elements: "target." By default, a followed link will open in the same browser tab, replacing one webpage with another. Giving an anchor element a "target" attribute of "_blank" will cause the link to open in a new browser tab instead:

```
<a href="https://www.google.com" target="_blank">dignis-
sim enim sit</a>
```

If you look back at the original HTML template from earlier, some of the elements there have common attributes: the <html> element has a "lang" attribute set to a value of "en," which helps make it clear that the HTML document's content will be in English; one of the <meta> elements in the <head> element uses a "char" attribute to specify the webpage's encoding so that a wider range of characters can be properly displayed.

The image element

<img>: Add an image to an HTML document. Like the <hr> and <br> elements, it's also empty, so it has no closing tag.

The image element uses an attribute, "src," to embed a local image file or an image accessed via a URL. It has another commonly used attribute, "alt," which is used to store what's known as "alternative text." This is generally a short description of the image that will appear in its place if it fails to load for some reason, or if someone consumes the page's content with a screen reader. Being sure to include this "alt" text is important when considering how accessible your webpage is.

Image elements also have other attributes that can modify the dimensions of the image like height and width, but we'll come back to those—they're better controlled through CSS.

Altogether, an image element may look like this to display a local JPEG image file in the same directory as the HTML file:

```
<img src="image.jpg" alt="A brief written description of
the image.">
```

Where CSS fits in, and how it works with HTML

CSS is short for "cascading style sheets"; like HTML, it is a language designed to target HTML elements, either broadly or very precisely, and describe how that content should appear when rendered by a web browser.

By writing CSS in tandem with HTML, you can make what would be only a basic webpage in HTML into something vibrant. Without it, what you see is dull: left-justified black text on a white background, using a serif font like Times New Roman.

While these style "directions" can be embedded directly into an HTML document and attached directly to HTML elements through a style attribute, keeping all that information together in one place isn't efficient.

For example, let's say all the paragraphs in your story should be colored light gray and use the Arial font—you would have to add those two styles to every single paragraph element, repeating it over and over. This is the least effective option, only changing the way that one element appears on your webpage.

You could also create a <style> element, written as CSS, in the <head> element of your HTML file. In doing this, you could apply the chosen styles to all paragraphs in the document at once, but there's a catch: It would only apply to the paragraphs in this one document. If you're trying to set the same look and feel for multiple webpages in a website, that `<style>` element would need to be copied to each HTML file.

And that may be fine to do—once. If you need to make any tweaks to any specific styles in the CSS, like darkening the shade of gray used for the paragraph text, that modification would need to be made to every document. Again, it's a more time-consuming way to make changes to a website.

Because of this, we generally keep all the CSS describing page styles in a separate, or external, CSS file (with a .css suffix). Some websites may even use more than one. But one separate CSS file can then be "linked" to multiple HTML files, allowing you to swiftly apply and update the same visual instructions to all of them. This is the method we'll focus on here.

A common file name convention for a primary CSS file is "main.css," and like an HTML file, you'll create this file using the Atom text editor, rather than a word processor. Just open a new tab or document in the same program you used for your HTML file.

But, how exactly do HTML and CSS files work together? Start by adding a `<link>` element to the `<head>` element in an HTML file to connect them together. The general format is this:

```
<link rel="stylesheet" href="main.css">
```

Here, the `<link>` element has two different attributes: "rel" describes the relationship for this outside resource that you're bringing in to the HTML document (it's a stylesheet), and the "href" attribute fulfills the same purpose that it does for an anchor element (`<a>`)—it's a hypertext reference, which in this case is just the name of the file itself rather than a full URL. We only need the file name when the HTML document and the CSS file are located in the same directory or folder.

Writing a CSS selector

CSS has its own format and structure, and it follows a different pattern than HTML. It has three key components:

1   A **selector**, which is meant to point at a specific HTML element. Selectors can be very broad as in the example above, applying to all paragraph elements. There are also ways to write selectors so that they will capture a smaller subset of HTML elements within a file. Another way to think about them is like a filter in a spreadsheet: You're defining the criteria needed to pick a certain group of HTML elements that you want to style.

2   A **property**, which is the name of the style that you want to modify, like the element's color, its top margin, or the font that it uses. While dozens of these CSS properties exist, there are only a relative handful of them that you will use with any frequency.

3   A **value**, which is the property's counterpart. For example, if you're defining an HTML element's color, this is where you would set the color.

The standard convention for writing CSS is the selector, followed by a space and then an opening curly brace ({) before beginning a new line. Each property/value pair is written on its own line and indented, ending in a semicolon (;). When all the specific styles are composed, the selector ends with a closing curly brace (}) on its own line:

```
selector {
  property: value;
}
```

While a browser can understand CSS written on one line without indentation, this standard format helps keep it more readable. But without the semicolon to separate property/value pairs, the browser won't be able to interpret them. To turn all the paragraphs in an HTML document light gray and give them a display font of Arial, the CSS selector could look like this:

```
p {
  color: lightgray;
  font-family: Arial, sans-serif;
}
```

To select and style all paragraphs, you use the paragraph element as the selector—you don't need to include any angle brackets here the way you would when writing it out as an HTML element.

At its core, a CSS file is made up of a list of these selectors, their properties, and values. You may have one selector that styles paragraphs, and another that makes any <h1> element headline 60 pixels tall:

```
p {
  color: lightgray;
  font-family: Arial, sans-serif;
}

h1 {
  font-size: 60px;
}
```

Some common CSS properties

Although there are many different style facets within your control, these are among the most regularly used for controlling the look of written content, especially when starting out. Since we've been dealing mainly with text-related HTML elements so far, most of these properties are specifically designed to style text, though properties having to do with color and alignment have wider uses:

- **font-family**: As mentioned previously, this property allows you to choose the preferred display font for text.[3] Always include a back-up generic font style in case the exact font isn't available for some reason. Commonly used fonts like Arial and Times New Roman are generally considered "web safe" meaning that regardless of a specific device's operating system, those fonts will be present for use. You can supply a comma-separated list of fonts to move through if the first choice isn't available, ending in a generic style. For example, to choose Arial as the displayed font, with sans-serif font as your backup:

```
font-family: Arial, sans-serif;
```

Also, if the font name has spaces in it, it will need to be enclosed in quotation marks:

```
font-family: "Times New Roman", serif;
```

- **font-size**: This allows you to choose the preferred size for font display. Although there are several ways to approach sizes and heights in CSS, a common one is to express text size in pixels; this is an absolute size measurement, corresponding with 1/96th of an inch. HTML element widths are also frequently discussed in terms of pixels. The default size for unstyled is generally 16px, or 16 pixels tall. For example, to change the text to 40 pixels tall:

```
font-size: 40px;
```

font-weight: This is the CSS way to make text bold rather than by enclosing it with a <strong> element in the HTML:

```
font-weight: bold;
```

- **font-style**: Italicizing text is considered a font style in CSS rather than a property dealing with the stroke weight of a typeface. This has the same visual effect as using the <em> element.

```
font-style: italic;
```

- **color** and **background-color**: Choose a foreground and background color for an HTML element. In the case of text, the **color** property will change the color of the typeface while **background-color** will do as the property describes—use the color as background behind the text, extending to the same height as the type. The value here can be a specific HTML color name,[4] of which there are more than 100, or a color hex code, which is a common way in web development to reproduce a very specific color and hue. For example, to turn the background of an HTML element blue using a hex code:

```
color: #0000FF
```

- **text-align**: This property is primarily used to specify the alignment of text elements on a webpage or within another element. By default, headings like `<h1>` elements and paragraph elements will be left justified. Common values for this are "left," "right," or "center." For example, to center an element:

```
text-align: center
```

Giving your CSS selectors more specific targets

In the previous examples, we've been applying style properties to all of a specific type of HTML element, like paragraphs or headings.

For one, if you're trying to apply the same style properties to more than one element, you don't have to type them all out again or copy and paste them into a new selector statement in your CSS file. The different elements that you want to style can be listed out, separated by commas. So, to give both `<h2>` heading and paragraph elements the Arial font, you could create a selector like this:

```
h2, p {
      font-family: Arial, sans-serif;
}
```

You can also get more specific with the elements you want to style based on what encloses them. Let's say you only wanted to change the color of anchor elements (`<a>`) that were present in a webpage's unordered lists (`<ol>`), as opposed to other hyperlinks that may be included in a paragraph or another element.

A way to do this is to separate the element and what encloses it with a space. In practice, a CSS selector like this would turn all hyperlinks located inside of an ordered list red while leaving the others alone:

```
ol a {
     color: red;
}
```

But think about how written content appears on different websites that you visit. A digital news publication may have paragraph text for stories styled with a specific font, color, and line spacing, but use a completely different set of styles for an image caption, or an article's summary blurb. In all these situations, the text content is still enclosed within a paragraph element, but we need more precise methods to select specific parts of an HTML document rather than apply styles with such a broad brush.

Styling HTML based on classes and IDs

One way to do this is by giving HTML elements either a **class** or **ID** attribute, which can then be pinpointed by a CSS selector.

Classes are like creating groups among your HTML elements. You can name them whatever you want, though making them more descriptive is better. ("Banana" would probably be a weak class name, while something like "story-top" is much more understandable.)

Adding a class attribute to an HTML element creates a sort of hook for managing styles because the same style properties can be applied to all members of the same class with one CSS selector.

If, for example, you wanted the paragraphs holding different image captions in a webpage to be smaller and italicized, you could add a class attribute to those paragraphs only:

```
<img src="image.png">
<p class="caption">An image caption.</p>

<p>A separate paragraph.</p>
```

Now, to apply those styles only to HTML elements with a class of "caption," you can create a selector that takes the format of a period (.) and then the class name:

```
.caption {
  font-size: 12px;
  font-style: italic;
}
```

It's also possible that the same class of "caption" has been assigned to other HTML elements beyond just paragraphs—classes can be a way to effectively group different types of HTML content, regardless of specific element.

To only target paragraph elements that have a class of caption, you'd need to make a small modification to the selector, putting the specific element type directly in front of the period:

```
p.caption {
  font-size: 12px;
  font-style: italic;
}
```

Any other members of the caption class would not take those styles.

IDs work in much the same way, except their values can't be reused among different HTML elements like classes can. An ID is assigned to one distinct element in an HTML file. So instead of having to figure out how to focus on a single element based on what kind of element it is or where it sits in the HTML tree, adding an ID offers the same kind of hook for a CSS selector as a class.

If a page has a single paragraph element that serves as an author's byline, an ID attribute identifying it as such can be applied to the element:

```
<p id="byline">By Jane Smith</p>
```

To center that text and make the typeface bold, it's selected much like a class—the syntactical difference is to replace the period (.) with a hashtag symbol (#):

```
#byline {
  text-align: center;
  font-weight: bold;
}
```

When CSS selectors clash

With all the different methods to choose which HTML elements to style, including classes and IDs, it's inevitable that the CSS you write will end up targeting more than one element at the same time. In these situations, the styles you see onscreen might be puzzling—and maybe a little frustrating—because the properties and values that you've assigned aren't being reflected in the web browser as you expect.

Knowing a little bit about how styles can supersede one another can be helpful for troubleshooting when things don't look right. Ultimately, when CSS selectors conflict with each other, one style has to win out. Paragraph text can't be light gray and black at the same time; a headline can't be 60 pixels in size and also 16 pixels in size.

One thing to keep in mind is that more specific CSS selectors will overtake less specific selectors, having their styles applied where more than one property value exists. For example, selecting HTML elements by a class name (like our "caption" class above) is going to be considered more specific than a selector pointed at all paragraph elements.

If a CSS selector for "caption"-class paragraphs are 12 pixels tall, italicized, and colored red, those properties will leapfrog over any clashing styles assigned to paragraphs in general.

```
p.caption {
  color: red;
  font-style: italic;
  font-size: 12px;
}

p {
  font-size: 20px;
  color: black;
  background-color: yellow;
}
```

In this case, there's a conflict between color and font size; the properties applied to the caption will prevail, making them red and 12 pixels in height.

But as these CSS selectors are written, the "caption"-class paragraphs will have a yellow background like all the other paragraphs. Why? There's no property defined for the captions selector that will overrule it; they will inherit the same yellow background color that all paragraphs have.

If, for some reason, selectors are written for the same type of element in the same stylesheet (e.g., two different selectors that apply the same style properties to all <h2> heading elements), the one further on in the stylesheet will overtake the one that comes before it.

Notes

1 Google. (2021, April 28). *HTML Formatting.* Google Developer Documentation Style Guide. https://developers.google.com/style/html-formatting.
2 MDN. (n.d.). *Empty Element.* MDN Web Docs. Retrieved January 3, 2022, from https://developer.mozilla.org/en-US/docs/Glossary/Empty_element.
3 MDN. (n.d.). *Font-family.* MDN Web Docs. Retrieved January 3, 2022, from https://developer.mozilla.org/en-US/docs/Web/CSS/font-family.
4 Dixon & Moe. (2021). *HTML Color Codes.* https://htmlcolorcodes.com/color-names/.

11 More advanced CSS

Layouts, Bootstrap, and more

* * *

In 2011, the Boston Globe introduced one of the news world's first responsive websites.[1] This was a revolutionary idea at the time—a news site that would actually "respond" to different screen types by dynamically altering its layout as the dimensions of the web browser changed.

Instead of a single webpage design that was meant to be consumed on a larger laptop or desktop screen, with its attendant breaking news headlines, splashes, sections, and story links, all arranged across a significant amount of visual real estate, the Globe now had a set of layouts meant for more than one type of device—and everything in between.

The Globe's switch was not long after the launch of the first iPad tablet; by 2012, Pew noted that nearly a quarter of U.S. adults were "multiscreen," consuming news on more than one device,[2] a trend that's deepened with the march of time.

And the idea behind a "responsive" website is just that: The way its various HTML elements are arranged and rendered will change depending on screen width. Today, responsive websites that look right no matter the screen size are the standard rather than the exception, and most of those responsive abilities are governed by a webpage's CSS.

To approach webpage layout, it helps to have a better understanding of how CSS can control HTML elements—not just properties like colors and fonts, but how much space they take up on a page and how they fit together with other elements on a webpage.

We'll take two approaches. The first is a purely vertical layout that will adapt in width for smaller screens, balancing the need for keeping page content inside of a comfortable visual span. No one wants to read a paragraph of text that stretches to each side of a 27-inch monitor.

The other is using an open-source framework for websites and webpages called Bootstrap, which greatly simplifies the process of content layouts that intermix vertical and horizontal positioning of elements. It includes a responsive grid system for arranging page content as columns within rows; by making changes to class names, you can quickly choose how content should be arranged on small, medium, and large screens, without the need for writing a ton of CSS from scratch to govern all these behaviors.

DOI: 10.4324/9781003182238-11

Block vs. inline display

So far, most of the HTML elements we've been using, like paragraphs and head-ings, display as "**block**." Put simply, a paragraph element inside of a webpage's body element is going to take up the full width available to it by default—it's going to fill in a "block" of the webpage. This is true even if a paragraph element encloses a single word. Add another paragraph element after it, and it will appear below, rather than next to, the preceding paragraph.

Contrast this with elements that have an "**inline**" display. Take anchor ele-ments, for example. When you create a hyperlink, it's only as wide as it needs to be.

These aren't the only manners of display, but we're primarily going to be deal-ing with these block elements, where we can use CSS properties to control their width, size, and spacing.

The "box model" in HTML

In addition to taking up the full width available, the block elements we've been using are as tall vertically as the text content inside them—increase the pixel size of a font in a paragraph element, and the height of the element will adjust accordingly.

Beyond the content they hold, the space a block element takes up is split up into three parts: its padding, border, and margin. **Padding** describes the space between the content itself and its outside edge; the **border** is the outside edge; and **margin** describes the space between the outside edge of an element and other elements above, below, or to either side of it.

For these block elements, each of these parts can be thought of as boxes that surround each other and together are known as the CSS "box model."

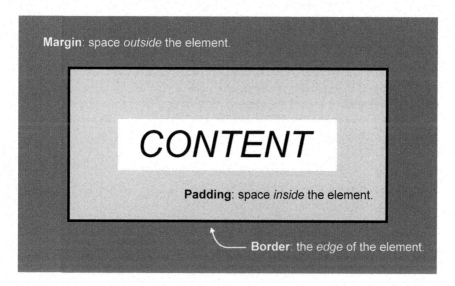

Figure 11.1 A diagram of the box model, showing where padding, the border, and margins are situated around content in an HTML element.

Each aspect is accessed through a CSS selector that defines (or overrides) existing properties.

The border

Let's start with the border, which comprises the outside edge of an element. By default, it's going to be invisible—it has no color or width. It's up to us to assign values to properties to make that border visible if we want it to be seen.

In this case, it's probably helpful: Having a visible border provides a clear visual delineation between what's inside the element and the space that falls outside.

An element's border has three different properties that can be assigned: **border-color, border-style,** and **border-width.**

The border-color property works in much the same way as previously described CSS properties for color: it can be a named color in HTML, or it can be a hex color code.

But without a border-style property, it still won't be visible. This sets the type of border that appears around the element. A common one is "solid"—that will turn the border into an unbroken line around the element's outside edge. But there are other possibilities, too, like "dashed" or "dotted."

Finally, you can specify a border-width by assigning a specific numerical thickness and a measurement unit together, like 2px for two pixels.

To add a dashed black border to paragraph elements that's a single pixel in width, the CSS selector would look like this:

```
p {
  border-color: black;
  border-style: dashed;
  border-width: 1px;
}
```

This applies the border to all four sides of paragraph elements. Individual sides can be accessed by expanding the property name to include the specific side, immediately following the word "border."

So, to only have this dashed black border appear on the top and bottom of each paragraph, with no border present on the left or right sides:

```
p {
  border-top-color: black;
  border-top-style: dashed;
  border-top-width: 1px;
  border-bottom-color: black;
  border-bottom-style: dashed;
  border-bottom-width: 1px;
}
```

The padding

Inside that border is the padding area, which occupies the space between the border and the content itself.

Unlike the border, there's only one property to consider here: How much padding should there be? The amount of padding can be controlled on each side individually with properties like **padding-top**. So, keeping the dashed border from earlier intact, but to also give all paragraph elements a 50-pixel padding on each side:

```
p {
    border-color: black;
    border-style: dashed;
    border-width: 1px;
    padding-top: 50px;
    padding-right: 50px;
    padding-bottom: 50px;
    padding-left: 50px;
}
```

With these styles applied, paragraph elements still take up the full width of the browser window, but the text content is going to be squeezed in on each side by 50 pixels. The paragraph elements aren't getting any smaller, but the content is getting narrower. Also, having this padding on the top and bottom is also going to make the element taller by a total of 100 pixels.

Among the uses for padding are to give a bit of space between the content and what's around it, especially when the margins are small. It can make text content more readable and provide a bit of a buffer for images and graphics that are close together.

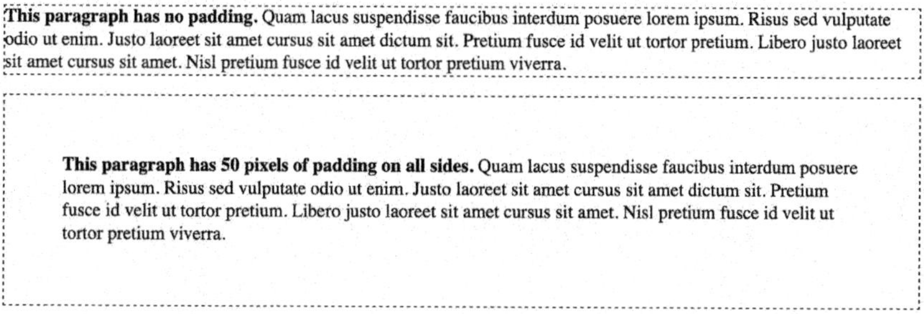

This paragraph has no padding. Quam lacus suspendisse faucibus interdum posuere lorem ipsum. Risus sed vulputate odio ut enim. Justo laoreet sit amet cursus sit amet dictum sit. Pretium fusce id velit ut tortor pretium. Libero justo laoreet sit amet cursus sit amet. Nisl pretium fusce id velit ut tortor pretium viverra.

This paragraph has 50 pixels of padding on all sides. Quam lacus suspendisse faucibus interdum posuere lorem ipsum. Risus sed vulputate odio ut enim. Justo laoreet sit amet cursus sit amet dictum sit. Pretium fusce id velit ut tortor pretium. Libero justo laoreet sit amet cursus sit amet. Nisl pretium fusce id velit ut tortor pretium viverra.

Figure 11.2 A paragraph with 50 pixels of padding on all sides, creating space between the text content and its outside edge. Above, another paragraph that has no padding property defined, for comparison.

The margin

Beyond the outside edge of our elements, we can also define a margin for each. Some of the HTML elements we've covered have an innate margin, even though you've never set it as a style.

Paragraph elements have an automatic top and bottom margin—it's the reason that if you create two paragraphs, vertical space exists between them. In the example above, that default margin is still present between the outside edges of the paragraphs, even with a considerable amount of padding added to paragraphs.

Through CSS, you can add margins on each side and overwrite those built-in values. Adding to the margin on the right and left sides makes the paragraph element narrower, keeping a set distance between the sides of its enclosing element. The property uses the same naming convention as padding, like **margin-top** and **margin-right**.

```
p {
    border-color: black;
    border-style: dashed;
    border-width: 1px;
    margin-top: 20px;
    margin-bottom: 50px;
}
```

Instead of creating this 50 pixels of space between the content and its outside edge (here, the text and the dashed black border), it repels other elements above and below, keeping them at 50 pixels of distance.

Simple responsiveness for block elements using width

For block elements placed on top of each other, setting CSS properties that control the **width** of these elements is among the most straightforward ways to make them respond to screen size.

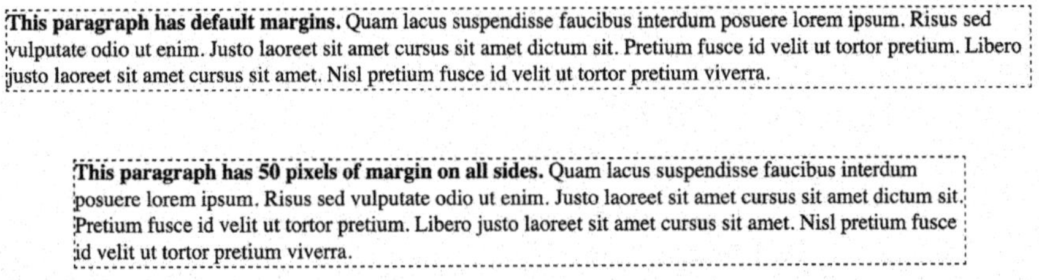

This paragraph has default margins. Quam lacus suspendisse faucibus interdum posuere lorem ipsum. Risus sed vulputate odio ut enim. Justo laoreet sit amet cursus sit amet dictum sit. Pretium fusce id velit ut tortor pretium. Libero justo laoreet sit amet cursus sit amet. Nisl pretium fusce id velit ut tortor pretium viverra.

This paragraph has 50 pixels of margin on all sides. Quam lacus suspendisse faucibus interdum posuere lorem ipsum. Risus sed vulputate odio ut enim. Justo laoreet sit amet cursus sit amet dictum sit. Pretium fusce id velit ut tortor pretium. Libero justo laoreet sit amet cursus sit amet. Nisl pretium fusce id velit ut tortor pretium viverra.

Figure 11.3 A paragraph with 50 pixels of margin on all sides, creating space between its outside edge (in this case, a dashed black border) and its enclosing element. Above, another paragraph that has no specific margin property defined, for comparison.

By default, the elements we've discussed here, like paragraphs, headings, horizontal rules, and others, will run the full width of the body element.

You may have noticed that even without writing any CSS, these block elements don't quite touch the edges of the browser window—they actually fall a little short. This is another example of default CSS properties existing for certain HTML elements: A body element has 8 pixels of margin on all sides. So, the outside edge of the body element remains slightly inside the browser window, and content placed within it will be, at minimum, 8 pixels from the top, bottom, and sides as well.

Generally, you're going to set a width for an HTML element without worrying about setting a **height**. The reason: The necessary height of the element, based on its content and padding, is going to be recalculated and rendered automatically. If you set a height for an element that's lower than what is necessary to display the content that it holds, like a 75-pixel height on a paragraph that needs 150 pixels of vertical space, the content will overrun the element, even overlapping into the next block element if there's not enough room.

Studies have shown that longer line lengths—meaning, more words stretched across a page before breaking to the next line—negatively affect people's ability to read quickly and understand the information they're reading.[3] Having set margins around content increases reading comprehension.

Controlling margins and maximum width (using the CSS property **max-width)** are critical concepts when writing CSS for these basic responsive designs that are essentially a "tower" of HTML elements stacked vertically on top of each other. Without adjusting those styles, the content will take up the full width of the browser window, making it almost unreadable for the average consumer.

Why max-width instead of just defining a width for one or more elements?

Let's say you put a hard stop on paragraph elements, keeping them at 600 pixels, which is the width of many story paragraphs in New York Times's online articles.

```
p {
    width: 600px;
}
```

When using a smartphone's web browser and a responsive page, the idea is generally that it's a seamless vertical scrolling experience—the user scrolls downward to see additional content, rather than having to go side-to-side to view other parts of the webpage that exceed the window's horizontal dimensions.

On a tablet, much like on a desktop or laptop screen, the paragraphs would likely look fine. But on a smartphone, the words would run off the right-hand side of the screen, forcing the user to constantly navigate back and forth.

And that's where max-width comes into play. Defining this property tells the element that it can't exceed that width—but it can narrow on smaller screens.

```
p {
    max-width: 600px;
}
```

With a maximum width of 600 pixels, the text content will wrap and increase in height to fit. As the screen gets wider, eventually it crosses that 600-pixel threshold and stops.

Content divisions

So far, we've just been stacking HTML block elements on top of one another. But to take our page design and layout to the next level, we'll want to use CSS to alter the page layout.

Content division elements (`<div>`), which we'll refer to as "div" elements, exist to compartmentalize content. Without any styling, they are invisible boxes that can enclose and hold different HTML elements together. Many websites use a complex network of these div elements to control the layout and various styles of elements on the page—not only can CSS properties added to div elements control where various sections of text, images, and multimedia elements appear, but how they will look.

If the actual page content is the scenery in a theater production, the div elements work behind the scenes, like unseen rigging, holding everything in its proper place. The audience doesn't always see these div elements (unless they've been given a background color or some other CSS property that would make them visible), but they're essential to creating a dynamic website with a pleasing layout.

For our purposes, you may package elements that contain a story's headline, subheader, and author byline inside of a div element, give the div element a class attribute, and then write a CSS selector that applies a specific font to all of the text content inside of that div; or that gives that div element a deeper margin along the bottom to separate it from another div element below it which holds an article's lead image.

So, one way they can be helpful is as a place to apply styles that then are passed down to the HTML elements and contents within. This can be easier and faster to write than having to target each individual element with its own CSS selector and apply the same styles repeatedly.

```
<h1>A headline</h1>
<p>The first paragraph in a story. ...</p>
<p>The second paragraph in a story. ...</p>
<p>The third paragraph in a story. ...</p>
...
```

For a simple structure like this, with an h1 heading element followed by a series of paragraphs, if we wanted to adjust the font family used, text size, maximum width, and side padding, those CSS properties would have to be written out at least twice in a selector—once for the heading and again for the paragraphs. Even then, you would have to think about whether you wanted those styles to apply to all the paragraphs on the page. If not, you would have to assign each of these paragraph elements a class attribute to offer a more precise target in the CSS to leave the non-story paragraphs alone.

With a div element enclosing these HTML elements, this becomes a more straightforward prospect:

```
<div class="story-main">
  <h1>A headline</h1>
  <p>The first paragraph in a story. …</p>
  <p>The second paragraph in a story. …</p>
  <p>The third paragraph in a story. …</p>
  …
</div>
```

```
.story-main {
  font-family: Arial, sans-serif;
  font-size: 20px;
  padding-left: 10px;
  padding-right: 10px;
  margin-top: 40px;
  max-width: 600px;
}
```

In this case, some of these properties will apply to the contents of the div element with the class "story-main" (font-family and font-size), while others will change the div element itself (padding, margin, and max-width).

The font family and font size are inherited by the text content inside the div element: Paragraph text becomes 20 pixels tall, and h1 headings, which normally appear at twice the size of the base font size, will now be 40 pixels tall.

The headings and paragraphs now run the full width of the div element rather than the webpage's body element, and the div stops at 600 pixels in width. The "story-main" div element has become a very simple responsive container on the webpage that holds other content. As a screen's width drops below 600 pixels, the div element will shrink with it.

Repositioning a content division element using margins

Setting a maximum width can provide more comfortable sizes for div elements and their enclosed contents on large screens, but by default, div elements are going to be left aligned. This isn't really noticeable on a small screen, but on anything wider, there's going to be a considerable amount of unused space on the right side of the screen.

One way to overcome this is by repositioning a content division using the CSS margin properties. And rather than setting a specific margin value, like 50 pixels, we can take advantage of the fact that margins can be calculated automatically based on the width of the browser window using the value "auto."

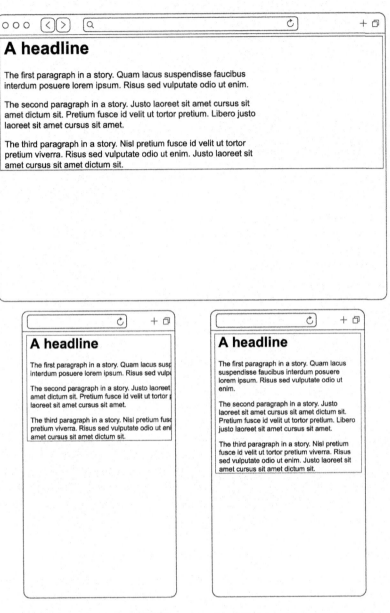

Figure 11.4 Top: An example of HTML rendered in full-sized web browser; with a width or max-width property for paragraphs and a headline set to 600 pixels, the text content will stop at 600 pixels, even though more horizontal space is available. Bottom left: On mobile, a width of 600 pixels is wider than the screen, so text content will spill off to the right, forcing a user to scroll. Bottom right: A max-width of 600 pixels, though, means that the paragraphs and headline will narrow along with the screen.

The idea here is that the browser looks at the horizontal space available between an element and whatever encloses it—in this case, the body element—and adjusts the margin value accordingly.

To center this div element within the body, you would set an "auto" margin on both the left and right sides: The 600-pixel wide div is pushed to the middle, and the margins on the side are calculated to share the remaining space.

```
.story-main {
  font-family: Arial, sans-serif;
  font-size: 20px;
  padding-left: 10px;
  padding-right: 10px;
  margin-top: 40px;
  margin-left: auto;
  margin-right: auto;
  max-width: 600px;
}
```

To move this div element all the way to the right instead, you only need to have the left margin property set to "auto," though it won't hurt to set the right margin to 0 pixels. This sets up a situation where all the remaining space is added to the left margin, regardless of screen (and body element) width.

```
.story-main {
  font-family: Arial, sans-serif;
  font-size: 20px;
  padding-left: 10px;
  padding-right: 10px;
  margin-top: 40px;
  margin-left: auto;
  margin-right: 0px;
  max-width: 600px;
}
```

Nesting div elements

Maximum widths and automatic margins are important considerations for basic vertical layouts that are responsive. But keeping all the webpage content in a single "column," so to speak, that doesn't vary in width and can only sit at the left, right, or center of the window might be considered a little too basic.

In our news story example, you could potentially have separate div elements to hold content like headlines, bylines, subheads, article text, and graphics. It may be the case that you want the headline and lead image to be wider and more visually dominant than the article content below; or that photos and their captions should be inset as they're interspersed throughout a story, appearing narrower than the surrounding text.

The idea of nesting becomes key here: Content division elements can be placed inside one another, and a property like margin will then be calculated based on how much space exists between the enclosed div and the outside edge of the div that it occupies.

This kind of "box within a box (within a box)" structure helps determine where and how web content is placed on the pages of many websites.

So let's say rather than having content within a div centered on the page when viewed on a desktop or laptop, you wanted it off-center, with a significant margin of around 150 pixels on the left and the remainder of the page space to the right— all while keeping the enclosed text content at 600 pixels. One way to achieve this kind of responsive layout is by nesting div elements that have different maximum widths and automatic margins.

The HTML structure, with one div enclosing another, would look like this:

```
<div class="outside">
  <div class="inside">
    <h1>A headline</h1>
    <p>The first paragraph in a story. …</p>
    <p>The second paragraph in a story. …</p>
    <p>The third paragraph in a story. …</p>
    …
  </div>
</div>
```

The goal would be to assign the same CSS properties as before to the div element with a class of "inside." Giving it a margin-left of "auto" causes it to adhere to the right-hand side of whatever element encloses it; in this case, it's another div that belongs to the class "outside."

```
.inside {
  font-family: Arial, sans-serif;
  font-size: 20px;
  padding-left: 10px;
  padding-right: 10px;
  margin-left: auto;
  margin-right: 0px;
  max-width: 600px;
}

.outside {
  max-width: 750px;
}
```

The "outside" div element, which is left-aligned within the webpage's body element by default, won't ever exceed 750 pixels in width. The "inside" div element

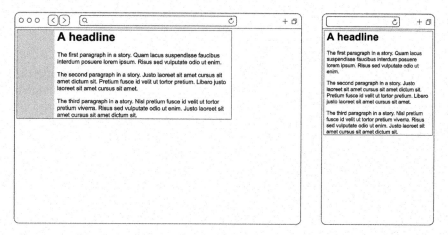

Figure 11.5 Text content inside of two div elements with different max-widths set. The outside div is wider at 750 pixels (colored gray for emphasis); the inside div is 600 pixels wide, and has an automatic left margin and a zero-pixel right margin, right-justifying itself within the outside div. On a narrower mobile screen, the margins fall away and both divs conform to the available browser width.

is narrower, having a max-width of 600 pixels, so the content stays on the right side of the "outside" div.

As the screen gets narrower, the space to the right of the "outside" div element disappears first; once it dips below 750 pixels, the automatic margin to the left of the "inside" div element will shrink; finally, once the screen dimensions are below 600 pixels in width, the content will simply take up the full window.

Keeping images in check

You may have noticed a tendency for any images to default to their native dimensions. Often, in an era of high-resolution screens, these dimensions can be considerable, greatly exceeding the size of a browser window.

One way to constrain image size is by controlling its width through CSS, much in the same way as other HTML elements.

Rather than setting the width property to a specific value, like a number of pixels, you can use a relative measurement, like a percentage.

Giving an image a width of 100% means that it will take up the full width of whatever element it's enclosed by. In turn, the height of the image will change automatically—it will retain its original aspect ratio, preventing the image from looking pinched or squashed.

```
<img id="my-image" src="image.png" alt="Alt text for the
image.">
```

```
#my-image {
  width: 100%;
}
```

Now, instead of a large image directly in the body element overflowing the page, forcing a user to scroll to the right (and likely downward to see additional content), it's limited to 100% of the body element. It may still be quite large, especially on a desktop-size screen, but the full width of the image will be in view.

This holds true for an image inside of a narrower div element, like the one we'd given a maximum width of 600 pixels. The image would take up 100% of its enclosure, and it would get smaller below that 600-pixel threshold.

But something to note: While shrinking the dimensions of an image so that it conforms to its enclosing element works well for a large image, it will stretch a smaller image to take up 100% of the element's width. This can cause an image to lose its crispness.

In this situation, you can find a higher-resolution image or set a max-width of 100% instead:

```
#my-image {
  max-width: 100%;
}
```

For an image that displays smaller than its enclosing element, it will appear at its normal size; once that containing element grows narrower than the image within, then the image will shrink along with it.

Shorthand properties for margins, padding, and borders

Defining margin, padding, and border properties for all sides of an HTML element can be time-consuming to write and potentially more difficult to parse and read, especially if a particular CSS selector has a bunch of other properties defined.

To streamline these properties, you can use shorthand for their values, which allows you to define multiple parts at once.

So instead of having three separate properties to control the color, thickness, and style of an element's entire border, they call all be set on a single line of CSS:

```
p {
  border: 1px solid red;
}
```

It doesn't matter which order the values for the "border" property go in, if all three of them are present and separated by a space character. (As long as the border style is defined, like "solid" or "dashed," the browser will render something.)

Similarly, padding and margin for an element can be set on a single line as well. Instead of having to define those styles separately:

```
p {
  padding-top: 30px;
  padding-right: 15px;
  padding-bottom: 30px;
  padding-left: 15px;
}
```

You can define all four at once through the property "padding," following an order of top, right, bottom, and left:

```
p {
  padding: 30px 15px 30px 15px;
}
```

And here, the shorthand values can even be reduced further because the top and bottom share the same amount of padding (30 pixels), as do the sides (15 pixels). In a situation like this, you only need to define two values: one for the top and bottom, followed by one for the sides.

```
p {
  padding: 30px 15px;
}
```

Given this pattern, as you might expect, giving a "margin" or "padding" property a single value will apply to all sides of the element.

Content divisions and the semantic web

If you inspect the source HTML for other websites, you may notice other elements we haven't discussed, like `<section>`, `<article>`, `<navbar>`, `<footer>`, and others. These elements in particular are HTML content divisions with names that make them easier to interpret by other web developers, screen readers, and search.

These semantic elements can help accessibility technologies parse different kinds of content divisions and give pages an advantage online, allowing search engines like Google to index the most important parts of the page correctly.

For our purposes, we'll stick to using the div element to keep this process less confusing. Just know that when you see these other elements in HTML, they are, at their core, just content divisions functioning in the same way as a div. The element names are there to give them more context.

Creating more complex webpage layouts with the Bootstrap Grid

With HTML and CSS, you can design a useful, visually pleasing, responsive website—but it takes a lot of time to individually code each element you'd need to best organize the content on your pages.

That's where Bootstrap comes in.

What is Bootstrap?

Bootstrap is an open-source CSS framework that's free to use. That framework includes prewritten CSS for many complex situations. To put it simply, it makes the layout process easier.

Think of it like making a meal: Writing all the CSS from scratch is like starting the process with farming and raising livestock just to get the ingredients you need to cook. Working within Bootstrap's framework is more like going to the store to pick what you need off the shelf—it frees you up to focus on the more big-picture concerns, like page layouts, without having to agonize over every single styling choice and creating everything yourself.

Bootstrap has many different abilities—it's a veritable superstore—but for our purposes, we'll focus on its grid system for responsive content, which largely works within a predefined, 12-column grid that you can quickly modify by adding Bootstrap's classes to certain HTML elements. These classes control the behavior of content division elements, enabling webpage layouts where content stacks vertically on small screens and spreads out horizontally on a larger one. And it can all be done without having to write much CSS: You can rely on Bootstrap to do much of the heavy lifting.

Again, you could accomplish something similar without using the Bootstrap framework, but using it will allow you to make fairly sophisticated layouts with a lot less work.

Figure 11.6 An example of a webpage layout using the Bootstrap grid; on a desktop or laptop screen, content elements are arranged horizontally as well as vertically. On a smaller mobile screen, the layout collapses to a simpler, vertical arrangement, making for a better scrolling experience.

Adding Bootstrap to your webpage

One way to access Bootstrap is by linking it to a webpage through the head element. It's similar and uses the same overall method as accessing a CSS file. When the webpage is loaded in a browser window, the Bootstrap-specific CSS and other files are retrieved from the URL, making all its functionality immediately accessible.

The specific link element is available to copy from the Bootstrap website; at the time of this writing, this would need to be placed within the head element of a webpage:

```
<link
href="https://cdn.jsdelivr.net/npm/bootstrap@5.1.3/dist/css/
bootstrap.min.css" rel="stylesheet" integrity="sha384-
1BmE4kWBq78iYhFldvKuhfTAU6auU8tT94WrHftjDbrCEXSU1oBoqy
l2QvZ6jIW3" crossorigin="anonymous">
```

(The "href" and "rel" attributes are probably familiar, holding the remote URL for the Bootstrap CSS and describing the type of file. Don't worry too much about the others—one's like a code word to help ensure that you're getting unadulterated versions of the CSS over the internet.)

Other Bootstrap abilities use JavaScript, a programming language that's executed in the browser (enabling all manner of dynamic behaviors, among other things). Because of this, a script element also needs to be copied and pasted into the body element of the webpage, preferably after the rest of the HTML content, but before the body element's closing tag.

Note: You can also download your own copy of the Bootstrap framework files if you prefer not to always retrieve them from the internet.

How the Bootstrap grid works: using containers, rows, and columns

By using Bootstrap, you can generate complex website layouts consisting of many different elements that automatically collapse and stack on top of each other on a mobile screen. But how does it work?

The system uses a set of three classes that can be added to div elements. Together, they form the Bootstrap grid: A "container" to hold the whole arrangement, "rows" that span the container and sit atop one another in a vertical stack, and one or more "cols" (columns) within a row to hold the HTML content.

The framework effectively splits a webpage into 12 equal columns that serve as a basis for how wide the "cols" will be and how they will share each "row."

But the thing to remember right off the bat is that these classes are designed to nest inside one another: A container encloses rows, and a row encloses columns.

Don't worry if that doesn't make sense yet. First, let's discuss these classes individually:

Container: The outside element, this class is key for accessing the Bootstrap grid and making the content divisions that go inside it responsive. A container div will automatically resize at different screen widths, maintaining a margin on either side of the container, extending to the edges of the body element, and centering the content.

```
<body>
  <div class="container">

  </div>
  ...
</body>
```

There's also a **container-fluid** class that can be used instead: This allows the container to fill the full width of the webpage from side to side, without the presence of those left and right margins. It's still responsive in the same way, but the content in the rows and columns will generally extend to the sides of the browser window.

Row: The next content division within a container div element. These enclose columns, allowing you to spread content horizontally on the page.

```
<body>
  <div class="container">
    <div class="row">

    </div>
  </div>
  ...
</body>
```

Col (column): These div elements are intended to hold the HTML elements we're accustomed to, like images and paragraphs. By default, a single column inside a row will spread out, taking up the full horizontal space. But these columns are important to making a layout responsive: By making changes to the class name, you give Bootstrap instructions on how columns should behave at different screen sizes. How they share the row, when they stack instead of appearing side by side—these are all things you're able to control.

```
<body>
  <div class="container">
    <div class="row">
      <div class="col">

      </div>
    </div>
  </div>
  ...
</body>
```

For example, an arrangement of five column divs across two rows—with two on the top row and three in the bottom row—would be written out like this:

```
<body>
  <div class="container">
    <div class="row">
      <div class="col">
        <p>Column 1 in Row 1.</p>
      </div>
      <div class="col">
        <p>Column 2 in Row 1.</p>
      </div>
    </div>
    <div class="row">
      <div class="col">
        <p>Column 1 in Row 2.</p>
      </div>
      <div class="col">
        <p>Column 2 in Row 2.</p>
      </div>
      <div class="col">
        <p>Column 3 in Row 2.</p>
      </div>
    </div>
  </div>
...
</body>
```

Rendered in a web browser, that arrangement would look like this:

Column classes

As mentioned above, a single column will take up an entire row; when a row holds more than one column, each of those columns will share a row evenly.

Under the 12-column system the Bootstrap grid uses, if two columns are present inside of a row, each will share the row equally, taking up 6 out of the

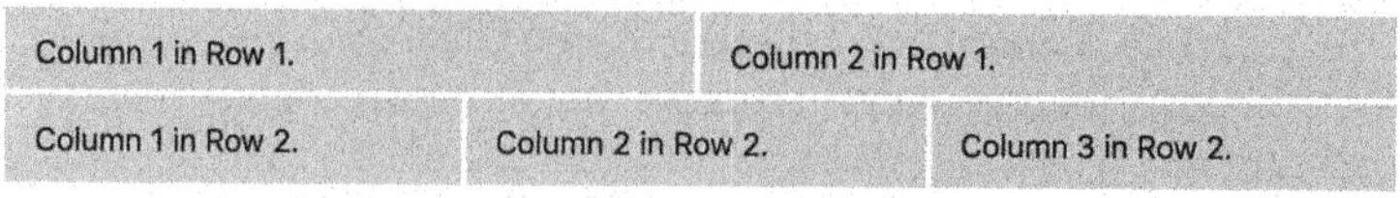

Figure 11.7 A simple two-row layout using the Bootstrap grid: By default, column divs (shaded gray for visibility) will share the available 12 columns of horizontal space equally. Where two are present, each will take up six columns of space; three will use four columns; etc.

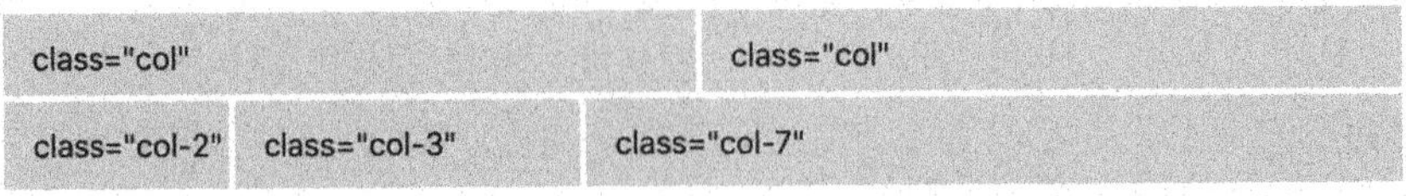

class="col"		class="col"
class="col-2"	class="col-3"	class="col-7"

Figure 11.8 Column divs can have their classes modified to conform to a specific width.
In the top row, column divs will share the space equally; in the bottom row,
a specific width has been set on each of the column divs. A class of "col-3"
means that the column div will take up 3 of the 12 available columns.

12 available columns. Three columns in a row would each take up four columns,
and so on.

That's helpful for building an evenly spaced horizontal layout of content, but
it's not truly responsive on its own. No matter how narrow the screen gets—even
if it makes the content really small and difficult to view—those columns will, by
default, still appear next to each other and share the row.

By adding to the column's class value, you're able to control two primary things:

1   **Width**: How wide each column should be (meaning, how many of the 12
available columns within the grid should the individual column take up).

2   **Breakpoint**: At what screen width should columns within a row stack on top
of one another instead of appearing side by side.

The general format for providing these two instructions through the class is **col-
[breakpoint]-[width]**. The "col" class name is essentially extended, adding these
extra details separated by hyphens (-).

Both breakpoint and width don't need to be defined at the same time—
depending on what you need the column to do, it can be one or the other (or, as
you've seen in previous examples, neither): **col-[width]** or **col-[breakpoint]**.

For example, **col-[width]** by itself will set a number of columns on the grid that
a column div will use, regardless of screen width. In this case, making the class
attribute `col-8` tells Bootstrap that the column element should take up the first
two-thirds of the row only—8 of the 12 available columns.

```
<body>
  <div class="container">
    <div class="row">
      <div class="col-8">
        <h1>A heading inside a column.</h1>
        <p>A paragraph inside a column.</p>
      </div>
    </div>
  </div>
  ...
</body>
```

Or let's say you have two columns in a row, but you want one of them to take up those first eight columns and the other to use the rest of the space, which is four columns on the grid:

```
<body>
  <div class="container">
    <div class="row">
      <div class="col-8">
        <h1>A heading inside a column.</h1>
        <p>A paragraph inside a column.</p>
      </div>
      <div class="col-4">
        <h1>Another heading inside a column.</h1>
        <p>Another paragraph inside a column.</p>
      </div>
    </div>
  </div>
...
</body>
```

But this still doesn't solve the responsiveness issue—the desired behavior is for these column divs to collapse and stack as the screen shrinks.

So, we add a **size breakpoint**. It's exactly as it sounds: The point at which you want the arrangement of column divs to switch from a more vertical layout to a more horizontal one across a row as the screen size expands.

Bootstrap has different breakpoints that change the default behavior of a column div, using a "small" through "extra large" sizing system: **sm**, **md**, **lg**, **xl**, and **xxl**. The two you will likely end up using most frequently are the "small" breakpoint, which is at 576 pixels wide, and the "large" breakpoint, which is at 992 pixels wide.

It's certainly not exact, but the small breakpoint can be thought of as the transition point between a mobile display and a larger device. For example, a modern iPhone has a browser display width of roughly 400 pixels (depending on the model), while a tablet may be approximately twice the width or more—so a better candidate for the large threshold.

But let's cover how this works. Setting specific widths aside for a moment, let's say you have two column divs in a row, and both of them specify the small breakpoint as a part of the class name: col-sm.

```
<body>
  <div class="container">
    <div class="row">
      <div class="col-sm">
        <h1>A heading inside a column.</h1>
        <p>A paragraph inside a column.</p>
```

```
    </div>
    <div class="col-sm">
      <h1>Another heading inside a column.</h1>
      <p>Another paragraph inside a column.</p>
    </div>
  </div>
</div>
...
</body>
```

On mobile-size screen, these column divs and their content will stack vertically on top of each other. Even though one appears above the other, they are still contained within the same row div. And this is what we want because there's not much horizontal space available, and having them appear beside each other would be far too cramped.

As the screen gets wider on a larger device, you'll reach the small breakpoint, which sits at 576 pixels. Upon crossing that threshold, those columns no longer stack, appearing next to each other and each using half of the available row space.

Setting that breakpoint tells Bootstrap where it should make this transition and unstack content, ideally unleashing the full horizontal layout because the screen size now allows for it.

Note: A desktop or laptop browser provides two methods for checking out responsiveness for yourself. One easy way is to manually narrow it until you see the expected changes to layout based on the HTML and CSS that you've written. It's not very precise, but it can serve as a quick test to ensure things are working properly. The other

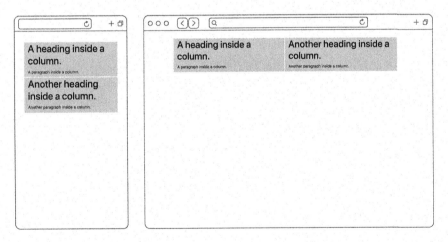

Figure 11.9 Column breakpoints set the threshold for which column divs will change from stacking vertically to appearing side by side. With a small ("sm") breakpoint set, on a screen narrower than 576 pixels, the columns will stack; on one wider, they will appear next to each other.

way is to use developer tools: Browsers like Mozilla Firefox and Google Chrome have a developer tools section that allows you to emulate the window dimensions of common mobile devices.

Because you're most likely writing HTML on a full-sized screen and seeing the webpage rendered in a browser window taking up a laptop or desktop-sized screen width, it may be a little bit more difficult to understand how these breakpoints work. Don't think of it as an instruction for how a column should alter its display as the screen shrinks. Reverse the order—it describes how a column should look as the screen widens, after the breakpoint is crossed.

Combining a breakpoint with a width controls the column div behavior as the screen size expands beyond the threshold. A class of `col-md-8` means that below the medium threshold—a window narrower than 768 pixels—the column will take up the entire width, appearing stacked above or below any columns that are also in the row. Once the screen is wider, and after it's larger than that medium threshold, then it will take up eight columns of space.

And if you add width values to classes in the Bootstrap grid that would total more than the 12 available columns in a row, the column divs will "wrap," starting a new line underneath. They'll remain in the same row div, of course, but their display and layout at a width larger than the specified breakpoint will be modified this way to accommodate the specific widths.

So, for three column divs within the same row, with their classes all set to `col-md-5`, for example:

```
<div class="row">
  <div class="col-md-5">
    <h1>A heading inside a column.</h1>
    <p>A paragraph inside a column.</p>
  </div>
  <div class="col-md-5">
    <h1>Another heading inside a column.</h1>
    <p>Another paragraph inside a column.</p>
  </div>
  <div class="col-md-5">
    <h1>Another heading inside a column.</h1>
    <p>Another paragraph inside a column.</p>
  </div>
</div>
```

Below the medium breakpoint, these three column divs stack vertically. But above it, they would take up 15 columns of space, three more than are available through the grid system. As soon as this happens, the column div that doesn't have enough space available will overflow, wrapping below. The first two divs in this row would only take up 10 of the 12 available columns leaving the rightmost two columns unused.

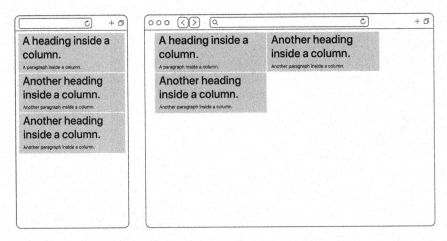

Figure 11.10 If column divs within a row div have been set up to take up more than 12 columns of space, they will wrap below.

Giving instructions for more than one breakpoint

As mentioned in the previous chapter, an HTML element can have multiple classes—they just need to be separated by a space.

With the Bootstrap grid, we can take advantage of this fact to layer different behaviors onto a single-column div, controlling how it looks at more than one screen width. Instead of giving it two different "looks"—one for a window narrower than the breakpoint and another layout when it's wider—you could create different arrangements meant for phones, tablets, and full-size computing devices.

For a row layout like this, column divs would begin stacked vertically on a mobile device, moving to sharing the row equally on tablet-sized screens. Finally, it settles on a desktop arrangement where the first and third column divs take up three columns of space, while the second column div is a bit more of a centerpiece element, taking up five columns.

```
<div class="row">
  <div class="col-sm col-lg-3">
    <h1>A heading inside a column.</h1>
    <p>A paragraph inside a column.</p>
  </div>
  <div class="col-sm col-lg-5">
    <h1>Another heading inside a column.</h1>
    <p>Another paragraph inside a column.</p>
  </div>
  <div class="col-sm col-lg-3">
    <h1>Another heading inside a column.</h1>
    <p>Another paragraph inside a column.</p>
  </div>
</div>
```

Aligning and distributing content

The fact that HTML elements can have more than one class also means that you can add alignment and justification instructions through Bootstrap for column divs, determining where content sits as columns shift.

By default, everything is positioned to the top and left: When column divs don't take up all 12 columns within a row, for example, they begin from the left and leave an open gap to the right; if the column div's content doesn't take up the full vertical space that it has available, it hugs the top of the row, leaving space below.

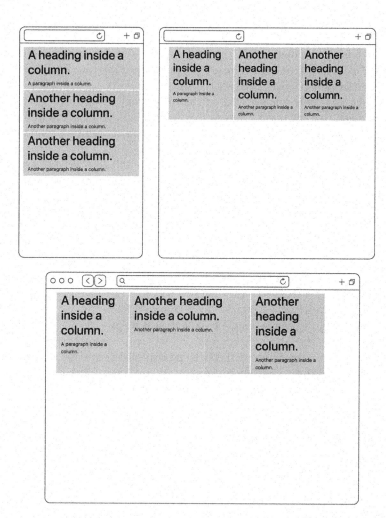

Figure 11.11 Top left: Below the "small" breakpoint, the column divs will stack. Top right: On a larger mobile device screen, like a tablet, that falls between the "small" and "large" breakpoints, the column divs will share the space equally. Bottom: On a full-size display, wider than the "large" breakpoint, the column divs will follow the instructions in the other class that's been applied, resizing their widths accordingly.

Bootstrap offers three overarching class types to change how your column divs are positioned within the rows: Two of them deal with vertical alignment, and another handles horizontal justification to the left and right.

Align items: This class is added to *rows* and changes the vertical alignment of all enclosed column divs. The format is **align-items-[position]**.

Align self: This class is applied to individual column divs, changing their vertical alignment within a row. Different column divs may have different alignments. The format is **align-self-[position]**.

For vertical alignment, whether for one column div or for all of them, the default position at the top of a row is considered the "start"—column divs can also be aligned at the "center" or the "end," which is the equivalent of the bottom of a row.

So, to have all columns sit in the center of one row, you would add the appropriate class to the one that already exists, defining the row; `class="row"` becomes `class="row align-items-center"`.

To make it so only one selected column div would move to the center of a row, you'd add the "align self" class to that specific column rather than the row: `class="col"` becomes `class="col align-self-center"`, and leaves any other columns in the row untouched.

Setting an alignment on an individual column div will also override any "align items" directions set for the row. So, using the example from above, with three horizontal columns that adjust their layout beyond different breakpoints, all column divs could be centered by adding the `align-items-center` class to the row, and then the middle column could be set to aligned to the bottom of the row by adding the `align-self-end` class to it:

```
<div class="row align-items-center">
  <div class="col-sm col-lg-3">
    <h1>A heading inside a column.</h1>
    <p>A paragraph inside a column.</p>
  </div>
  <div class="col-sm col-lg-5 align-self-end">
    <h1>Another heading inside a column.</h1>
    <p>Another paragraph inside a column.</p>
  </div>
  <div class="col-sm col-lg-3">
    <h1>Another heading inside a column.</h1>
    <p>Another paragraph inside a column.</p>
  </div>
</div>
```

Justify content: This class is also applied to rows and changes the horizontal positioning of all enclosed column divs.

This only really matters if the column div(s) on a row have widths set that keep them from using the full 12-column width available. If columns are either automatically sharing the entire row or have widths that total 12 combined, changing the justification won't be visible.

Just like with alignment, columns can be justified at the start, center, or end, which behave like left, middle, and right; the default positioning for all column divs will be to the start.

In addition to moving columns on the horizontal axis to the left or right, they can also be distributed across a row equally. So, if there are two column divs using a total of eight columns of space, the remaining four would be spread between them and at the left and right sides using "evenly": `class="row justify-content-evenly"`.

When moving content around in this way, the effect you see with alignment is going to depend on the HTML content enclosed in the column divs. As mentioned previously, HTML elements expand along with the content inside of them, unless specific dimensions have been set. Constrained in its ability to expand horizontally, an element will grow vertically. In turn, this will increase the amount of vertical space inside of a row. So, in some configurations and screen sizes, alignment and justification choices may barely be noticeable; in others, they will be starkly visible.

Next Bootstrap steps

Beyond the grid, the Bootstrap framework includes many predefined capabilities, including navbars, buttons, and accordions for showing and hiding text. Many of these features are accessed in the same way that we've built simple responsive layouts—by adding Bootstrap's existing classes to different HTML elements. Getting into the details of how all these features can be added to a project exceeds what can be discussed in this chapter, but Bootstrap has significant documentation online along with templates and examples.[4]

* * *

Iris Lee uses web development skills to better tell stories

Iris Lee was a successful business development and sales executive for a large company before deciding she wanted to do something different. After years in the working world, she took a few community college classes in journalism and realized she wanted to pursue it full-time, eventually going back to school to get a Master's Degree. She's now a data journalist for the Los Angeles Times.

Lee considers herself a highly logical person. As a child, she built her own computers. She was a chemistry major who loved math – not the usual profile of a future journalist. But after discovering how web development could be used along with data to tell stories, she was hooked.

"It just satisfied my natural inclination towards those things. That, I mean – it was like an 'aha' moment," Lee said. "It was like, wow, I could do this while doing journalism."

She approached the task of learning code as though it were any foreign language, forgiving herself for not understanding everything immediately, taking her time and slowly gaining confidence.

And much like understanding any other language, Lee said learning to code and comprehend data has helped her better interpret information from a source she might otherwise struggle to interview.

"At the end of the day, especially in data journalism, the data we work with is data that's collected by people, about people … and you have to interview the data like you would any person," she said.

Notes

1 Sonderman, J. (2011, September 12). How the Boston Globe Built an All-in-One Website, Web App and Mobile Site. Poynter. https://www.poynter.org/reporting-editing/2011/how-the-boston-globe-built-an-all-in-one-website-web-app-and-mobile-site/.

2 Mitchell, A., Rosenstiel, T., & Christian, L. (2012, March 18). Mobile Devices and New Consumption: Some Good Signs for Journalism. Pew Research Center. https://www.pewresearch.org/journalism/2012/03/18/mobile-devices-and-news-consumption-some-good-signs-for-journalism/.

3 Nanavati, A. A., & Bias, R. G. (2005). Optimal Line Length in Reading – A Literature Review. Visible Language, 39 (2), 120–144.

4 Getbootstrap.com. (n.d.). Introduction: Get Started with Bootstrap, the World's Most Popular Framework for Building Responsive, Mobile-First Sites, with JsDelivr and a Template Starter Page. Retrieved December 16, 2021, from https://getbootstrap.com/docs/5.0/getting-started/introduction/.

12 Where to learn more

* * *

We've covered a lot of ground together in this book. We talked about the importance of data journalism in holding the powerful accountable; knowing how to use data and records to make your reporting stronger; and how to get data you can use in your investigations. We covered using spreadsheets to better understand and analyze your data or taking your analysis a step further with R and the tidyverse. You learned how to create data visualizations to make your findings clearer to your reader, and how to make basic webpages using HTML, CSS, and the Bootstrap framework.

By this point, you may recognize this text for what it is—a book that lays a foundation for how to do this work, with strong starting points that cover what journalists primarily care about. It's written with the expectation that you'll want to learn more and stretch some of these newfound skills a bit further. You may want to know where to turn next for more specialized information about computer programming, web development, and advanced statistical techniques that can be used for journalism.

Among the topics you may want to explore further: Web scraping to collect data from webpages using languages like R, Python, or JavaScript; data analysis using SQL and traditional database managers; different frameworks for building data-driven web applications; and more complex code-based visualizations with packages and libraries like D3.js.

Luckily, information abounds on these topics as they become more essential to everyday journalism. Here are some opportunities to find out more:

Records and investigative journalism: If you're interested in the different types of information out there that have been used to build meticulous investigative stories, consider *The Investigative Reporter's Handbook: A Guide to Documents, Databases, and Techniques.*[1]

More with programming in R, Python, and/or JavaScript: Learning to code can be as complicated as learning any other language, but you started on the basics in this book—concepts like variables, code interpreters, and scripts are transferable.

DOI: 10.4324/9781003182238-12

For more information on using R in journalism, read *Practical R for Mass Communication and Journalism*[2] by Sharon Machlis and *R for Data Science*[3] by Hadley Wickham and Garrett Grolemund.

If you'd rather try a different programming language than R, Python may be more your speed. It has outside packages that allow journalists to perform data analysis and visualization as well. To get a better grounding with how it all works, you can learn to *Automate the Boring Stuff with Python* using Al Sweigart's aptly named book.[4]

For more general information, Paul Bradshaw's *Scraping for Journalists*[5] gives a solid overview of several web scraping tools (coding-based and otherwise).

More with front-end web development: If reading the HTML and CSS chapters were your favorite parts of this book, try *CSS in Depth*[6] by Keith J. Grant. As the title suggests, you'll find a deeper dive into the world of front-end development and design.

SQL and database managers: Understanding how to use SQL, a data querying language used by databases, will allow you to manipulate data in many new ways. That includes batch updates to data you're keeping in a large database and queries—or asking questions of—large databases to quickly retrieve information. For SQL basics, try *Practical SQL: A Beginner's Guide to Storytelling with Data*.[7]

Data visualization with code: Although we covered the basics of using R for data visualization, you've no doubt realized we only skimmed the surface of those capabilities. If you're looking for quick, simple, and effective R graphs, check out *R Graphics Cookbook*[8] by Winston Chang. This cookbook-style manual offers "recipes" to solve various problems, plus notes on how those recipes can be applied to your work.

To dive into the more complex end of the data-visualization-using-code realm, a heavyweight is the JavaScript library D3, which news organizations rely on to turn data sets into charts, maps, and other interactive experiences. Become familiar with D3 by reading *Interactive Data Visualization for the Web: An Introduction to Designing with D3*.[9]

* * *

Of course, these are just several of the many books that discuss various aspects of the wide world of data and presentation. But the more you understand about data—its analysis, interpretation, and capabilities—the less daunting using data for reporting, research, and investigation becomes.

Notes

1 Houston, B. (2020). *The Investigative Reporter's Handbook: A Guide to Documents, Databases and Techniques* (6th ed.). Bedford/St. Martin's.
2 Machlis, S. (2018). *Practical R for Mass Communication and Journalism.* Chapman and Hall/CRC.
3 Wickham, H., & Grolemund, G. (2017). *R for Data Science.* O'Reilly Media.

4 Sweigart, A. (2015). *Automate the Boring Stuff with Python: Practical Programming for Total Beginners*. No Starch Press.

5 Bradshaw, P. (2017). *Scraping for Journalists: How to Grab Data from Hundreds of Sources, Put it in a Form You Can Interrogate – and Still Hit Deadlines* (2nd ed.). Leanpub.

6 Grant, K. (2018). *CSS In Depth*. Manning.

7 DeBarros, A. (2022). *Practical SQL: A Beginner's Guide to Storytelling with Data* (2nd ed.). No Starch Press.

8 Chang, W. (2018). *R Graphics Cookbook* (2nd ed.). O'Reilly Media.

9 Murray, S. (2013). *Interactive Data Visualization for the Web: An Introduction to Designing with D3*. O'Reilly Media.

Index

Note: *Italic* page numbers refer to figures.

absolute change 47
absolute *vs.* relative data 18–19
accessibility 31–32
adding new categories based on condition 83–85, *84*
Adobe Color 99
aggregation 59
annotations 95
anti join 133–134
approximations 18
area charts 89, *90*
arguments 49, 108, 111
ascending order 53, 118, 119
autofill 46–49

bar chart 88, *88*
blanks or zeros 14–15
block *vs.* inline display 155
Booleans 39, 84
Bootstrap 168–180, *168*; adding to webpage 169; aligning and distributing content 177–179, *177*; column 170–171, *171*, *172*; column classes 171–176, *174*, *176*; container 170; more than one breakpoint, instructions for 176; row 170
borders 156; shorthand properties for 166–167
"box model," in HTML 155–158, *155*; border 156, 166–167; margin 158; padding 157, *157*

cascading style sheets (CSS) 6, 146–180; block *vs.* inline display 155; Bootstrap 168–180; content division element using margins, repositioning 161–163, *162*; content divisions 160–161; in HTML 146–147; content divisions and semantic web 167; keeping images in check 165–166; margins, padding, and borders, shorthand properties for 166–167; nesting div elements 163–165, *165*; properties 148–149; selector, writing 147–148; targeting more than one element 152; targets 150; width, responsiveness for block elements 158–160
categorical data 55
cell 38; contents, combining and separating 76; reference 38; at specific positions, splitting 81–83, *83*
chatter 97–98, *99*
checklist 17
choropleth maps 91
cleaned values, adding columns for 72–74, *73*
cleaning column 72; functions for 74–75
cleaning text, functions for 74
clustered columns 88
collection standards 17
color in data visualizations 98–100
column 38, 126; Bootstrap 170–171, *171*, *172*; chart 87, 88; classes, in Bootstrap 171–176, *174*, *176*; clustered 88; headers, changing 118; paired 88; reference 45
comma-separated values (CSV) 77; simple data table from CSV, importing 111
common data problems, spotting: blanks or zeros 14–15; duplication 15–16; outliers 14; standardization 13, *14*
conclusion 98
content divisions 160–161; element using margins, repositioning 161–163, *162*; and semantic web 167
CSS *see* cascading style sheets (CSS)

CSS3 8
CSV *see* comma-separated values (CSV)

data analysis 5–6; building blocks of
  51–69; R for, using 117–138
database manager 109
Data Color Picker 99
data display, navigation of 44–45
data journalism 7–8; definition of 2
data representation 6–7
data set, exploration of 45–50, *47, 48, 50*
data structure, controlling 44–45
data tables 113–115
data universe, problems with: collection
  standards 17; missing data 16
data visualization 86–102; chatter 97–98,
  99; color in, using 98–100; credit
  98, 99; deviations in 100–101; extra
  explanatory information, for clarity and
  context 95–96, *95, 96*; graphics, publish
  of 97; headlines 97–98, 99; notes 98, 99;
  online 97; process of creating 92–97;
  right form, choosing 93–94, *94*; shaping
  of data 93; source 98, 99; thinking
  through details 94; types of 86–92
Datawrapper 92, 93
descending order 53
duplication 15–16; full 15; mixing of levels
  15; partial 16; spreadsheets 41

"Empowerment Scholarship" program 12

filter(s/ing) 54–58, *55*; by condition
  56–57; menu 70–72, *71*; pivot table 67,
  68; by values 55–56, 70–71
finding data 3–4
Flourish 92
FOIA *see* U.S. Freedom of Information
  Act (FOIA)
formula 39, *40*; bar 39
freezing 44
frequency tables 70–72, *71*
full join 132–133, *133*
function 49, *50*; for cleaning column
  74–75; for cleaning text 74; nesting
  75–76
functionality 36

GDELT *see* Global Database of Events,
  Language, and Tone (GDELT)
Geographic Information Systems 6
geospatial charts 91–92, *92*
Global Database of Events, Language, and
  Tone (GDELT) 12

Google Drive 37, 42–44
Google Maps 6
Google Sheets 5, 7; arguments 49; autofill
  46; booleans 39; data set, exploration
  of 45–50, *47, 48, 50*; cell reference 38;
  cells 38; column reference 45; columns
  38; data display, navigation of 44–45;
  data set, exploration of 45–50, *47, 48,
  50*; data structure, controlling 44–45;
  delimiters 43; duplication 15, 41; filter
  menu 70–72; filters 54–58, *55*; formula
  bar 39; formulas 39; frequency tables
  70–72; function 49, 50; functionality
  36; getting data into 42–44, *43*; header
  rows 40; interface components 38;
  lag 36; multiple sheets 41; name box
  41; numbers 38; pivot tables 58–69;
  quicksum menu 41; ranges 41; rows 38;
  sorting 51–54, *52, 53*; space 36; table
  40; text 38; text qualifier 43

header rows 40
headlines 97–98, 99
HTML 6, 97, 139–147, *140*; attributes
  145–146; "box model" in 155–158,
  155, 157; CSS in 146–147; element,
  parts of 142–143; hyperlinks 145–146;
  image element 146; properties 148–149;
  requirements to create 141–142; styling,
  based on classes and IDs 150–151; text
  elements 144–145
HTML5 8
hyperlinks 145–146

Infogram 92
inner join 132, *132*
interpreter 104

JavaScript 6
join: anti 133–134; full 132–133, *133*;
  inner 132, *132*; left 131–132, *131*; types
  of 130–134

Learn UI Design: Data Color Picker 99
left join 131–132, *131*
line charts 88–89, 89
literal 97–98

margins 158; content division element
  using, repositioning 161–163, *162*;
  shorthand properties for 166–167
merging values 80, *81*
Microsoft Access 5
Microsoft Excel 5

missing data 16
MySQL 5

name box 41
nesting div elements 163–165, *165*
Non-public data 30–31
numbers 38

official request, writing 26–30; charge
    for data 29; communication 30;
    expectations 29–30; format 28–29; open
    records law 27; type of records 27–28;
    where and to whom 27
open records 23; law, writing official
    request in 27
outliers 14, 51

padding 157, *157*; shorthand properties for
    166–167
paired columns 88
"Paste special" 75
percentage change 47
Pew Research Center 32
pipes in tidyverse, using 122–123
Pivot Table Editor 60
pivot tables 58–69; creation of 59–61,
    60, *61*; elements 61; filtering 67, 68;
    flexibility of 65–66, *66*; grouping of data
    67–69, *69*; meaningful groups, finding
    59; from a question, building 61–63, *62*;
    sorting 65; summarizing data sets with
    58–59; summary types 63–64, *64*
public data, routes to 22–23

quicksum menu 41

R 7, 104–138; analysis into new columns,
    expanding 123–124; for data analysis,
    using 117–138; data's column headers,
    changing 118; data set by different
    groups, summarizing 125–129; data
    tables 113–115; data types, adjusting
    113–115; duplicated data 136–137;
    environment 105; expanding, with
    outside packages 108–109; joins, types
    of 130–134; merging with populations
    134–136; read_csv() 112–113; simple
    data table from CSV, importing
    111; tibbles 113–115; tidyverse 109,
    118–123, 129–130; variables 107–108;
    working directory 112, *113*
ranges 41
RCFP *see* Reporters Committee for
    Freedom of Press (RCFP)

read_csv() 112–113
record retention schedules 24–26, *25, 26*;
    general schedules 24; specific schedules
    24
regular expressions 121
relative change 47
Reporters Committee for Freedom of Press
    (RCFP) 31
right form, choosing 93–94, *94*
rows 12–13, 38; Bootstrap 170
RStudio 105–106, *106*; installing and
    loading packages within 109–111, *110*;
    sorting and filtering data in 118–122

SAS 5
scatter charts 90–91, *91*
semantic web, content divisions and 167
shaping of data 93
Social Security Administration 3
sorting 51–54, *52, 53*; ascending order 53;
    descending order 53; pivot table 65
space 36
"Split text to columns," using 77–80,
    77–80
spreadsheets *see* Google Sheets
SPSS 5
SQL 109
stacked bar chart 88
stacked column chart 88
standardization 13, *14*

table, data 40
text 38
thresholds, power 19
tibbles 113–115
tidyverse 109; joining data sets using
    column with shared values 129–130;
    sorting and filtering data in 118–122;
    using "pipes" in 122–123
tooltips 95, 96

understanding of data 10–12, 17
Urban Institute 100
U.S. Census 15, 39
U.S. Freedom of Information Act (FOIA)
    3, 27, 32, 33

variable 107–108
vector 108, 122
verification 10
Voice of San Diego 12

width, responsiveness for block elements
    158–160

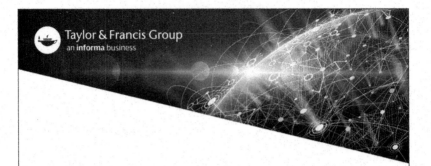

Taylor & Francis eBooks

www.taylorfrancis.com

A single destination for eBooks from Taylor & Francis
with increased functionality and an improved user
experience to meet the needs of our customers.

90,000+ eBooks of award-winning academic content in
Humanities, Social Science, Science, Technology, Engineering,
and Medical written by a global network of editors and authors.

TAYLOR & FRANCIS EBOOKS OFFERS:

A streamlined
experience for
our library
customers

A single point
of discovery
for all of our
eBook content

Improved
search and
discovery of
content at both
book and
chapter level

REQUEST A FREE TRIAL
support@taylorfrancis.com

 Routledge
Taylor & Francis Group

 CRC Press
Taylor & Francis Group